Stochastic Calculus for Finance

This book focuses specifically on the key results in stochastic processes that have become essential for finance practitioners to understand. The authors study the Wiener process and Itô integrals in some detail, with a focus on results needed for the Black–Scholes option pricing model. After developing the required martingale properties of this process, the construction of the integral and the Itô formula (proved in detail) become the centrepieces, both for theory and applications, and to provide concrete examples of stochastic differential equations used in finance. Finally, proofs of the existence, uniqueness and the Markov property of solutions of (general) stochastic equations complete the book.

Using careful exposition and detailed proofs, this book is a far more accessible introduction to Itô calculus than most texts. Students, practitioners and researchers will benefit from its rigorous, but unfussy, approach to technical issues. Solutions to the exercises are available online.

MAREK CAPIŃSKI has published over 50 research papers and eleven books. His diverse interests include mathematical finance, corporate finance and stochastic hydrodynamics. For over 35 years he has been teaching these topics, mainly in Poland and in the UK, where he has held visiting fellowships. He is currently Professor of Applied Mathematics at AGH University of Science and Technology in Kraków, Poland, where he established a Master's programme in mathematical finance.

EKKEHARD KOPP is Emeritus Professor of Mathematics at the University of Hull, UK, where he taught courses at all levels in analysis, measure and probability, stochastic processes and mathematical finance between 1970 and 2007. His editorial experience includes service as founding member of the Springer Finance series (1998–2008) and the Cambridge University Press AIMS Library series. He has taught in the UK, Canada and South Africa, and he has authored more than 50 research publications and five books.

JANUSZ TRAPLE is Professor of Mathematics in the Faculty of Applied Mathematics at AGH University of Science and Technology in Kraków, Poland. His former positions and visiting fellowships include the Jagiellonian University in Kraków, Scuola Normale in Pisa, University of Siena and University of Florence. He has taught courses in differential equations, measure and probability, and the theory of Markov processes, and he is the author of more than 20 research publications.

Mastering Mathematical Finance

Mastering Mathematical Finance (MMF) is a series of short books that cover all core topics and the most common electives offered in Master's programmes in mathematical or quantitative finance. The books are closely coordinated and largely self-contained, and can be used efficiently in combination but also individually.

The MMF books start financially from scratch and mathematically assume only undergraduate calculus, linear algebra and elementary probability theory. The necessary mathematics is developed rigorously, with emphasis on a natural development of mathematical ideas and financial intuition, and the readers quickly see real-life financial applications, both for motivation and as the ultimate end for the theory. All books are written for both teaching and self-study, with worked examples, exercises and solutions.

[DMFM]   *Discrete Models of Financial Markets*,
Marek Capiński, Ekkehard Kopp

[PF]   *Probability for Finance*,
Ekkehard Kopp, Jan Malczak, Tomasz Zastawniak

[SCF]   *Stochastic Calculus for Finance*,
Marek Capiński, Ekkehard Kopp, Janusz Traple

[BSM]   *The Black–Scholes Model*,
Marek Capiński, Ekkehard Kopp

[PTRM]   *Portfolio Theory and Risk Management*,
Maciej J. Capiński, Ekkehard Kopp

[NMFC]   *Numerical Methods in Finance with C++*,
Maciej J. Capiński, Tomasz Zastawniak

[SIR]   *Stochastic Interest Rates*,
Daragh McInerney, Tomasz Zastawniak

[CR]   *Credit Risk*,
Marek Capiński, Tomasz Zastawniak

[FE]   *Financial Econometrics*,
Marek Capiński, Jian Zhang

[SCAF]   *Stochastic Control Applied to Finance*,
Szymon Peszat, Tomasz Zastawniak

Series editors Marek Capiński, *AGH University of Science and Technology, Kraków*; Ekkehard Kopp, *University of Hull*; Tomasz Zastawniak, *University of York*

Stochastic Calculus for Finance

MAREK CAPIŃSKI
AGH University of Science and Technology, Kraków, Poland

EKKEHARD KOPP
University of Hull, Hull, UK

JANUSZ TRAPLE
AGH University of Science and Technology, Kraków, Poland

CAMBRIDGE
UNIVERSITY PRESS

CAMBRIDGE
UNIVERSITY PRESS

University Printing House, Cambridge CB2 8BS, United Kingdom

One Liberty Plaza, 20th Floor, New York, NY 10006, USA

477 Williamstown Road, Port Melbourne, VIC 3207, Australia

314-321, 3rd Floor, Plot 3, Splendor Forum, Jasola District Centre, New Delhi - 110025, India

79 Anson Road, #06-04/06, Singapore 079906

Cambridge University Press is part of the University of Cambridge.

It furthers the University's mission by disseminating knowledge in the pursuit of education, learning and research at the highest international levels of excellence.

www.cambridge.org
Information on this title: www.cambridge.org/9780521175739

First published 2012

A catalogue record for this publication is available from the British Library

Library of Congress Cataloging in Publication data
Capinski, Marek, 1951–
Stochastic calculus for finance / Marek Capinski, Ekkehard Kopp, Janusz Traple.
p.   cm. – (Mastering mathematical finance)
Includes bibliographical references and index.
ISBN 978-1-107-00264-7 (hardback : alk. paper) – ISBN 978-0-521-17573-9
(pbk. : alk. paper)
1. Finance – Mathematical models.   2. Stochastic processes.
3. Options (Finance) – Mathematical models.
I. Kopp, P. E., 1944–   II. Traple, Janusz.   III. Title.
HG106.C364   2012
332.01´51922 – dc23   2012024342

ISBN   978-1-107-00264-7   Hardback
ISBN   978-0-521-17573-9   Paperback

Additional resources for this publication at www.cambridge.org/9780521175739

Contents

Preface

In this volume of the series 'Mastering Mathematical Finance' we develop the essential tools from stochastic calculus that will be needed in later volumes for the rigorous development of the Black–Scholes option pricing model and various of its extensions. Our motivation, and hence our choice of material, is again taken from the applications we have in mind: we develop only those parts of the theory that will be indispensable for the financial models discussed in this series. The Itô integral, with the Wiener process as its driving force, forms the heart of the text, with the Itô formula, developed in stages until we reach a sufficiently general setting, as the principal tool of our calculus.

The initial chapter sets the scene with an account of the basics of martingale theory in discrete time, and a brief introduction to Markov chains. The focus then shifts to continuous time, with a careful construction and development of the principal path, martingale and Markov properties of the Wiener process, followed by the construction of the Itô integral and discussion of its key properties. Itô processes are discussed next, and their quadratic variations are identified. Chapter 4 focuses on a complete proof of the Itô formula, which is often omitted in introductory texts, or presented as a by-product of more advanced treatments. The stringent boundedness assumptions required by an elementary treatment are removed by means of localisation, and the role of local martingales is emphasised. Applications of the Itô formula to the exponential martingale, the Feynman–Kac formula and integration by parts complete the chapter. The final chapter deals with existence and uniqueness of stochastic differential equations, motivated by the solution of the Black–Scholes equation and related examples.

The treatment throughout seeks to be thorough rather than comprehensive, and proofs are given in detail – sometimes deferred to the end of a chapter in order not to disrupt the flow of key ideas. The exercises form an integral part of the text; solutions and further exercises and solutions may be found at www.cambridge.org/9781107002647. Throughout, the reader is referred to the previous volumes in the series: to [DMFM] for initial motivation and to [PF] for basic results on measure and probability.

We wish to thank all who have read the drafts and provided us with feedback, especially Rostislav Polishchuk for very valuable comments.

1

Discrete-time processes

Our study of stochastic processes, motivated by their use in financial modelling, begins with discrete-time models, including and generalising the models studied in detail in *Discrete Models of Financial Markets* [DMFM], where the typical 'process' was simply a finite sequence of random variables defined on some finite sample space. We generalise this in two directions, by considering a general probability space $(\Omega, \mathcal{F}, P)$ and allowing our processes to be infinite sequences of random variables defined on this space. Again the key concept is that of martingales, and we study the basic properties of discrete martingales in preparation for our later consideration of their continuous-time counterparts. We then briefly consider how another basic class of discrete-time processes, Markov chains, enters into the study of credit ratings, and develop some of their simple properties. Throughout, we will make extensive use of the fundamental properties of probability measures and random variables described in *Probability for Finance* [PF], and we refer the reader to that text for any probabilistic notions not explicitly defined here.

1.1 General definitions

We take a discrete time scale with $n = 0, 1, 2, \ldots$ denoting the number of consecutive steps of fixed length $h > 0$, so time instants are $t = nh \in [0, \infty)$. In contrast to [DMFM], where we had finitely many times, we allow infinitely many steps as a prelude to the continuous case, where $t \in [0, \infty)$ is arbitrary, which we study in the subsequent chapters.

We assume that a probability space $(\Omega, \mathcal{F}, P)$ is available, sufficiently rich to accomodate the various collections of random variables we wish to define. We have to allow infinite Ω to be able to discuss random variables without restricting their values to some finite set. Thus Ω is an arbitrary set, while $\mathcal{F}$ is a σ-field, and P a countably additive probability measure.

From the financial perspective, a random variable is a mathematical object modelling an unknown quantity such as a stock price. A sequence of random variables will correspond to its future evolution with no limiting horizon, as described in the next definition.

Definition 1.1
A **discrete-time stochastic process** is a sequence of random variables, that is an $\mathcal{F}$-measurable function

$$X(n) : \Omega \to \mathbb{R} \text{ for } n \geq 0,$$

and we assume that $X(0)$ is constant.

We employ the notation $X = (X(n))_{n \geq 0}$ but often we refer to 'the process $X(n)$' and alternatively we will use X to denote an arbitrary random variable, thus risking a lack of precision. This allows us, for instance, to indicate the time variable and to keep the presentation brief and free of pure formalism. In the same spirit, we will often drop the expression 'almost surely' after any relation between random variables.

Example 1.2
A classical example of a probability space, which, as it will turn out, is sufficiently rich for all our purposes, is $\Omega = [0, 1]$, $\mathcal{F} = \mathcal{B}([0, 1])$ – Borel sets, $P = m$ – Lebesgue measure (a construction can be found in [PF]).

Example 1.3

Consider a binomial tree, discussed in detail in [DMFM], determined by two single-step returns $D < U$. We define a sequence of returns

$$K(n) : [0, 1] \to \mathbb{R},$$

$n = 1, 2, \ldots$, by

$$K(n, \omega) = U\mathbf{1}_{A_n}(\omega) + D\mathbf{1}_{[0,1]\setminus A_n}(\omega),$$

$$A_n = \left[0, \frac{1}{2^n}\right) \cup \left[\frac{2}{2^n}, \frac{3}{2^n}\right) \cup \cdots \cup \left[\frac{2^n - 2}{2^n}, \frac{2^n - 1}{2^n}\right),$$

and clearly

$$P(K(n) = U) = P(K(n) = D) = \frac{1}{2}.$$

For instance,

$$K(2) = \left\{ \begin{array}{l} U \text{ if } \omega \in [0, \frac{1}{4}) \cup [\frac{1}{2}, \frac{3}{4}), \\ D \text{ if } \omega \in [\frac{1}{4}, \frac{1}{2}) \cup [\frac{3}{4}, 1]. \end{array} \right.$$

The stock prices are defined in a familiar way by

$$S(n) = S(n - 1)(1 + K(n)),$$

$n = 1, 2, \ldots$, with $S(0)$ given, deterministic.

Exercise 1.1 Show that for each n, the random variables $K(1), \ldots, K(n)$ are independent.

Exercise 1.2 Redesign the random variables $K(n)$ so that $P(K(n) = U) = p \in (0, 1)$, arbitrary.

Example 1.4

A version of a binomial tree with additive rather than multiplicative changes is called a **symmetric random walk** and is defined by taking $Z(0)$

given and

$$Z(n) = Z(n-1) + L(n),$$

$$L(n) = \pm 1, \text{ each with probability } \frac{1}{2}.$$

The sequence $L(n)$ defining a symmetric random walk can conveniently be regarded as representing a sequence of independent tosses of a fair coin. The outcome of each coin toss might determine whether a gambler gains or loses one unit of currency, so that the random variable $Z(n) = Z(0) + \sum_{i=1}^{n} L(i)$ describes his fortune after n games if he starts with $Z(0)$. Alternatively, it could describe the position on the line reached after n steps by a particle starting at position $Z(0)$ and, at the ith step (for each $i \leq n$), moving one unit to the right if $L(i) = 1$, or to the left if $L(i) = -1$. If the particle moves with constant velocity between the changes of direction, its path can be visualised by joining subsequent points $(n, Z(n))$ in the plane with line segments.

Information given by an initial segment $X(0), \ldots, X(n)$ of the sequence X can be captured by means of a filtration of partitions if the number of possible values of random variables is finite. We exploited this in [DMFM], but here we take a more general approach, replacing partitions by σ-fields, which allows us to consider arbitrary random variables.

Definition 1.5
The **filtration generated** by a discrete-time process $(X(n))_{n \geq 0}$ (also known as its **natural** filtration) is a family of σ-fields

$$\mathcal{F}_n^X = \sigma(\{X(k)^{-1}(B) : B \in \mathcal{B}(\mathbb{R}), k = 0, \ldots, n\}),$$

where for any family of sets $\mathcal{A}$, $\sigma(\mathcal{A})$ is the smallest σ-field containing $\mathcal{A}$, and $\mathcal{B}(\mathbb{R})$ is the σ-field of Borel sets on the real line.

Observe that the same result would be obtained by taking B to run through all intervals, or, indeed, all intervals of the form $(-\infty, a]$ for $a \in \mathbb{R}$. Since all elements of the sequence $X(n)$ are $\mathcal{F}$-measurable, $\mathcal{F}_n^X \subset \mathcal{F}$ for each n. In addition, $X(n)$ is clearly $\mathcal{F}_n^X$-measurable.

Note that, by its definition, the sequence $\mathcal{F}_n^X$ is increasing with respect to set inclusion $\subset$. This motivates introducing a general notion to indicate this

Definition 1.6
A **filtration** is a sequence of σ-fields $\mathcal{F}_n$ such that $\mathcal{F}_n \subset \mathcal{F}$ and $\mathcal{F}_n \subset \mathcal{F}_{n+1}$. A process X is **adapted** if each $X(n)$ is $\mathcal{F}_n$-measurable. If an arbitrary filtration $(\mathcal{F}_n)_{n\geq 0}$ has been fixed, we call $(\Omega, \mathcal{F}, (\mathcal{F})_{n\geq 0}, P)$ a **filtered probability space**.

Note that for any process its natural filtration is the smallest filtration to which it is adapted.

As we wish $X(0)$ to be constant (almost surely, of course!), we assume that $\mathcal{F}_0$ is **trivial**; that is, it is simply made up of all P-null sets and their complements.

Example 1.7
Consider $K(n)$ as given in Example 1.3. Clearly, for every $n \geq 1$

$$\{K(n)^{-1}(B) : B \in \mathcal{B}(\mathbb{R})\} = \{\emptyset, [0, 1], A_n, [0, 1] \setminus A_n\}$$

and the σ-field $\mathcal{F}_n$ consists of all null sets and all possible unions of intervals of the form $[\frac{i-1}{2^n}, \frac{i}{2^n})$, $i = 1, \ldots, 2^n - 1$ and $[\frac{2^n-1}{2^n}, 1]$ (This is an example of a field generated by so-called **atoms**.)

Exercise 1.3 Find the filtration in $\Omega = [0, 1]$ generated by the process $X(n, \omega) = 2\omega \mathbf{1}_{[0, 1 - \frac{1}{n}]}(\omega)$.

Example 1.8
The previous exercise illustrates the idea of flow of information described by a filtration. With increasing n, the shape of some function defined on Ω (here $\omega \mapsto 2\omega$) is gradually revealed. The values of X, if known, allow us to make a guess about the location of ω. If for instance $X(2, \omega) = \frac{1}{2}$, we know that $\omega = \frac{1}{4}$, but if $X(2, \omega) = 0$, we only know that $\omega \in (\frac{1}{2}, 1]$. Clearly, our information about ω, given the value of X, increases with n.

1.2 Martingales

We prepare ourselves for the estimation of some random variable Y after we observe a process X up to some future time n. The information obtained will be reflected in the σ-field $\mathcal{G} = \mathcal{F}_n$. The idea of the approximation of Y given the information contained in $\mathcal{G}$ is explained in the next definition (see [PF] for more details).

Definition 1.9
The **conditional expectation** of Y given $\mathcal{G}$ is a random variable $\mathbb{E}(Y|\mathcal{G})$, which is:

1. $\mathcal{G}$-measurable,
2. for all $A \in \mathcal{G}$,

$$\int_A \mathbb{E}(Y|\mathcal{G})dP = \int_A Y\,dP.$$

Example 1.10
In $\Omega = [0, 1]$, take the σ-field

$$\mathcal{G} = \left\{ B \subset \left[0, \frac{1}{2}\right) : B \in \mathcal{B}(\mathbb{R}) \right\} \cup \left\{ B \cup \left[\frac{1}{2}, 1\right] : B \subset \left[0, \frac{1}{2}\right), B \in \mathcal{B}(\mathbb{R}) \right\}$$

and $Y(\omega) = \omega^2$. Condition 1 imposes the constraint that the conditional expectation be constant on $[\frac{1}{2}, 1]$ but it can be arbitrary on $[0, \frac{1}{2})$. If so, Y will be the best approximation of itself on $[0, \frac{1}{2})$, while the constant c is given by condition 2 with $A = [\frac{1}{2}, 1]$ by solving $cP([\frac{1}{2}, 1]) = \int_{[\frac{1}{2},1]} \omega^2 dP$ and so

$$\mathbb{E}(Y|\mathcal{G})(\omega) = \begin{cases} \omega^2 & \text{if } \omega \in [0, \frac{1}{2}), \\ \frac{7}{12} & \text{if } \omega \in [\frac{1}{2}, 1]. \end{cases}$$

With increasing information about the future, as captured by a filtration $\mathcal{F}_n$, the accuracy of prediction improves, which follows from the important **tower property** of conditional expectation

$$\mathbb{E}(Y|\mathcal{F}_n) = \mathbb{E}(\mathbb{E}(Y|\mathcal{F}_{n+1})|\mathcal{F}_n).$$

Writing $M(n) = \mathbb{E}(Y|\mathcal{F}_n)$ above, we have an example of the following notion, crucial in what follows:

Definition 1.11
A process M is a **martingale** with respect to the filtration $\mathcal{F}_n$ if, for all

$n \geq 0$, $\mathbb{E}(|M(n)|) < \infty$, and

$$M(n) = \mathbb{E}(M(n + 1)|\mathcal{F}_n).$$

Note that a martingale is $\mathcal{F}_n$-adapted, by the definition of conditional expectation.

Exercise 1.4 Working on $\Omega = [0, 1]$, find (by means of concrete formulae and sketching the graphs) the martingale $\mathbb{E}(Y|\mathcal{F}_n)$, where $Y(\omega) = \omega^2$ and $\mathcal{F}_n$ is generated by $X(n, \omega) = 2\omega\mathbf{1}_{[0,1-\frac{1}{n}]}(\omega)$ (see Exercise 1.3).

Exercise 1.5 Show that the expectation of a martingale is constant in time. Find an example showing that constant expectation does not imply the martingale property.

Exercise 1.6 Show that martingale property is preserved under linear combinations with constant coefficients and adding a constant.

Exercise 1.7 Prove that if M is a martingale, then for $m < n$

$$M(m) = \mathbb{E}(M(n)|\mathcal{F}_m).$$

Another classical example of a martingale is the random walk $Z(n) = Z(n-1)+L(n)$, with filtration generated by $L(n)$. The proof of the martingale property of a random walk is exactly the same as that of the general result below.

Proposition 1.12
The sequence obtained by sums of independent random variables with zero mean is a martingale with respect to the filtration it generates.

Proof Assume that $L(n)$ is an arbitrary sequence of independent random variables with $\mathbb{E}(L(n)) = 0$, and write

$$Z(n) = Z(0) + \sum_{j=1}^{n} L(j),$$

$$\mathcal{F}_n = \sigma(Z(k) : 0 \leq k \leq n).$$

The properties of the conditional expectation immediately give the result:

$$
\begin{aligned}
\mathbb{E}(Z(n+1)|\mathcal{F}_n) &= \mathbb{E}(Z(n) + L(n+1)|\mathcal{F}_n) \quad \text{(definition of } Z) \\
&= \mathbb{E}(Z(n)|\mathcal{F}_n) + \mathbb{E}(L(n+1)|\mathcal{F}_n) \quad \text{(linearity)} \\
&= Z(n) + \mathbb{E}(L(n+1)) \quad \text{(definition of } \mathcal{F}_n, \text{ independence)} \\
&= Z(n).
\end{aligned}
$$

$\square$

We now develop a method of producing new martingales from a given one, which was already exploited in [DMFM], where we discussed the value process of a trading strategy. The result we wish to highlight is sometimes called a theorem on discrete stochastic integration. As we shall see later, the name is well deserved. To state this theorem, we need one more definition, which codifies an important property of trading strategies: recall that, for $n > 0$, an investor's decision to hold $x(n)$ units of stock throughout the period between trading dates $n - 1$ and n was based on his knowledge of the behaviour of the stock price up to time $n - 1$, so that the random variable $x(n)$ is $\mathcal{F}_{n-1}$-measurable. Such a process $x(n)$ was said to be predictable, and we use this idea for a general definition:

Definition 1.13
A process $X = (X(n))_{n \geq 1}$ is **predictable** relative to a given filtration $(\mathcal{F}_n)_{n \geq 0}$ if for every $n \geq 1$, $X(n)$ is $\mathcal{F}_{n-1}$-measurable.

Note that the sequence starts at $n = 1$, so there is no $X(0)$. Recall also that we take the σ-field $\mathcal{F}_0$ to be trivial. Thus if X is predictable, $X(1)$ is a constant function.

As we saw for trading strategies, predictability means that the variable $X(n)$ is 'known' by time $n - 1$, so we can 'predict' future values of X one step ahead. This property is incompatible with the martingale property unless the process is constant.

Proposition 1.14
A predictable martingale is constant.

Proof By definition of martingale $M(n-1) = \mathbb{E}(M(n)|\mathcal{F}_{n-1})$, which equals $M(n)$ if M is predictable. $\square$

We return to our stock price example. Having bought $x(n)$ shares at time $n-1$, we are of course interested in our gains. When Ω is finite and $P(\omega) > 0$ for each ω in Ω we know that, under the No Arbitrage Principle, the pricing model admits a risk-neutral probability Q, with $Q(\omega) > 0$ for each

ω (as discussed in [DMFM]). This means that, assuming that investment in a risk-free asset attracts a constant return $R \geq 0$, the discounted stock prices $\tilde{S}(n) = (1 + R)^{-n}S(n)$ follow a martingale under Q. Working with discounted values is a sound concept since the alternative risk-free investment provides a natural benchmark for returns. Our discounted gain (or loss) at the nth step will be $x(n)[\tilde{S}(n) - \tilde{S}(n - 1)]$. It is natural to consider the gains accumulated from time zero:

$$G(n) = V(0) + \sum_{i=1}^{n} x(i)[\tilde{S}(i) - \tilde{S}(i - 1)].$$

As we will see, the resulting process, expressing the discounted values, remains a martingale. In other words, the fairness of the discounted stock prices expressed by means of martingale property – the 'best guess' of future prices is the current price – is preserved by the strategy, so this market cannot be 'second-guessed' legally to ensure a profit by making cleverly chosen purchases and sales of the stock.

Theorem 1.15
Let M be a martingale and H a predictable process. If H is bounded, or if both H and M are square-integrable, then $X(0) = 0$,

$$X(n) = \sum_{j=1}^{n} H(j)[M(j) - M(j - 1)]\, for\, n > 0,$$

defines a martingale.

Proof This is proved in [DMFM] in a multi-dimensional setting for a finite Ω. The only change needed now is to observe that the conditions imposed here ensure the integrability of $X(n)$, trivially in the first case and by the Cauchy–Schwarz inequality in the second. You should fill in the details by writing out the easy proof of this result yourself, recalling that $H(j)$ is $\mathcal{F}_{j-1}$-measurable). □

The next exercise provides a converse to the theorem in an important special case.

Exercise 1.8 Let M be a martingale with respect to the filtration generated by $L(n)$ (as defined for a random walk), and assume for simplicity $M(0) = 0$. Show that there exists a predictable process H such that $M(n) = \sum_{i=1}^{n} H(i)L(i)$ (that is $M(n) = \sum_{i=1}^{n} H(i)[Z(i) - Z(i - 1)]$, where

$Z(i) = \sum_{j=1}^{i} L(j)$. (We are justified in calling this result a representation theorem: each martingale is a discrete stochastic integral).

Adding a constant to the sum on the right in the above theorem preserves the martingale property – unlike non-linear operations, which typically destroy it.

Exercise 1.9 Show that the process $Z^2(n)$, the square of a random walk, is not a martingale, by checking that $\mathbb{E}(Z^2(n+1)|\mathcal{F}_n) = Z^2(n) + 1$.

Recall the **Jensen inequality**: If $\varphi : \mathbb{R} \to \mathbb{R}$ is a convex function and $\varphi(X) \in L^1(P)$, then we have

$$\mathbb{E}(\varphi(X)|\mathcal{G}) \geq \varphi(\mathbb{E}(X|\mathcal{G})).$$

Applied to $\varphi(x) = x^2$, $X = M(n+1)$, $\mathcal{G} = \mathcal{F}_n$, this gives the following property of the square of a martingale

$$\mathbb{E}(M^2(n+1)|\mathcal{F}_n) \geq (\mathbb{E}(M(n+1)|\mathcal{F}_n))^2 = M^2(n).$$

This leads to some useful general notions.

Definition 1.16
A process $X(n)$-adapted to a filtration $\mathcal{F}_n$ with all $X(n)$ integrable, is
  1. a **submartingale** if $\mathbb{E}(X(n+1)|\mathcal{F}_n) \geq X(n)$,
  2. a **supermartingale** if $\mathbb{E}(X(n+1)|\mathcal{F}_n) \leq X(n)$.

Clearly, a martingale is a sub- and supermartingale. A process which is both, sub- and supermartingale, is a martingale. The above application of Jensen's inequality shows that the square of a martingale is a submartingale.

Exercise 1.10 Show that if X is a submartingale, then its expectations increase with n:

$$\mathbb{E}(X(0)) \leq \mathbb{E}(X(1)) \leq \mathbb{E}(X(2)) \leq \cdots,$$

and if X is a supermartingale, then its expectations decrease as n increases:

$$\mathbb{E}(X(0)) \geq \mathbb{E}(X(1)) \geq \mathbb{E}(X(2)) \geq \cdots .$$

Exercise 1.11   Let $X(n)$ be a martingale (submartingale, supermartingale). For a fixed m, consider the sequence $X'(k) = X(m + k) - X(m)$, $k \geq 0$, Show that X' is a martingale (submartingale, supermartingale) relative to the filtration $\mathcal{F}'_k = \mathcal{F}_{m+k}$.

1.3   The Doob decomposition

We know that the square of a martingale M is a submartingale. An intriguing question arises: is it possible to change – to compensate – the submartingale M^2 in a way to make the resulting process a martingale? The answer is positive. Since the sequence $\mathbb{E}(M^2(n))$ is increasing, we will need to subtract an increasing process from $M^2(n)$ to achieve our goal.

Definition 1.17
A process $A = (A(n))_{n \geq 0}$ is **increasing** if $A(n) \leq A(n + 1)$ for all $n \geq 0$.

For simplicity, the term 'increasing' is used instead of the more correct 'non-decreasing'. As with predictable processes, this property is incompatible with the martingale property.

Proposition 1.18
Any increasing martingale is constant.

Proof   If M is increasing, then $M(n) - M(n - 1) \geq 0$, but, since the expectation of a martingale is constant, $\mathbb{E}(M(n) - M(n - 1)) = 0$. This implies $M(n) - M(n - 1) = 0$ since a non-negative random variable with zero integral vanishes almost surely. □

An equivalent version of the next theorem was also discussed in [DMFM]; for completeness we remind the reader of the main idea of the proof given there.

Theorem 1.19 Doob decomposition
If $Y(n)$ is a submartingale with respect to some filtration, then there exist,

for the same filtration, a martingale $M(n)$ and a predictable, increasing process $A(n)$ with $M(0) = A(0) = 0$ such that

$$Y(n) = Y(0) + M(n) + A(n).$$

This decomposition is unique. We call the process A the **compensator** *of the submartingale Y.*

Proof The proof given in [DMFM] for supermartingales can easily be adapted to the present case since $-Y$ is a supermartingale. Thus the recursive formula for the compensator becomes, for $n \geq 1$,

$$A(n) = A(n-1) + \mathbb{E}(Y(n) - Y(n-1)|\mathcal{F}_{n-1}) \qquad (1.1)$$

and the form of M is implied by our target relation

$$M(n) = -A(n) + Y(n) - Y(0).$$

It is not difficult to see that A and M have the desired properties.

For the uniqueness property, suppose that $Y(n) = Y(0) + M'(n) + A'(n)$ is another decomposition, where M' is a martingale and A' is a predictable increasing process. It follows that

$$M(n) - M'(n) = A'(n) - A(n) = Z(n),$$

where $Z(n)$ is a predictable martingale, hence by Proposition 1.14 it is constant; in fact, $Z(n) = 0$ for all $n \geq 0$ because $Z(0) = 0$. Thus the decomposition is unique.   □

Exercise 1.12   Prove the Doob decomposition for submartingales from first principles.

Exercise 1.13   Let $Z(n)$ be a random walk (see Example 1.4), $Z(0) = 0, Z(n) = \sum_{j=1}^{n} L(j)$, $L(j) = \pm 1$, and let $\mathcal{F}_n$ be the filtration generated by $L(n)$, $\mathcal{F}_n = \sigma(L(1), \ldots, L(n))$. Verify that $Z^2(n)$ is a submartingale and find the increasing process A in its Doob decomposition.

A case of particular interest to us is the square of a martingale.

Proposition 1.20
Suppose $M(n) \in L^2(\Omega)$ is a martingale with $M(0) = 0$. Then for $n > m$

$$\mathbb{E}([M(n) - M(m)]^2|\mathcal{F}_m) = \mathbb{E}(M^2(n) - M^2(m)|\mathcal{F}_m).$$

Proof The equality seems to defy 'normal' algebra, but it is very easy to prove:

$$\mathbb{E}([M(n) - M(m)]^2|\mathcal{F}_m)$$
$$= \mathbb{E}(M^2(n)|\mathcal{F}_m) - 2M(m)\mathbb{E}(M(n)|\mathcal{F}_m) + M^2(m)$$
$$= \mathbb{E}(M^2(n)|\mathcal{F}_m) - 2M^2(m) + M^2(m) \quad (M \text{ is a martingale})$$
$$= \mathbb{E}(M^2(n) - M^2(m)|\mathcal{F}_m).$$

$\square$

Recall that the discrete stochastic integral of a predictable process H with respect to the martingale M is defined by

$$X(n) = \sum_{k=1}^{n} H(k)[M(k) - M(k-1)],$$

with $X(0) = 0$, and by Theorem 1.15 it is a martingale. Below we assume that $X(n)$ is square-integrable, which holds, for example, when each $M(n)$ is square-integrable and each $H(n)$ is bounded.

Proposition 1.21 (Discrete Itô isometry)
If $X(n)$ is square-integrable, then

$$\mathbb{E}(X^2(n)) = \mathbb{E}\left(\sum_{k=1}^{n} H^2(k)[A(k) - A(k-1)]\right),$$

where A is the compensator of M^2.

Proof We begin with simple algebra on the left

$$\mathbb{E}(X^2(n)) = \mathbb{E}\left(\sum_{k=1}^{n}\sum_{j=1}^{n} H(j)[M(j) - M(j-1)]H(k)[M(k) - M(k-1)]\right)$$
$$= \sum_{k=1}^{n}\sum_{j=1}^{n} \mathbb{E}(H(j)[M(j) - M(j-1)]H(k)[M(k) - M(k-1)]).$$

Consider terms in the last sum separately. When $j < k$, we introduce carefully chosen conditioning to use the measurability properties for handling the product:

$$\mathbb{E}(H(j)[M(j) - M(j-1)]H(k)[M(k) - M(k-1)])$$
$$= \mathbb{E}(\mathbb{E}(H(j)[M(j) - M(j-1)]H(k)[M(k) - M(k-1)]|\mathcal{F}_{k-1}))$$
$$= \mathbb{E}(H(j)[M(j) - M(j-1)]H(k)\mathbb{E}([M(k) - M(k-1)]|\mathcal{F}_{k-1}))$$
$$= 0$$

since M is a martingale, so $\mathbb{E}([M(k) - M(k-1)]|\mathcal{F}_{k-1}) = 0$. The terms with $j > k$ vanish by a similar argument.

On the diagonal, $j = k$, we have:

$$\mathbb{E}(H^2(k)[M(k) - M(k-1)]^2)$$
$$= \mathbb{E}(\mathbb{E}(H^2(k)[M(k) - M(k-1)]^2|\mathcal{F}_{k-1}))$$
$$= \mathbb{E}(H^2(k)\mathbb{E}([M(k) - M(k-1)]^2|\mathcal{F}_{k-1})) \quad (H^2 \text{ is also predictable})$$
$$= \mathbb{E}(H^2(k)\mathbb{E}(M^2(k) - M^2(k-1)|\mathcal{F}_{k-1})) \quad (\text{Proposition 1.20}).$$

Next, since A is the compensator of M^2,

$$\mathbb{E}(M^2(k) - M^2(k-1)|\mathcal{F}_{k-1})) = A(k) - A(k-1)$$

since the successive differences of the martingale part of the Doob decomposition of M^2 vanish under this conditional expectation and A is predictable. □

Exercise 1.14 Using the Doob decomposition, show that if Y is a square-integrable submartingale (respectively, supermartingale) and H is predictable with bounded non-negative $H(n)$, then the stochastic integral of H with respect to Y is also a submartingale (respectively, supermartingale).

1.4 Stopping times

Suppose an investor decides to sell his shares in stock S if its value falls below 50% of its current (time zero) price. Thus he sells his shares at the random time $\tau(\omega) = \inf\{n : S(n, \omega) \le \frac{1}{2}S(0)\}$. This is known as a 'stop-loss' strategy. Note that it is possible that the stock will never be sold, $\{n : S(n, \omega) \le \frac{1}{2}S(0)\}$ can be empty for a particular ω, so we must allow $\tau(\omega) = +\infty$, employing the convention $\inf \emptyset = +\infty$, and we need the extended set of non-negative integers for the values of τ. Clearly, unless the investor is prescient, his decision will be based on information available by time n, which is represented by $\mathcal{F}_n = \sigma(S(i) : i \le n)$. Thus we should require that $\{\omega : \tau(\omega) = n\} \in \mathcal{F}_n$. This leads us to a general definition.

Definition 1.22
A random variable $\tau : \Omega \to \{0, 1, 2, \ldots\} \cup \{\infty\}$ is a **stopping time** relative to a given filtration $(\mathcal{F}_n)_{n \ge 0}$ if for every $n \ge 0$ the event $\{\omega : \tau(\omega) = n\}$ belongs to $\mathcal{F}_n$.

The requirement in this definition is equivalent to $\{\tau \leq n\} \in \mathcal{F}_n$. To see this, notice that since $\mathcal{F}_k \subset \mathcal{F}_n$ for $k < n$, we have, on the one hand,

$$\{\tau \leq n\} = \bigcup_{k \leq n}\{\tau = k\} \in \mathcal{F}_n,$$

while, on the other, if $\{\tau \leq k\} \in \mathcal{F}_k$ for all $k \geq 0$, then for all n

$$\{\tau = n\} = \{\tau \leq n\}\backslash \bigcup_{k < n}\{\tau \leq k\} \in \mathcal{F}_n.$$

We shall use both versions interchangeably.

Remark 1.23
To deal with the set $\{\tau = \infty\}$, we introduce the σ-field $\mathcal{F}_\infty = \sigma(\bigcup_{n=0}^\infty \mathcal{F}_n)$. If we know that $\{\tau = n\} \in \mathcal{F}_n$ for each finite $n \geq 0$, the sets $\{\tau = n\}$ all belong to $\mathcal{F}_\infty$; hence so does $\{\tau = \infty\}$, which is the complement of their union. So this case does not need to be checked separately.

Example 1.24
The first hitting time τ_B of a Borel set $B \subset \mathbb{R}$ by an adapted process X is defined by setting

$$\tau_B(\omega) = \inf\{n : X(n, \omega) \in B\}.$$

It is a stopping time because for every $n \geq 0$ we have

$$\{\tau_B \leq n\} = \bigcup_{k \leq n}\{X(k) \in B\} \in \mathcal{F}_n.$$

On the other hand, the last hitting time, that is

$$\nu_B(\omega) = \sup\{n : X(n, \omega) \in B\}$$

will not be a stopping time in general. For this, observe that

$$\nu_B(\omega) = n \text{ iff } \omega \in \{X(n) \in B\} \cap \bigcap_{k > n}\{X(k) \notin B\}$$

and the sets in the last intersection do not need to belong to $\mathcal{F}_n$.

Exercise 1.15 Let τ be a stopping time relative to the filtration $\mathcal{F}_n$. Which of the random variables $\tau + 1$, $\tau - 1$, τ^2 is a stopping time?

> **Exercise 1.16**   Show that the constant random variable, $\tau(\omega) = m$ for all ω, is a stopping time relative to any filtration.

Given two stopping times τ and v, we adopt the notation: $\tau \vee v = \max\{\tau, v\}$, $\tau \wedge v = \min\{\tau, v\}$.

Proposition 1.25
If τ, v are stopping times relative to the filtration $\mathcal{F}_n$, then $\tau \vee v$ is also a stopping time relative to $\mathcal{F}_n$.

Proof   For the maximum to be at the level m, at least one of the functions must hit it, while the other must not exceed m, so

$$\{v \vee \tau = m\} = \{v = m, \tau \leq m\} \cup \{v \leq m, \tau = m\}.$$

Each of the sets on the right is in $\mathcal{F}_m$ as the intersection of elements of $\mathcal{F}_m$.   □

> **Exercise 1.17**   Show that if τ and v are as in the Proposition, then $\tau \wedge v$ is also a stopping time.

Proposition 1.26
Let v_k, $k = 1, 2, \dots$ be a convergent sequence of stopping times. Then $v = \lim_{k \to \infty} v_k$ is a stopping time.

Proof   The range of any stopping time is contained in $\{0, 1, 2, \dots\} \cup \{+\infty\}$, so for a sequence $v_n(\omega)$ to converge to $m < +\infty$, we must have $v_n(\omega) = m$ eventually, that is for all $n \geq N$ for some N, hence

$$\{v = m\} = \bigcup_{N \in \mathbb{N}} \bigcap_{n \geq N} \{v_n = m\}.$$

The set on the right is clearly in $\mathcal{F}_m$.   □

Stopped processes

If the stopping time $\tau : \Omega \to \mathbb{N} \cup \{\infty\}$ is P-a.s. finite, that is $P(\{\tau = \infty\}) = 0$, we can consider the function $X(\tau) : \Omega \to \mathbb{R}$ defined by $\omega \to X(\tau(\omega), \omega)$ on $\{\tau < \infty\}$ and 0 on $\{\tau = \infty\}$. We then have

$$X(\tau) = \sum_{m \geq 0} X(m) \mathbf{1}_{\{\tau = m\}} \tag{1.2}$$

since the sets $\{\tau = m\}$, $m = 0, 1, 2, \ldots$ are pairwise disjoint. This is a random variable, since for each $m \geq 0$, $X(m)\mathbf{1}_{\{\tau=m\}}$ is $\mathcal{F}_m$-measurable, and $\mathcal{F}_m \subset \mathcal{F}$.

Let us briefly consider situations where this arises naturally in the management of investments. As before, we are guided by the results obtained in [DMFM], and model the (discrete-time) evolution of a risky asset, such as a stock, by a sequence $(S(n))_{n \geq 0}$ of random variables satisfying $S(n) > 0$ for all n. We combine our holdings of $x(n)$ units of stock with $y(n)$ units of the (riskless) money market account, which is taken as 1 at time zero, and increases with each step at the riskless return R, so that at time n the value of our holdings is

$$V(n) = x(n)S(n) + y(n)(1 + R)^n.$$

Example 1.27
Freezing an investment at a fixed level. An investor may set himself a target in advance for the wealth he wishes to extract from a given investment. Recall from [DMFM] that, given an initial investment $V(0)$, we follow some self-financing strategy $x(n)$, $y(n)$ (the choice of $y(n)$ is secondary). Assume for simplicity that the riskless return R is zero. If the value of our total holdings arrives at the prescibed level M, we may wish to close the position, and we define

$$\tau = \min\{n : V(n) \geq M\}$$

so that closing the position means liquidating our stock holdings and keeping all the funds in cash (at zero interest) at a trading date determined by τ. Then the value of our investment is frozen after time τ :

$$V_\tau^{\text{frozen}}(n) = \begin{cases} V(n) \text{ if } n < \tau, \\ V(\tau) \text{ if } n \geq \tau. \end{cases}$$

The values of our original strategy $V(n)$ follow a martingale with respect to a risk-neutral probability Q. In particular, the Q-expectation of $V(n)$ remains constant. We might ask whether the same remains true of V_τ^{frozen}, that is whether a judicious choice of target wealth will improve our prospects on average? The intuition that a martingale represents a 'completely random' process suggests otherwise; we suspect that the 'frozen' value process remains a Q-martingale, and thus has constant expectation.

Example 1.28

Exercising an American put option. Suppose we hold an American put option with strike K, expiry N, on a stock S. We again keep the riskless rate at zero. In considering trading strategies, we need to consider an extended market, where a strategy is a triple (x, y, z), with $x(n)$ denoting the number of shares, $y(n)$ the units in the money market, and $z(n)$ the number of options held at time n. In this case, we have $z(n) = 1$ until exercise of the option. We know that the option payoff at time $n \leq N$ is given by $I(n) = (K - S(n))^+$ and that the option price $P(n)$ can be found from $I(n)$ by backward induction via $P(N) = I(N)$, $P(n-1) = \max[I(n-1), \mathbb{E}_Q(P(n)|\mathcal{F}_{n-1})]$ for $n < N$. It is optimal to exercise the option at the first possible opportunity, that is define

$$\tau = \min\{n : I(n) = P(n)\}$$

and then the option ceases to exist and the position is terminated (in effect, the holding $z(n)$ is liquidated at time τ). In the setting of [DMFM], it is also shown that a stopping time ν is optimal if and only if $I(\nu) = P(\nu)$ and the stopped process (which we define immediately below) is a martingale. This principle underlies delta hedging of an American option: the hedging is terminated at the random time decided by the option holder. Up to this moment, the value of the strategy follows a martingale, which is frozen at the exercise time. Again we would expect the resulting process to remain a martingale.

Guided by these examples we show how to stop any adapted process at a stopping time.

Definition 1.29

For an adapted process X and a stopping time τ, the **stopped process** $X_\tau = (X_\tau(n))_{n \geq 0}$ is defined by the formula

$$X_\tau(n, \omega) = X(n \wedge \tau(\omega), \omega).$$

Note that for each ω, X_τ truncates (freezes) the path $\{X(n, \omega) : n \geq 0\}$ at the level $X(\tau(\omega))$.

Proposition 1.30

The process X_τ is adapted.

Proof For $\omega \in \Omega$ with $\tau(\omega) < \infty$, there are two possibilities:

First, $\tau(\omega) = m < n$. Here $X_\tau(n, \omega) = X(m, \omega)$.

Second, $\tau(\omega) = m \geq n$ which gives $X_\tau(n, \omega) = X(n, \omega)$.

The sets $\{\tau = m\}, m = 0, 1, 2, \ldots, n$ and $\{\tau \geq n\}$ are pairwise disjoint, so the value of $X_\tau(n)$ can be written compactly in the form

$$X_\tau(n) = \sum_{m<n} X(m)\mathbf{1}_{\{\tau=m\}} + X(n)\mathbf{1}_{\{\tau \geq n\}}.$$

On the right, each term is $\mathcal{F}_n$-measurable, since $\{\tau \geq n\} = \Omega \setminus \{\tau < n\}$. $\quad\square$

Our discussion of financial examples illustrates the importance of the requirement that the martingale property is preserved under stopping – we now prove that this is the case.

Theorem 1.31

Let M be a martingale. If τ is a stopping time, then the stopped process M_τ is also a martingale.

Proof As observed above

$$M_\tau(n) = \sum_{m<n} M(m)\mathbf{1}_{\{\tau=m\}} + M(n)\mathbf{1}_{\{\tau \geq n\}}.$$

We have shown that M_τ is an adapted process, and since the above sum involves only finitely many terms, $M_\tau(n)$ is integrable for all n. Finally,

$$\mathbb{E}(M_\tau(n)|\mathcal{F}_{n-1}) = \mathbb{E}\left(\sum_{m<n} M(m)\mathbf{1}_{\{\tau=m\}}|\mathcal{F}_{n-1}\right) + \mathbb{E}(M(n)\mathbf{1}_{\{\tau \geq n\}}|\mathcal{F}_{n-1})$$

$$= \sum_{m<n} M(m)\mathbf{1}_{\{\tau=m\}} + \mathbf{1}_{\{\tau \geq n\}}\mathbb{E}(M(n)|\mathcal{F}_{n-1})$$

$$(\text{since } \mathbf{1}_{\{\tau \geq n\}} = 1 - \mathbf{1}_{\{\tau < n\}} \text{ is } \mathcal{F}_{n-1}\text{-measurable})$$

$$= \sum_{m<n-1} M(m)\mathbf{1}_{\{\tau=m\}} + M(n-1)\mathbf{1}_{\{\tau=n-1\}} + \mathbf{1}_{\{\tau \geq n\}}M(n-1)$$

$$= \sum_{m<n-1} M(m)\mathbf{1}_{\{\tau=m\}} + M(n-1)\mathbf{1}_{\{\tau \geq n-1\}}$$

$$= M_\tau(n-1).$$

$\quad\square$

Corollary 1.32

For a martingale, the expectation is preserved under stopping, that is in general for a martingale M, a stopping time τ, and $n \geq 0$,

$$\mathbb{E}(M_\tau(n)) = \mathbb{E}(M(0)) = \mathbb{E}(M(n)).$$

Exercise 1.18 Deduce the above theorem from Theorem 1.15 by considering $H(k) = \mathbf{1}_{\{\tau \geq k\}}$.

Exercise 1.19 Using the Doob decomposition show that a stopped submartingale is a submartingale (and similarly for a supermartingale). Alternatively, use the above representation of the stopped process and use the definition to reach the same conclusions.

Optional sampling for bounded stopping times

We now consider properties of the random variable $X(\tau)(\omega) = X(\tau(\omega), \omega)$ described at (1.2). Given a finite-valued stopping time τ and any Borel set $B \subset \mathbb{R}$, we see that $\{X(\tau) \in B\} = \bigcup_{m \geq 0} (\{X(m) \in B\} \cap \{\tau = m\})$. This suggests that we should define the σ-field generated by the random variable $X(\tau)$ as follows:

Definition 1.33

Let τ be a finite-valued stopping time. The collection of subsets of $\mathcal{F}$ given by

$$\mathcal{F}_\tau = \{A \in \mathcal{F} : A \cap \{\tau = m\} \in \mathcal{F}_m \text{ for all } m \in \mathbb{N}\}$$

is called the σ-field of **events known at time** τ.

Exercise 1.20 Show that $\mathcal{F}_\tau$ is a sub-σ-field of $\mathcal{F}$.

When $\tau = n_0$ is constant, we have $\mathcal{F}_\tau = \mathcal{F}_{n_0}$, since $\{\tau = m\} \cap A = A$ when $m = n_0$ and is empty otherwise.

Suppose that τ, v are stopping times, with associated σ-fields $\mathcal{F}_\tau$, $\mathcal{F}_v$. These are increasing, as the next exercise shows – using $\{\tau \leq m\}$ rather than $\{\tau = m\}$ is useful here.

Exercise 1.21 Show that if τ, v are stopping times with $\tau \leq v$, then $\mathcal{F}_\tau \subset \mathcal{F}_v$.

Note that as a result we have $\mathcal{F}_{\tau \wedge v} \subset \mathcal{F}_\tau \subset \mathcal{F}_{\tau \vee v}$.

Exercise 1.22 Show that any stopping time τ is $\mathcal{F}_\tau$-measurable.

Proposition 1.34
Let τ and $X(n)$ be, respectively, a finite-valued stopping time and a process adapted to $\mathcal{F}_n$. Then $X(\tau)$ is $\mathcal{F}_\tau$-measurable.

Proof To show that $X(\tau)$ is $\mathcal{F}_\tau$-measurable, we must show that for every $s \in \mathbb{R}$ and for every $k \geq 0$

$$U = \{X(\tau) < s\} \cap \{\tau \leq k\} \in \mathcal{F}_k.$$

But $U = \bigcup_{n=0}^{k}(\{X_n < s\} \cap \{\tau = n\})$ and for each $n \leq k$, $\{X_n < s\} \cap \{\tau = n\} \in \mathcal{F}_n \subset \mathcal{F}_k$, so the result follows. $\qquad\square$

In financial applications we often have a finite time horizon, N. For such applications, we can restrict ourselves to bounded stopping times. This has the advantage that $X(\tau)$ is automatically integrable, and we can apply Theorem 1.15 to show that the martingale property is preserved when bounded stopping times replace constant times. This is the simplest form of Doob's optional sampling theorem for martingales.

Theorem 1.35
If M is a martingale and $\tau \leq \nu$ are bounded stopping times, then

$$M(\tau) = \mathbb{E}(M(\nu)|\mathcal{F}_\tau).$$

Proof Fix A in $\mathcal{F}_\tau$. We have to show that $\int_A M(\nu)dP = \int_A M(\tau)dP$ according to the definition of conditional expectation. This goal can be written in the form

$$\mathbb{E}(\mathbf{1}_A(M(\nu) - M(\tau))) = 0.$$

If $\nu(\omega) = \tau(\omega)$, then the random variable under the expectation is zero. Otherwise we write the increment as a (telescopic) sum

$$M(\nu(\omega), \omega) - M(\tau(\omega), \omega) = \sum_{k=\tau(\omega)+1}^{\nu(\omega)} [M(k, \omega) - M(k-1, \omega)].$$

This gives us a clue: write the random variable in question as the value of a discrete stochastic integral with zero initial value so that its martingale property does the trick. So

$$\mathbf{1}_A(\omega)(M(\nu(\omega), \omega) - M(\tau(\omega), \omega)))$$

$$= \sum_{k=\tau(\omega)+1}^{\nu(\omega)} \mathbf{1}_A(\omega)[M(k, \omega) - M(k-1, \omega)]$$

$$= \sum_{k=0}^{\nu(\omega)} \mathbf{1}_A(\omega)\mathbf{1}_{\{\tau(\omega)<k\}}[M(k, \omega) - M(k-1, \omega)]. \qquad (1.3)$$

If we can show that the sequence $H(k) = \mathbf{1}_A\mathbf{1}_{\{\tau<k\}}$ is predictable, then the right-hand side of (1.3) is $X_\nu(N) = X(N \wedge \nu)$, where

$$X(n) = \sum_{k=1}^{n} H(k)[M(k) - M(k-1)]$$

is a martingale with $X(0) = 0$, so $\mathbb{E}(X_\nu(N)) = 0$ as required (a stopped martingale is a martingale).

Predictability of H boils down to proving that $A \cap \{\tau < j\} \in \mathcal{F}_{j-1}$ but this is immediate since

$$\{\tau < j\} = \bigcup_{m=0}^{j-1} \{\tau = m\}$$

and we know that $A \cap \{\tau = m\} \in \mathcal{F}_m$ for all m as $A \in \mathcal{F}_\tau$.   □

We may interpret this result as follows: suppose our investor does not keep in close touch with market information, but chooses to observe the stock price S at random times. His information 'up to time τ' is then contained in $\mathcal{F}_\tau$, and the optional sampling theorem confirms that the martingale property of the stock price is maintained, so that the expected value, given $\mathcal{F}_\tau$, of a randomly chosen future stock price is still the current value.

Exercise 1.23   Extend the optional sampling theorem to supermartingales.

1.5   Doob's inequalities and martingale convergence

The following important inequality will be used frequently in what follows. It allows us to control the size of maximum of a process, a random variable whose distribution is difficult to tackle. The final estimate, although less exact, only involves expectations, which are often easy to compute or estimate.

Theorem 1.36 (Doob's maximal inequality)
If $M(n)$ is a non-negative submartingale, then for each $n \in \mathbb{N}$ and $\lambda > 0$

$$P(\max_{k \leq n} M(k) \geq \lambda) \leq \frac{1}{\lambda} \int_{\{\max_{k \leq n} M(k) \geq \lambda\}} M(n)dP \leq \frac{1}{\lambda}\mathbb{E}(M(n)). \qquad (1.4)$$

Proof Let $A = \{\max_{k \leq n} M(k) \geq \lambda\}$. Then $A = \bigcup_{k=0}^{n} A_k$, where $A_0 = \{M(0) \geq \lambda\}$ and, for $k = 1, 2, \ldots, n$, $A_k = (\bigcap_{j=0}^{k-1}\{M(j) < \lambda\} \cap \{M(k) \geq \lambda\}$ consists of the ω in Ω, where $M(k, \omega)$ is at least λ for the first time. The sets in this union are disjoint. The set A_k is in $\mathcal{F}_k$, since M is adapted, and we obtain

$$\lambda P(A_k) \leq \int_{A_k} M(k)dP \quad \text{(since } M(k) \geq \lambda \text{ on } A_k)$$

$$\leq \int_{A_k} M(n)dP \quad (M \text{ is a submartingale}).$$

Sum these inequalities over $k = 0, 1, ..., n$ to obtain the first claimed inequality (since measures are additive and the union is disjoint) in the form:

$$\lambda P(A) \leq \int_A M(n)dP.$$

Since $M(n)$ is non-negative, $\int_A M(n)dP \leq \int_\Omega M(n)dP$, which implies the second inequality. $\qquad \square$

Jensen's inequality enables us instantly to improve this estimate as follows:

Exercise 1.24 Suppose that, with $M(n)$ and λ as in the Theorem, $(M(n))^p$ is integrable for some $p > 1$. Show that we can improve (1.4) to read

$$P(\max_{k \leq n} M(k) \geq \lambda) \leq \frac{1}{\lambda^p} \int_{\{\max_{k \leq n} M(k) \geq \lambda\}} M^p(n)dP \leq \frac{1}{\lambda^p}\mathbb{E}(M^p(n)).$$

The maximal inequality allows us to find a simple upper bound for the L^2-norm of the random variable $\sup_{n \geq 0} M(n)$ for a non-negative submartingale. The inequality is again due to Doob.

Theorem 1.37 (Doob's L^2-inequality)

Let $M(n)$ be a non-negative submartingale with $\mathbb{E}(M^2(n))$ finite for each $n \geq 0$. Then

$$\mathbb{E}(\max_{k \leq n} M(k))^2 \leq 4\mathbb{E}(M^2(n)).$$

If $M(n)$ is bounded in L^2-norm, for some $c > 0$ we have $\mathbb{E}(M^2(n)) < c$ for all $n \geq 0$, then $\sup_{n \geq 0} M(n)$ is in $L^2(\Omega)$ and

$$\mathbb{E}[(\sup_{n \geq 0} M(n))^2] \leq 4 \sup_{n \geq 0} \mathbb{E}(M^2(n)).$$

The continuous-time version of this inequality is crucial in stochastic calculus, as we shall see. We wish to apply the maximal inequality in the proof. To show that the hypothesis of that inequality is satisfied, we first need a simple lemma from integration theory, using Fubini's theorem (see [PF]):

Lemma 1.38

Suppose we have non-negative random variables X, Y such that Y is in $L^2(\Omega)$ and for all $x > 0$,

$$xP(X \geq x) \leq \int_{\{X \geq x\}} Y\,dP.$$

Then X is in $L^2(\Omega)$ and

$$\mathbb{E}(X^2) \leq 4\mathbb{E}(Y^2).$$

Proof   See page 34.   □

Proof of the theorem   The Doob L^2-inequality follows, since, using the maximal inequality with $Y = M_n$ and $X = \max_{k \leq n} M(k)$, we have

$$\lambda P(X \geq \lambda) \leq \int_{(X \geq \lambda)} Y\,dP,$$

hence the Lemma tells us that

$$\mathbb{E}[(\max_{k \leq n} M(k))^2] \leq 4\mathbb{E}(M^2(n)),$$

which is our first claim, while the second follows from the monotone convergence theorem, since $\max_{k \leq n} M^2(k) \nearrow \sup_{n \geq 0} M^2(n)$ as $n \to \infty$.   □

Exercise 1.25 Extend the above Lemma to L^p for every $p > 1$, to conclude that for non-negative $Y \in L^p$, and with its relation to $X \geq 0$ as stated in the Lemma, we obtain $\|X\|_p \leq \frac{p}{p-1} \|Y\|_p$. (Hint: the proof is similar to that given for the case $p = 2$, and utilises the identity $p \int_{\{z \geq x\}} x^{p-1} dx = x^p$.)

We are ready for our martingale convergence theorem. Our first simple example of a martingale was the sequence $(\mathbb{E}(Y|\mathcal{F}_n))_{n \geq 0}$ for some integrable random variable Y. It turns out that under some regularity conditions, each martingale is of this form. Here we restrict our attention to the special case of martingales uniformly bounded in L^2-norm, where the existence of such a Y is easy to prove and which is sufficient for the applications we have in mind. In the literature, the limit Y is often denoted by M_∞.

Theorem 1.39
Let M be an L^2-bounded martingale; that is, for some constant c we have $\mathbb{E}(M^2(n)) \leq c$ for all $n \geq 0$. Then there exists a random variable Y with $\mathbb{E}(Y^2) \leq c$ such that:
  1. *$P(\lim_{n \to \infty} M(n) = Y) = 1$ (in other words, $M(n)$ converges almost surely to Y),*
  2. *$\lim_{n \to \infty} \mathbb{E}(M(n) - Y)^2) = 0$ (so $M(n)$ converges to Y in L^2-norm),*
  3. *$M(n) = \mathbb{E}(Y|\mathcal{F}_n)$ for each $n \geq 0$.*

Proof The idea of the proof of the first claim is to show that the set on which the sequence $M(n, \omega)$ does not converge has probability zero:

$$P(\{\omega : \liminf_{n \to \infty} M(n, \omega) < \limsup_{n \to \infty} M(n, \omega)\}) = 0.$$

Consider the sets

$$A_{ab} = \{\omega : \liminf_{n \to \infty} M(n, \omega) \leq a < b \leq \limsup_{n \to \infty} M(n, \omega)\},$$

where $a < b$ are arbitrary rational numbers.

We will prove $P(A_{ab}) = 0$ and then we will achieve our goal by taking the union of all A_{ab}.

For fixed $a < b$, take $\varepsilon = (b - a)/6$ and fix any m. If $\omega \in A_{ab}$, then for some $i \geq m$, $M(i, \omega) < a + \varepsilon$, for some $j \geq m$, $M(j, \omega) > b - \varepsilon$, and the distance between $M(i, \omega)$ and $M(j, \omega)$ is at least 4ε. Therefore, either $|M(i, \omega) - M(m, \omega)| > 2\varepsilon$ or $|M(j, \omega) - M(m, \omega)| > 2\varepsilon$, hence

$$\sup_{k \geq m} |M(k, \omega) - M(m, \omega)| > \varepsilon.$$

Write

$$A_{ab}^m = \{\omega : \sup_{k \geq m}[M(k, \omega) - M(m, \omega)]^2 > \varepsilon^2\}$$

so that $A_{ab} \subset A_{ab}^m$ for all m, and the task will be accomplished if we show

$$P(A_{ab}^m) \to 0 \text{ as } m \to \infty.$$

If $\sup_{k \geq m}(M(k, \omega) - M(m, \omega))^2 > \varepsilon^2$, then for some n

$$\max_{m \leq k \leq m+n} [M(k, \omega) - M(m, \omega)]^2 \geq \varepsilon^2.$$

The sequence $(M(k) - M(m))_{k \geq m}$ is a martingale (Exercise 1.11), hence $([M(k) - M(m)]^2)_{k \geq m}$ is a submartingale (see the discussion preceding Definition 1.16). By Doob's maximal inequality

$$P(\max_{m \leq k \leq m+n} [M(k, \omega) - M(m, \omega)]^2 \geq \varepsilon^2) \leq \frac{1}{\varepsilon^2}\mathbb{E}[M(n) - M(m)]^2$$

so

$$P(A_{ab}^m) \leq \frac{1}{\varepsilon^2}\mathbb{E}[M(n) - M(m)]^2.$$

To tackle the right-hand side, we employ the martingale property

$$\mathbb{E}((M(n) - M(m))^2)$$
$$= \mathbb{E}(\mathbb{E}([M(n) - M(m)]^2|\mathcal{F}_m))$$
$$= \mathbb{E}(\mathbb{E}(M^2(n) - M^2(m)|\mathcal{F}_m)) \text{ (by Proposition 1.20)}$$
$$= \mathbb{E}(M^2(n) - M^2(m))$$
$$= \sum_{k=m+1}^{n} \mathbb{E}(M^2(k) - M^2(k-1))$$
$$= \sum_{k=m+1}^{n} \mathbb{E}([M(k) - M(k-1)]^2) \text{ (again by Proposition 1.20).}$$

By our assumption, the left-hand side is bounded by the constant c for all n, m, as $\mathbb{E}(M^2(n) - M^2(m)) \leq \mathbb{E}(M^2(n)) \leq c$, so the series $\sum_{k=1}^{\infty} \mathbb{E}([M(k) - M(k-1)]^2)$ is convergent and

$$\mathbb{E}[(M(n) - M(m))^2] \leq \sum_{k=m+1}^{\infty} \mathbb{E}([M(k) - M(k-1)]^2) \to 0 \text{ as } m \to \infty.$$

So we have shown that $P(A_{ab}) = 0$. The set $\Omega \setminus \bigcup_{a<b, a, b \in \mathbb{Q}} A_{ab}$ has probability one and on this set the sequence $M(n, \omega)$ converges. Denote the limit by $Y(\omega)$ and extend it to the whole of Ω by setting $Y(\omega) = 0$ for ω in A_{ab}, for every such pair (a, b) of rationals.

For the second assertion, apply Fatou's lemma to the sequence $([M(n) - M(m)]^2)_{n \geq m}$ so that

$$\mathbb{E}(\lim_{n \to \infty} \inf [M(n) - M(m)]^2) \leq \lim_{n \to \infty} \inf \mathbb{E}[M(n) - M(m))]^2 \to 0 \text{ as } m \to \infty$$

as observed above. The sequence $M(n)$ is Cauchy in $L^2(\Omega)$, hence it converges and its almost sure and L^2-limits must agree.

To prove 3 note that, applying the Jensen inequality to $X\mathbf{1}_A$ with $\phi(x) = x^2$, we obtain $(\int_A X dP)^2 \leq \int_A X^2 dP$ for any A in $\mathcal{F}$. Taking A in $\mathcal{F}_n$ for fixed n and $k > n$, we have $\int_A M(n) dP = \int_A M(k) dP$ by the martingale property, so with $X = |Y - M(k)|$ we obtain, for all $k > n$,

$$\left(\int_A |Y - M(n)| dP \right)^2 = \left(\int_A |Y - M(k)| dP \right)^2 \leq \int_A (Y - M(k))^2 dP.$$

By 2, the right-hand side is bounded above by $\mathbb{E}[(Y - M(k))^2]$, which goes to 0 as $k \to \infty$. Thus $\int_A Y dP = \int_A M(n) dP$ for each A in $\mathcal{F}_n$, that is $M(n) = \mathbb{E}(Y|\mathcal{F}_n)$. $\qquad\square$

Having established this convergence theorem we can extend our optional sampling theorem to general stopping times: Our earlier restriction to finite-valued stopping times is not essential for the definition of $M(\tau)$. We can simply assume that, in addition to the adapted sequence $M(n)$, we are given an $\mathcal{F}_\infty$-measurable random variable Y and a stopping time τ, then $M(\tau) = \sum_{k \geq 0} M(k)\mathbf{1}_{\{\tau=k\}} + Y\mathbf{1}_{\{\tau=\infty\}}$ and our claims for $M(\tau)$ remain valid. The role of Y is usually played by the limit of the sequence $M(n)$, as in the previous result.

Theorem 1.40 (Optional sampling)
Let M be an L^2-bounded martingale with $M(n) = \mathbb{E}(Y|\mathcal{F}_n)$ for each n, where Y is square-integrable. If τ, v are stopping times with $\tau \leq v$, then

$$\mathbb{E}(M(v)|\mathcal{F}_\tau) = M(\tau).$$

Proof By Theorems 1.35 and 1.39, we know that for any n

$$\mathbb{E}(Y|\mathcal{F}_n) = M(n) \text{ and } \mathbb{E}(M(n)|\mathcal{F}_{\tau \wedge n}) = M(\tau \wedge n).$$

The tower property of conditional expectations then gives, since $\mathcal{F}_{\tau \wedge n} \subset \mathcal{F}_n$, that

$$\mathbb{E}(Y|\mathcal{F}_{\tau \wedge n}) = \mathbb{E}(\mathbb{E}(Y|\mathcal{F}_n)|\mathcal{F}_{\tau \wedge n}) = \mathbb{E}(M(n)|\mathcal{F}_{\tau \wedge n}) = M(\tau \wedge n). \qquad (1.5)$$

When A is in $\mathcal{F}_\tau$, we know that for each $m \geq 0$, $A \cap \{\tau = m\} \in \mathcal{F}_m$. On $A \cap \{\tau \leq n\} \cap \{\tau \wedge n = m\}$, we see that $\tau \wedge n = \tau$, hence this set equals $A \cap \{\tau = m\}$. Therefore $B_n = A \cap \{\tau \leq n\} \in \mathcal{F}_{\tau \wedge n}$ and (1.5) yields

$$\int_{B_n} Y dP = \int_{B_n} M(\tau \wedge n) dP = \int_{B_n} M(\tau) dP.$$

Now suppose that $Y \geq 0$ (the general case follows from this by taking positive and negative parts separately). This means that $M(n) \geq 0$ for all n. Now the increasing sequence $(M(\tau)\mathbf{1}_{B_n})_{n \geq 0}$ converges almost surely to $M(\tau)\mathbf{1}_{A \cap \{\tau < \infty\}}$, so we can apply the monotone convergence theorem to conclude that

$$\int_{A \cap \{\tau < \infty\}} Y dP = \int_{A \cap \{\tau < \infty\}} M(\tau) dP.$$

On $\{\tau = \infty\}$ we have $M(\tau) = Y$ and $A \in \mathcal{F}_\tau$ was arbitrary, so we have shown that $\mathbb{E}(Y|\mathcal{F}_\tau) = M(\tau)$. The same argument applies with v, and since $\mathcal{F}_\tau \subset \mathcal{F}_v$ the tower property gives

$$M(\tau) = \mathbb{E}(Y|\mathcal{F}_\tau) = \mathbb{E}(\mathbb{E}(Y|\mathcal{F}_v)|\mathcal{F}_\tau) = \mathbb{E}(M(v)|\mathcal{F}_\tau).$$

$\square$

Corollary 1.41
If M is L^2-bounded, and τ is a stopping time, then $M(\tau)$ is square-integrable and $\mathbb{E}(M(\tau)) = \mathbb{E}(M(0))$.

1.6   Markov processes

Look at a snapshot of a car taken at time n and think of a model for its positions at $n + 1$. We say 'model' since we assume random behaviour of the driver, which is reasonable, owing to our lack of knowledge about his intentions. Suppose that the length of the time step is quite short, a second, say. Clearly, the position alone does not enable us to make any sensible prediction: the car may be stationary or it may be moving fast. If we also know its position at the previous instant $n - 1$, we have a better chance (as would the police if they wanted to prove a speeding offence). Information about the change of position between times $n - 1$ and n now enables us to estimate velocity, but this may be still too rough if the driver is accelerating ferociously or braking desperately. The key factor to consider is inertia, as is typical for the motion of physical objects.

Asset prices are mental constructs rather than physical objects. We may ask whether knowledge of a price at time n allows us to build a model of possible prices at the next time. The answer depends on the model we assume, but is definitely positive in binomial trees. Here, in order to analyse the prices at time $n + 1$, their history (the prices at time $n - 1$ or earlier) is irrelevant, and no inertia is present. However, there is a quite popular belief that, in real markets, the history is relevant if we wish to model future market behaviour, and inevitably we land in trouble – the model then has to become more complex.

Price history does often play a role in discussing the prices of derivatives: note that in the binomial model, the call option price depends only on the current (final) stock price, whereas Asian option pricing involves the price history of the stock (see [DMFM]).

The Markov property

The upshot of the above discussion is that irrelevance of past data is related to model simplicity. Let us begin with a simple example.

Example 1.42
Consider a symmetric random walk, where by definition $Z(n + 1) = Z(n) + L(n + 1)$ does not depend on $Z(k)$, with $k < n$. Let $\mathcal{F}_n^Z$ be the filtration generated by Z (being the same as $\mathcal{F}_n^L$) and as we know $\mathbb{E}(Z(n + 1)|\mathcal{F}_n) = Z(n)$. On the other hand, consider the σ-field $\mathcal{F}_{Z(n)}$ generated by just $Z(n)$ and by the same token $\mathbb{E}(Z(n + 1)|\mathcal{F}_{Z(n)}) = Z(n)$, so

$$\mathbb{E}(Z(n + 1)|\mathcal{F}_n) = \mathbb{E}(Z(n + 1)|\mathcal{F}_{Z(n)}).$$

We can do better than that: consider a bounded Borel function f and write $f(Z(n + 1)) = f(Z(n) + L(n + 1)) = F(Z(n), L(n + 1))$ where $F(x, y) = f(x + y)$. Then since $Z(n)$ is $\mathcal{F}_n$-measurable and $L(n + 1)$ is independent of $\mathcal{F}_n$,

$$\mathbb{E}(f(Z(n + 1))|\mathcal{F}_n) = \mathbb{E}(F(Z(n), L(n + 1))|\mathcal{F}_n) = G(Z(n))$$

where $G(x) = \mathbb{E}(F(x, L(n + 1)))$ (see a general fact recalled for convenience below). Similarly, $\mathbb{E}(f(Z(n+1))|\mathcal{F}_{Z(n)}) = \mathbb{E}(F(Z(n), L(n+1))|\mathcal{F}_{Z(n)}) = G(Z(n))$ so

$$\mathbb{E}(f(Z(n + 1))|\mathcal{F}_n) = \mathbb{E}(f(Z(n + 1))|\mathcal{F}_{Z(n)}).$$

Lemma 1.43
Let $\mathcal{G}$ be a σ-field, $\mathcal{G} \subset \mathcal{F}$. If X is $\mathcal{G}$-measurable, Y is independent of $\mathcal{G}$,

then for any Borel bounded $F : \mathbb{R} \times \mathbb{R} \to \mathbb{R}$

$$\mathbb{E}(F(X, Y)|\mathcal{G}) = G(X),$$

where $G(x) = \mathbb{E}(F(x, Y))$.

Proof See [PF].   □

This example gives a motivation for the next definition.

Definition 1.44
We say that a stochastic process $(X(n))_{n \geq 0}$ has the **Markov property** if for all Borel bounded functions $f : \mathbb{R} \to \mathbb{R}$

$$\mathbb{E}(f(X(n + 1))|\mathcal{F}_n^X) = \mathbb{E}(f(X(n + 1))|\mathcal{F}_{X(n)}), \qquad (1.6)$$

where $\mathcal{F}_n^X = \sigma(X(0), X(1), \ldots, X(n))$ and $\mathcal{F}_{X(n)} = \sigma(X(n))$. We then say that X is a **Markov process**.

Proposition 1.45
The Markov property is equivalent to the following condition: (1.6) *holds with $f = \mathbf{1}_B$ for all Borel sets B.*

Proof One direction is obvious since $\mathbf{1}_B$ is a bounded measurable function. For the reverse implication, we are given (1.6) for indicators. This can be extended by linearity to simple functions and, since any bounded measurable f can be approximated pointwise by step functions, the dominated convergence theorem completes the argument.   □

Example 1.46
Consider a symmetric random walk with $Z(0) = 0$ for simplicity. If $Z(n) = x$, then either $Z(n + 1) = x + 1$ or $Z(n + 1) = x - 1$, each with probability $\frac{1}{2}$ so the probabilities

$$P(Z(n + 1) \in B|Z(n) = x)$$

are zero if $x + 1 \notin B$ and $x - 1 \notin B$, they are equal $\frac{1}{2}$ if precisely one of $x + 1$, $x - 1$ is in B and one if both belong there. Clearly, the above expression is a probability measure as a function of B (of the form $\frac{1}{2}\delta_{x+1} + \frac{1}{2}\delta_{x-1}$ where δ_a is the Dirac measure concentrated at a, see [PF]).

Definition 1.47

We call a family of probability measures $\{\mu_n(x, B)\}_{x \in \mathbb{R}, n \geq 0}$, defined on Borel sets, measurable as functions of x for each B, and such that

$$P(X(n + 1) \in B | \mathcal{F}_{X(n)}) = \mu_n(X(n), B)$$

transition probabilities of Markov process $(X(n))_{n \geq 0}$. We say that the Markov process is **homogeneous** if μ_n does not depend on n; so there is a single transition probability μ such that

$$\mathbb{E}(\mathbf{1}_B(X(n + 1)) | \mathcal{F}_{X(n)}) = \mu(X(n), B)$$

for every $n \geq 0$ and $B \in \mathcal{B}$.

Exercise 1.26 Find the transition probabilities for the binomial tree. Is it homogeneous?

Exercise 1.27 Show that a symmetric random walk is homogeneous.

Exercise 1.28 Let $(Y(n))_{n \geq 0}$, be a sequence of independent integrable random variables on $(\Omega, \mathcal{F}, P)$. Show that the sequence $Z(n) = \sum_{i=0}^{n} Y(i)$ is a Markov process and calculate the transition probabilities dependent on n. Find a condition for Z to be homogeneous.

Let $X(n)$ be a homogenous Markov process with the transition probability μ. We find a relation between consecutive distributions:

$$\begin{aligned}
P_{X(n+1)}(B) &= \mathbb{E}(\mathbf{1}_B(X(n + 1))) \\
&= \mathbb{E}(\mathbb{E}(\mathbf{1}_B(X(n + 1)|\sigma(X(n))))) \quad \text{(tower property)} \\
&= \mathbb{E}(\mu(X(n), B)) \quad \text{(Markov property)} \\
&= \int_{\mathbb{R}} \mu(x, B) P_{X(n)}(dx)
\end{aligned}$$

for all $n \geq 0$, $B \in \mathcal{B}$, where $P_{X(n)}$ is the distribution of $X(n)$. Hence the initial distribution $P_{X(0)}$ and the transition probability μ recursively determine the whole sequence of distributions $(P_{X(n)})_{n \geq 0}$.

Markov chains

Markov processes are composed of random variables taking values in the set of real numbers. We now focus attention on the case when the variables $X(n)$ take values in a finite set.

A well-known financial example may be based on credit ratings. Various agencies evaluate companies and (increasingly) whole countries from the point of ability to fulfil their financial obligations. Let the rating of a company n be denoted by $X(n)$, where we have (as is conventional in practice)

$$X(n) \in \{AAA, AA, A, BBB, BB, B, CCC, CC, C, D\}$$

with AAA the highest, and D the lowest rating (D denotes the state of bankruptcy). For simplicity, we many rename the ratings so that $X(n) \in \{9, 8, \ldots, 1, 0\}$ – this set being an example of the **set of states** $\mathbb{S}$, the common range of all random variables $X(n)$. We assume that $X(n) \in \mathbb{S} = \{0, 1, \ldots, N\}$, and such a Markov process is called a **Markov chain**. From the point of view of the credit risk applications, we may be vitally interested in finding the probabilities $P(X(n + 1) = j | X(n) = i)$ of a change of the rating, in particular with $j = 0$, the probability of bankruptcy.

For random variables with finitely many values, a finite Ω is sufficient and partitions may be used instead of σ-fields. So the Markov property says

$$\mathbb{E}(f(X(n + 1)) | \mathcal{P}_n^X) = \mathbb{E}(f(X(n + 1)) | \mathcal{P}_{X(n)})$$

where $\mathcal{P}_n^X$ is the family of atoms of $\mathcal{F}_n^X$, the maximal sets on which all $X(0), \ldots, X(n)$ are constant, and similarly $\mathcal{P}_{X(n)}$ corresponds to $\mathcal{F}_{X(n)}$.

The sets in the partitions have the form

$$A_{s_0, s_1, \ldots, s_n} = \{\omega : X(0, \omega) = s_0, X(1, \omega) = s_1, \ldots, X(n, \omega) = s_n\} \in \mathcal{P}_n^X,$$
$$A_{s_n} = \{\omega : X(n) = s_n\} \in \mathcal{P}_{X(n)},$$

where $s_i \in \mathbb{S}$. Consider $f = \mathbf{1}_{\{k\}}$ with $k \in \mathbb{S}$. For $\omega \in A_{s_0, s_1, \ldots, s_n}$

$$\mathbb{E}(f(X(n + 1)) | \mathcal{P}_n^X) = \mathbb{E}(f(X(n + 1)) | A_{s_0, s_1, \ldots, s_n})$$
$$= P(X(n + 1) = k | A_{s_0, s_1, \ldots, s_n}),$$

and for $\omega \in A_{s_n}$

$$\mathbb{E}(f(X(n + 1)) | \mathcal{P}_{X(n)}) = \mathbb{E}(X(n + 1)) | A_{s_n})$$
$$= P(X(n + 1) = k | A_{s_n})$$

provided that the conditions have positive probabilities (which we always assume when conditional probabilities appear). Hence the Markov property for chains reads

$$P(X(n+1) = s_{n+1}|A_{s_0,s_1,\ldots,s_n}) = P(X(n+1) = s_{n+1}|A_{s_n}),$$

or, in other words,

$$P(X(n+1) = s_{n+1}|X(0) = s_0,\ldots,X(n) = s_n) = P(X(n+1) = s_{n+1}|X(n) = s_n).$$

Exercise 1.29 Show that a Markov chain is homogeneous if and only if for every pair $i, j \in \mathbb{S}$

$$P(X(n+1) = j|X(n) = i) = P(X(1) = j|X(0) = i) = p_{ij} \qquad (1.7)$$

for every $n \geq 0$.

A probability P on $\mathbb{S}$ is a row vector $P = (p_0, p_1, \ldots, p_N)$ of real numbers such that $0 \leq p_k \leq 1$ and $\sum_k p_k = 1$.

Assume that $(X(n))_{n \geq 0}$ is a homogeneous Markov chain and let $P(n)$ be the distribution of $X(n)$ for $n \geq 0$, so that $P(n) = (p_k(n))$, $p_k(n) = P(X(n) = k)$ for $k \in \mathbb{S}$. Then from the law of total probability we have

$$
\begin{aligned}
p_j(n+1) &= P(X(n+1) = j) \\
&= \sum_{i \in \mathbb{S}} P(X(n) = i)P(X(n+1) = j|X(n) = i) \\
&= \sum_{i \in \mathbb{S}} p_i(n)p_{ij}.
\end{aligned}
$$

This can be written in the form

$$P(n+1) = P(n)\mathbf{P} \quad \text{for all } n, \qquad (1.8)$$

where $\mathbf{P} = [p_{ij}]$ is called the **transition matrix**. Using (1.8) repeatedly, we can express the distribution of each $X(n)$ by a simple formula involving the initial distribution and the transition matrix:

$$P(n) = P(0)\mathbf{P}^n.$$

Write $p_{ij}(k) = P(X(k) = j|X(0) = i)$ for the transition probability of moving from state i to j in k steps.

Exercise 1.30 Prove that the transition probabilities of a homogeneous Markov chain satisfy the so-called **Chapman–Kolmogorov equation**

$$p_{ij}(k + l) = \sum_{r \in S} p_{ir}(k) p_{rj}(l).$$

This means that the transition probability of moving from state i to state j in $k + l$ steps is the same as the sum, over all states r, of moving from i to r in k steps and then from r to j in a further l steps.

1.7 Proofs

Lemma 1.38
Suppose we have non-negative random variables X, Y such that Y is in $L^2(\Omega)$ and for all $x > 0$,

$$xP(X \geq x) \leq \int_{\{X \geq x\}} Y dP.$$

Then X is in $L^2(\Omega)$ and

$$\mathbb{E}(X^2) \leq 4\mathbb{E}(Y^2).$$

Proof To prove the lemma, note first that we may take X to be bounded. For if the result holds in that case, we can apply it to $X_n = \min(X, n)$ to conclude that $\mathbb{E}(X_n^2) \leq 4\mathbb{E}(Y^2)$ for each n, and since X_n^2 increases to X^2 almost surely the monotone convergence theorem shows that $\mathbb{E}(X^2) \leq 4\mathbb{E}(Y^2)$. This proves the first assertion: we may take $X \in L^2(\Omega)$.

Now observe that $\frac{1}{2}z^2 = \int_0^z x dx = \int_{\{z \geq x\}} x dx$, so with $z = X(\omega)$ we integrate this over Ω to find

$$\mathbb{E}(X^2) = 2 \int_\Omega \frac{1}{2} X^2(\omega) dP(\omega)$$

$$= 2 \int_\Omega \left(\int_0^\infty \mathbf{1}_{\{X(\omega) \geq x\}} x dx \right) dP(\omega)$$

$$= 2 \int_0^\infty \left(x \int_\Omega \mathbf{1}_{\{X(\omega) \geq x\}} dP(\omega) \right) dx \text{ (by Fubini)}$$

$$= 2 \int_0^\infty xP(X \geq x) dx.$$

We can now use our hypothesis so that

$$\mathbb{E}(X^2) \le 2 \int_0^\infty \left(\int_{\{X(\omega) \ge x\}} Y(\omega) dP(\omega) \right) dx$$

$$= 2 \int_\Omega Y(\omega) \left(\int_0^{X(\omega)} dx \right) dP(\omega)$$

$$= 2\mathbb{E}(YX)$$

$$\le 2(\mathbb{E}(Y^2))^{\frac{1}{2}} (\mathbb{E}(X^2))^{\frac{1}{2}} \text{ (by the Schwarz inequality).}$$

Hence $\mathbb{E}(X^2)^{\frac{1}{2}} \le 2\mathbb{E}(Y^2)^{\frac{1}{2}}$, which proves the lemma for $X \ne 0$, since then $\mathbb{E}(X^2) > 0$. If X is identically zero, the result is obvious. □

2

Wiener process

2.1 Scaled random walk

As is the case throughout this series, the motivation for the mathematical results and techniques we discuss comes from their application to financial markets. It may seem reasonable to argue that discrete-time market models suffice for such applications, since every transaction takes a finite length of time, and this is what we did in [DMFM]. In practice, however, the problems with this approach multiply rapidly once one recognises the computational hazards involved in seeking to model a stock whose price may be adjusted every few minutes over a period of (say) three months. Keeping track of all the possible scenarios rapidly becomes infeasible and we seek recourse to approximating such large-scale finite discrete models by continuous-time idealisations which may provide qualitative and quantitative insights into the stochastic behaviour being observed.

We therefore turn to a study of continuous-time stochastic processes. Thus we shall allow an interval of the form $[0, T]$ as our time set and study the evolution of random variables $X(t)$, where $t \in [0, T]$. A family of random variables $(X(t))_{t \in [0,T]}$ is called a (continuous-time) stochastic process. The study of such processes has many applications beyond finance, of course, and it is customary to use the unbounded interval $[0, \infty)$ as the time set. For finance applications, it usually suffices to restrict attention to a finite time interval, because, as John Maynard Keynes famously observed: 'In the long run we are all dead.' This restriction has a number of advantages which we shall exploit in due course. For the development of basic definitions and our first results, however, we shall follow the convention that the time sets we consider include unbounded intervals

The most important example we study is the Wiener process, which is often called Brownian motion in the literature. In 1827, the botanist Robert Brown noticed that minute particles suspended in a liquid moved in highly irregular ways. The physics of this phenomenon was explained satisfactorily only 80 years later, independently by Einstein and Smoluchowski: in suspensions a small solid particle is hit randomly by molecules of liquid from different directions, and unless the crashes are perfectly balanced, they will cause chaotic migration of the particle through the suspension. It took a further 20 years before Wiener presented a fully rigorous mathematical model describing this physical phenomenon. We shall use the physical model purely for illustrative purposes, hence we prefer to use the term **Wiener process** for the key stochastic process we shall construct and analyse in this chapter. It forms the foundation for the calculus developed in the remainder of this volume.

In 1900, in his remarkable Ph.D. thesis 'Theorié de la Speculation', L. Bachelier anticipated both Einstein and Wiener by employing a (not quite rigorous) version of Brownian motion to describe the probabilistic dynamics of a model of stock prices, hoping to develop a sound basis for option pricing! His work was rediscovered some 60 years later by Samuelson, and this led indirectly to the vindication of his expectations in the Black–Scholes option pricing model, published in 1973.

We begin with recalling the definition of symmetric random walk, highlighting some of its key features. For a sequence of independent random variables $L(k) = \pm 1$, where each value is taken with probability $\frac{1}{2}$, we write

$$Z(0) = 0, \quad Z(n) = \sum_{k=1}^{n} L(k).$$

Remark 2.1

In the previous chapter, we defined the sequence $L(k)$ on the probability space $\Omega = [0, 1]$ with Lebesgue measure. Another possibility is to take $\Omega = \{-1, 1\}^{\mathbb{N}}$, representing infinite sequences of results of coin tossing, $\omega : \mathbb{N} \to \{-1, 1\}$. This allows a particularly simple definition of the random variables: at outcome $\omega \in \Omega$ the value of the kth random variable $L(k)$ is $L(k, \omega) = \omega(k)$; however, a direct construction of a suitable σ-field and probability measure is a bit tricky.

The sequence $(Z(n)_{n \geq 0}$ has the following properties:

(i) The increments $Z(k) - Z(j), Z(n) - Z(m)$ are independent ($0 \leq j < k \leq m < n$) since $Z(k) - Z(j) = \sum_{j+1}^{k} L(i)$, $Z(n) - Z(m) = \sum_{m+1}^{n} L(i)$ and the vectors $(L(j+1), \ldots, L(k))$ and $(L(m+1), \ldots, L(n))$ are independent. An arbitrary number of increments of Z can be dealt with similarly.

(ii) $\mathbb{E}(Z(n)) = 0$ since $\mathbb{E}(L(k)) = 0$, by the linearity of expectation.

(iii) $Z(n)$ is a martingale with respect to its natural filtration – see Definition 1.5. This follows from the previous properties and Proposition 1.12.

(iv) $\text{Var}(Z(n) - Z(m)) = \text{Var}(\sum_{k=m+1}^{n} L(k)) = n - m, 0 \leq m \leq n$ since the variance of the sum of independent random variables is the sum of the variances.

We cast the sequence $Z(n)$ into a continuous-time framework, based on the time set $[0, \infty)$, by interpreting the number n of the step as the time instant $t = nh$ for some fixed length $h > 0$, here taken as $h = 1$ in the first instance. We now build a modification, reducing the length of the time step and also reducing the size of the change of position in each step, but in a specific way, using the square root of the time step.

For simplicity, take $h = \frac{1}{N}$ for some integer N and write

$$L_h(k) = \sqrt{h}L(k) = \pm\sqrt{h}$$

denoting the resulting **scaled random walk** by

$$Z_h(t) = \begin{cases} \sum_{k=1}^{n} L_h(k) \text{ for } t = nh, \\ \text{linear for } t \in (nk, (n+1)h) \end{cases}$$

(by 'linear' we mean linear interpolation with segments linking consecutive points so that the resulting function is continuous). Clearly,

$$Z_h(nh) = \sqrt{h}Z(n),$$

and note that for small h, the change of the value of the walk is of much larger magnitude than the time step as $\sqrt{h}$ is much larger than h.

The scaled random walk inherits the following properties from Z:

(i) The increments $Z_h(s) - Z_h(r)$, $Z_h(u) - Z_h(t)$, where $r < s \leq t < u$ are all of the form nh, are independent. This is obvious since the scaled random walk is nothing but Z multiplied by a number. Independence of many increments also follows immediately.

(ii) $\mathbb{E}(Z_h(t)) = 0$, since $\mathbb{E}(Z(n))) = 0$ so $\mathbb{E}(Z_h(nh)) = 0$ and for intermediate instants the values are linear combinations of the values at integer multiplies of h.

(iii) The scaled random walk Z_h is a martingale (same argument as above).

(iv) $\text{Var}(Z_h(nh) - Z_h(mh)) = h\text{Var}(Z(n) - Z(m)) = h(n-m)$ (since $\text{Var}(aX) = a^2\text{Var}(X)$).

We define the **variation** of the sequence $(Z_h(kh, \omega))_{k \geq 1}$ in the interval $[s, t]$ with $s = mh$, $t = nh$, by

$$V_{[s,t]}(Z_h, \omega) = \sum_{k=m}^{n-1} |Z_h((k + 1)h, \omega) - Z_h(kh, \omega)|.$$

Observe that

$$\sum_{k=m}^{n-1} |Z_h((k + 1)h, \omega) - Z_h(kh, \omega)| = \sqrt{h}(n - m) = \frac{N}{\sqrt{N}}(t - s) = \sqrt{N}(t - s)$$

so $V_{[s,t]}(Z_h, \omega)$ does not depend on ω and

$$V_{[s,t]}(Z_h) \to \infty \quad \text{as } h \to 0.$$

The **quadratic variation** of $(Z_h(kh, \omega))_{k \geq 1}$ in $[s, t]$ is defined similarly by

$$V^2_{[s,t]}(Z_h, \omega) = \sum_{k=m}^{n-1} (Z_h((k + 1)h, \omega) - Z_h(kh, \omega))^2.$$

Since

$$\sum_{k=m}^{n-1} (Z_h((k + 1)h, \omega) - Z_h(kh, \omega))^2 = h \sum_{i=m}^{n-1} L_h^2(k, \omega) = \frac{n - m}{N} = t - s,$$

we again have a deterministic quantity, also independent of $h = \frac{1}{N}$, this time finite:

$$V^2_{[s,t]}(Z_h) = t - s.$$

If $s = 0$, the quadratic variation $V^2_{[0,t]}(Z_h)$ is often denoted by $[Z_h, Z_h](t)$.

As we know from Section 1.3, the sequence $(Z^2_h(nh))_{n \geq 1}$ is not a martingale but a submartingale. The fundamental property of the quadratic variation is that it acts as the compensator:

Proposition 2.2
The sequence $(Z^2_h(nh) - nh)_{n \geq 0}$ is a martingale.

Proof By Theorem 1.19 on the Doob decomposition, the compensator $A = (A(n))_{n \geq 0}$ is given inductively by

$$A(n) = A(n-1) + \mathbb{E}(Z^2_h(nh) - Z^2_h((n-1)h)|\mathcal{F}_{n-1})$$
$$= A(n-1) + \mathbb{E}((Z_h(nh) - Z_h((n-1)h))^2|\mathcal{F}_{n-1})$$
$$\text{(by Proposition 1.20)}$$
$$= A(n-1) + h$$

by the definition of the scaled random walk. Together with $A(0) = 0$, the above relation proves $A(n) = nh$. □

2.2   Definition of the Wiener process

A justification of the definition of the Wiener process is based on considering a limit of scaled random walks as $h \to 0$. Rigorous discussion of such a limit is not our goal and we will only indicate some rough ideas in this direction.

Consider scaled random walk at time $t = 1$, that is

$$Z_h(1) = \frac{1}{\sqrt{N}} \sum_{k=1}^{N} L(n), \quad h = \frac{1}{N}.$$

Exercise 2.1 Show that scalings other than by the square root lead nowhere by proving that $X(n) = h^\alpha L(n)$, $\alpha \in (0, \frac{1}{2})$, implies $\sum_{n=1}^{N} X(n) \to 0$ in L^2, while for $\alpha > \frac{1}{2}$ this sequence goes to infinity in this space.

We can apply the following fundamental result from probability theory, the Central Limit Theorem, which we recall in a general version (a proof can be found in [PF]).

Theorem 2.3
Let $X(n)$ be independent random variables, identically distributed with finite expectations and variances, let $Y(N) = \sum_{n=1}^{N} X(n)$, and write

$$T_N = \frac{Y(N) - \mathbb{E}(Y(N))}{\sqrt{\mathrm{Var}(Y(N))}}.$$

Then

$$\lim_{N \to \infty} P(a < T_N < b) = \frac{1}{\sqrt{2\pi}} \int_a^b e^{-\frac{1}{2}x^2} dx.$$

Take $X(n) = L(n)$, so that $T_N = Z_h(1)$ since $h = 1/N$. As $h \to 0$ we have $N \to \infty$, hence the random variables $Z_h(1)$ converge to a random variable with standard normal distribution. This motivates the second condition of the following definition, while the third is directly inherited from random walks.

Definition 2.4
A **Wiener process** (Brownian motion) is a mapping $W : [0, \infty) \times \Omega \to \mathbb{R}$ for some probability space $(\Omega, \mathcal{F}, P)$, measurable with respect to the product σ-field $\mathcal{B}([0, \infty)) \times \mathcal{F} = \sigma\{B \times A : B \in \mathcal{B}([0, \infty)), A \in \mathcal{F}\}$ (here $\mathcal{B}([0, \infty))$, is the σ-field of Borel subsets of $[0, \infty))$ and such that:
1. $W(0) = 0$, a.s. (P),
2. for $0 \le s < t < \infty$, $W(t) - W(s)$ has normal distribution with mean zero and standard deviation $\sqrt{t - s}$,
3. for all m and all $0 \le t_1 \le t_2 \le \cdots \le t_m$, the increments $W(t_{n+1}) - W(t_n)$, $n = 0, 1, ..., m - 1$, are independent,
4. for almost all $\omega \in \Omega$ the paths, that is the functions $t \mapsto W(t, \omega)$, are continuous.

We are faced with the problem whether such a process actually exists.

2.3 A construction of the Wiener process

Our first task is the choice of probability space. We shall take $\Omega = [0, 1]^{\mathbb{N}}$. The probability measure on this space was given in [PF]. The distribution of each random variable $\omega(n)$, $n \in \mathbb{N}$, is uniform over $[0, 1]$ and the $\omega(n)$ are independent. On this space we define a sequence G_n of independent random variables with standard normal distribution, for instance writing $G_n(\omega) = N^{-1}(\omega(n))$.

Remark 2.5

The probability on $[0, 1]^{\mathbb{N}}$ is defined as the distribution of a random sequence whose elements were all defined on $[0, 1]$. The upshot of this is that the version of the Wiener process W we are able to construct by means of these G_n can be regarded as living on $[0, 1]$ as the underlying sample space, which is remarkable in itself, given the complexity of the process W.

The Wiener process is a function of two variables, t and ω. The random variables G_n will take care of ω and to describe the dependence on t we define a sequence of real-valued functions $\psi_n(t)$ defined for $t \in [0, 1]$. The first one is the building block for the others

$$\psi_1(t) = \begin{cases} 2t & \text{for } 0 \le t < \tfrac{1}{2}, \\ 2 - 2t & \text{for } \tfrac{1}{2} \le t < 1, \\ 0 & \text{otherwise,} \end{cases}$$

and its graph is shown Figure 2.1.

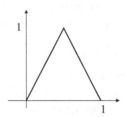

Figure 2.1

Any $n > 1$ can be written in the form $n = 2^j + k$ where $j > 0, 0 \le k < 2^j$ and we put

$$\psi_n(t) = \psi_1(2^j t - k).$$

These functions are best analysed from the point of view of j. For $j = 1$, $k = 0, 1$ so $n = 2, 3$ and the graphs of ψ_2, ψ_3 are shown in Figure 2.2.

For $j = 2$, k runs from 0 to 3 so $n = 4, 5, 6, 7$ with the graphs shown in Figure 2.3.

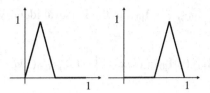

Figure 2.2

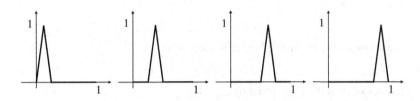

Figure 2.3

The pattern is maintained for the remaining n with the 'travelling' wave as k increases for fixed j, then with next j the new generation of waves is created with narrower base and steeper slope.

Additionally, we define

$$\psi_0(t) = \begin{cases} t & \text{for } 0 \le t < 1, \\ 0 & \text{otherwise.} \end{cases}$$

We will need some facts from basic Hilbert space theory (see [PF]). We define the sequence of **Haar functions** $H_n = a_n\psi_n'$: the function ψ_n is differentiable except at most at three points at which H_n has to be defined additionally, but the values assigned are irrelevant. It is easy to show that $(H_n)_{n\ge0}$ form an orthonormal basis of the space $L^2([0, 1])$, where we denote the inner product by $\langle f, g \rangle = \int_0^1 f(x)g(x)dx$. For $f, g \in L^2([0, 1])$, we have the Parseval identity

$$\langle f, g \rangle = \sum_{n=0}^{\infty} \langle f, H_n \rangle \langle g, H_n \rangle.$$

Lemma 2.6

Let $a_0 = 1$, $a_n = 2^{-(\frac{j}{2}+1)}$ for $n = 2^j + k$, $k = 0, 1, \ldots, 2^j - 1$. Then

$$\sum_{n=0}^{\infty} a_n^2 \psi_n(t)\psi_n(s) = \min\{t, s\}.$$

Proof Taking $f = \mathbf{1}_{[0,t)}$, $g = \mathbf{1}_{[0,s)}$ in the Parseval identity yields the result we seek: on the left

$$\langle f, g \rangle = \int_0^1 \mathbf{1}_{[0,t)}(x)\mathbf{1}_{[0,s)}(x)dx = \int_0^1 \mathbf{1}_{[0,t)\cap[0,s]}(x)dx = \min\{s,t\},$$

and on the right

$$\sum_{n=0}^{\infty} \int_0^t H_n(x)dx \int_0^s H_n(x)dx = \sum_{n=0}^{\infty} a_n^2 \psi_n(t)\psi_n(s).$$

$\square$

We come to the main result of this section.

Theorem 2.7
The process $(W(t))_{t\in[0,1]}$ *defined by*

$$W(t,\omega) = \sum_{n=0}^{\infty} a_n \psi_n(t) G_n(\omega)$$

is a Wiener process.

Proof See page 71. $\square$

Given the construction for $t \in [0,1]$ we can extend the process to longer intervals. For the extension to $t \in [0,2]$, let W_1, W_2 be independent Wiener processes in $[0,1]$ (note that they are zero outside the unit interval). These two processes can be defined on the same probability space $\Omega = [0,1]^{\mathbb{N}}$ since W_1 can be built using the odd indices of $\omega \in \Omega$, and W_2 using the even indices. Alternatively, we could take the product of two spaces following a general scheme of building independent random variables.

Put

$$W(t) = \begin{cases} W_1(t) \text{ for } t \in [0,1), \\ W_1(1) + W_2(t-1) \text{ for } t \in [1,2). \end{cases}$$

It is clear from the construction that the resulting process is continuous, the only tricky point being at $t = 1$. We have to show that the increments of W are independent and normally distributed. If we consider any sequence of times, $t_1 < t_2 < \cdots < t_n$ and the only problem is with the increment linking the intervals. So let $s \in [0,1)$, $t \in [1,2)$ and by definition of W, bearing in mind that $W_2(0) = 0$,

$$W(t) - W(s) = W_2(t-1) + W_1(1) - W_1(s)$$
$$= W_2(t-1) - W_2(0) + W_1(1) - W_1(s).$$

The random variables $W_2(t - 1) - W_2(0)$, $W_1(1) - W_1(s)$ are independent and have normal distribution, so the sum has normal distribution, as is well known.

The variance of the sum is the sum of variances so $\text{Var}(W(t) - W(s)) = t - s$ as needed. The extension to longer intervals is routine.

Remark 2.8

The choice of probability space is relevant when we wish to perform some simulation of the process. The random variables G_n can be considerd on $\Omega = [0, 1]$, but from the point of view of numerical simulations the relevance of this is somewhat restricted, however. Indeed, while the random selection of a number in $[0, 1]$ is very easy and such a number determines the whole path of the Wiener process, in practice we can obtain such a number only with limited accuracy, depending on the limitations of the computer. It is more feasible to draw a sequence of such numbers: each of these would determine the value of G_n in principle, and improved accuracy would result from many repetitions of the draw. So the main limitation here will be the running time of the programme, and with a bit of patience great accuracy is possible. Therefore it is better to regard G_n as defined on $\Omega = [0, 1]^{\mathbb{N}}$, approximated in practical experiments by $[0, 1]^N$ for large N. Figure 2.4 shows a graph of the function $t \mapsto \sum_{n=0}^{150} a_n \psi_n(t) N^{-1}(\omega(n))$, where $\omega(n) \in [0, 1]$ with uniform distribution.

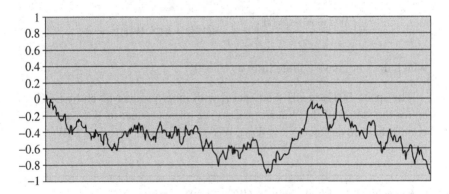

Figure 2.4

Remark 2.9

Other choices of the basis are possible. For instance,

$$\psi_n(t) = \sqrt{2} \sin\left(\left(n - \frac{1}{2}\right)\pi t\right), \quad a_n = 1 / \left(k - \frac{1}{2}\right)\pi$$

also generate a Wiener process (with a more advanced proof) and a remarkable feature is that the components here are smooth in t.

2.4   Elementary properties

We discuss various properties that follow directly from the definition, so are independent of any particular construction.

We begin with some simple mean-square properties. Since the random variables $W(t)$ have finite variances, the function $t \mapsto W(t)$ is a mapping from $[0, \infty)$ to $L^2(\Omega)$, the space of square-integrable random variables.

Proposition 2.10
As a function $W : [0, \infty) \to L^2(\Omega)$, the Wiener process is continuous and nowhere differentiable.

Proof   For any $t > 0$, we have

$$\|W(t + h) - W(t)\|^2_{L^2(\Omega)} = \mathbb{E}(W(t + h) - W(t))^2 = h \to 0$$

as $h \to 0$, with right continuity at $t = 0$.

For differentiability, consider the $L^2(\Omega)$-norm of the ratio

$$\mathbb{E}\left(\frac{W(t + h) - W(t)}{h}\right)^2 = \frac{1}{h^2}\mathbb{E}(W(t + h) - W(t))^2 = \frac{1}{h}$$

which does not have a finite limit as $h \to 0$.   □

The space $L^2(\Omega)$ is a Hilbert space, with inner product given by $\mathbb{E}(XY)$, so for the values of the Wiener process the inner product of $W(s)$ and $W(t)$ equals their covariance: $\text{Cov}(W(s), W(t)) = \mathbb{E}(W(s)W(t))$ since $\mathbb{E}(W(t)) = 0$.

Exercise 2.2   Show that $\text{Cov}(W(s), W(t)) = \min(s, t)$.

Exercise 2.3   Consider $B(t) = W(t) - tW(1)$ for $t \in [0, 1]$ (this process is called the Brownian bridge, since $B(0) = B(1) = 0$). Compute $\text{Cov}(B(s), B(t))$.

The Wiener process is not unique as it is defined by conditions concerned with distributions (apart from path-continuity). The underlying probability space is not specified, and there are several choices. So we could talk about the class of Wiener processes and it is interesting to see that this class is closed with respect to certain operations. The simplest of these is the mirror reflection of the paths: $X(t) = -W(t)$: intuitively, the reflected process is Wiener as well. Changing the time scale, $Y(t) = \frac{1}{c}W(c^2 t)$ again gives a Wiener process, which is related to fractal properties: the process considered in a short time interval is rich enough to observe its behaviour over a longer one.

Exercise 2.4 Show directly from the definition that if W is a Wiener process, then so are the processes given by $-W(t)$ and $\frac{1}{c}W(c^2 t)$ for any $c > 0$.

In the $L^2(\Omega)$ spirit, a convenient alternative characterisation of the Wiener process is possible. To prepare for this, we introduce Gaussian processes, defined as follows:

Definition 2.11
A stochastic process $X = (X(t))_{t \geq 0}$ is a **Gaussian process** if for every choice of $0 \leq t_1 \leq t_2 \leq \cdots \leq t_n$ the vector of increments $(X(t_2) - X(t_1), X(t_3) - X(t_2), \ldots, X(t_n) - X(t_{n-1}))$ is a Gaussian random vector.

For convenience, we recall the definition from [PF].

Definition 2.12
The n-dimensional random vector $\mathbf{Z} = (Z_1, Z_2, \ldots, Z_n)$ is **Gaussian** with (vector) mean $\mu = (\mu_1, \ldots, \mu_n)$ and covariance matrix $\Sigma = (\sigma_{ij})_{i,j \leq n}$ (with $\sigma_{ij} = \mathbb{E}[(Z_i - \mu_i)(Z_j - \mu_j)]$) if its density is given, for all $\mathbf{x}$ in $\mathbb{R}^n$, by

$$(2\pi)^{-\frac{n}{2}}(\det \Sigma)^{-\frac{1}{2}} \exp\left\{-\frac{1}{2}(\mathbf{x} - \mu)^{\mathrm{T}} \Sigma^{-1}(\mathbf{x} - \mu)\right\}.$$

Here det denotes the determinant and T the transpose.

The key property is that if Σ is a diagonal matrix, the random variables $(Z_i)_{i \leq n}$ are independent.

Now note that for any choice of t_i as above, the increments $W(t_{i+1}) - W(t_i)$ of the Wiener process are independent by definition, so they are uncorrelated. The covariance matrix $\Sigma = (\sigma_{ij})_{i,j \leq n}$ of the centred random vector $\mathbf{Z} = (Z_i)_{i \leq n}$ with $Z_i = W(t_{i+1}) - W(t_i)$ is therefore diagonal, with $\sigma_{ii} = t_{i+1} - t_i$

for each $i \leq n$. So $\det \Sigma$ is simply the product of these terms, and the form of the Gaussian density makes clear that the density of $\mathbf{Z}$ is just the product of the densities of the Z_i, so $\mathbf{Z}$ is a Gaussian vector. Exercise 2.2 shows that the Wiener process W is a Gaussian process with $X(0) = 0$, constant expectation, $\text{Cov}(W(s), W(t)) = \min(s, t)$ and almost all paths are continuous. The next result shows that the converse also holds.

Proposition 2.13

If X is a Gaussian process with $X(0) = 0$ and has constant expectation, almost surely continuous paths and $\text{Cov}(X(s), X(t) = \min(s, t)$, then X is a Wiener process.

Proof For condition 3 of the definition of the Wiener process, we must show that for given $0 \leq t_1 \leq t_2 \leq \cdots \leq t_n$ the increments $(X(t_2) - X(t_1), X(t_3) - X(t_2), \ldots, X(t_n) - X(t_{n-1}))$ are independent. By the above property of the multi-dimensional Gaussian distribution, we only need to show that the off-diagonal elements of the covariance matrix of the vector $(X(t_i))_{i \leq n}$ are zero. So for $i < j$ we compute

$$\mathbb{E}[(X(t_i) - X(t_{i-1}))(X(t_j) - X(t_{j-1}))]$$
$$= \mathbb{E}[(X(t_i)X(t_j)] - \mathbb{E}[(X(t_i)X(t_{j-1})] - \mathbb{E}[(X(t_{i-1})X(t_j)] + \mathbb{E}[(X(t_{i-1})X(t_{j-1})]$$
$$= t_i - t_i - t_{i-1} + t_{i-1} = 0.$$

Next we find the variance of $X(t) - X(s)$ for $s \leq t$:

$$\text{Var}[X(t) - X(s)] = \mathbb{E}[(X(t) - X(s))^2]$$
$$= \mathbb{E}[X(t)^2] - 2\mathbb{E}[X(s)X(t)] + \mathbb{E}[X(s)^2]$$
$$= t - 2\min(s, t) + s = t - s.$$

Thus X satisfies condition 2 of the definition of W as well, and the other two conditions are satisfied by the hypotheses of the proposition.   □

Exercise 2.5 Apply the above proposition to solve Exercise 2.4.

With this characterisation of the Wiener process, two further operations can also be seen to yield new Wiener processes. The first is a shift operation: after any fixed time $u > 0$, the shifted process $W^u(t) = W(u+t) - W(u)$ is again a Wiener process. Finally, we have a time inversion property: the inverted process $Y(t) = tW(\frac{1}{t})$ for $t > 0$ with $Y(0) = 0$ is again a Wiener process. Here the long-term and short-term behaviour are swapped.

Exercise 2.6 Show that the shifted Wiener process is again a Wiener process and that the inverted Wiener process satisfies conditions 2,3 of the definition. In fact, it is a Wiener process, although the proof of path-continuity at $t = 0$ needs some care, and is deferred until a later section.

2.5 Stochastic processes: basic definitions

We make an abstract detour to formalise some terminology. The Wiener process is an example of a stochastic process, which we often regard simply as a family of random variables $(X(t))_{t \in \mathbb{T}}$ indexed by time $t \in \mathbb{T}$ where either $\mathbb{T} = [0, \infty)$ or $\mathbb{T} = [0, T], 0 < T < \infty$. However, it is instructive to regard X as a single function on the space $\mathbb{T} \times \Omega$ equipped with the product σ-field $\mathcal{B}(\mathbb{T}) \times \mathcal{F} = \sigma(\{B \times A : B \in \mathcal{B}(\mathbb{T}), A \in \mathcal{F}\})$, and we make the following fundamental assumption – as indeed we did in defining W.

Definition 2.14
A mapping: $X : \mathbb{T} \times \Omega \to \mathbb{R}$ is called a **stochastic process** if X is measurable with respect to the product σ-field $\mathcal{B}(\mathbb{T}) \times \mathcal{F}$.

Let X be a stochastic process. Then, for all $t \in \mathbb{T}$, the mapping $X(t) = X(t, \cdot) : \Omega \to \mathbb{R}$ is a random variable, since the product σ-field is the smallest σ-field for which the projections onto the component spaces are measurable.

Definition 2.15
The maps from $\mathbb{T}$ to $\mathbb{R}$ given by $t \to X(t)(\omega) = X(t, \omega)$, for each fixed $\omega \in \Omega$, are called (sample) **paths** of the stochastic process X. The **finite-dimensional distributions** of a stochastic process are the family of probabilities

$$P_{t_1, \dots, t_n}(A_1 \times \cdots \times A_n) = P(X(t_1) \in A_1, \dots, X(t_n) \in A_n)$$

given for every choice of $t_1, \dots, t_n \in \mathbb{T}, A_1, \dots, A_n \in \mathcal{B}(\mathbb{R})$.

Random variables are regarded as identical if they agree on a set of probability one. A natural extension of this idea to stochastic processes is to demand that for every t in $\mathbb{T}$ the random variables $X(t)$, $Y(t)$ should be equal almost surely.

Definition 2.16

If $X = (X(t))_{t \in \mathbb{T}}$, $Y = (Y(t))_{t \in \mathbb{T}}$ are stochastic processes defined on the same probability space, then Y is said to be a **version** (also called a **modification**) of X if, for each $t \in \mathbb{T}$, $P(\{\omega : X(t, \omega) = Y(t, \omega)\}) = 1$.

It then follows that X and Y have the same finite-dimensional distributions, that is

$$P(X(t_1) \in A_1, \ldots, X(t_k) \in A_k) = P(Y(t_1) \in A_1, \ldots, Y(t_n) \in A_k).$$

These distributions provide limited information about the underlying process.

Example 2.17

The random variables $W(t)$ have the same distributions as $\sqrt{t}Z$, where Z is standard normal. However, the process $X(t) = \sqrt{t}Z$ is not a Wiener process.

Exercise 2.7   Show that $X(t) = \sqrt{t}Z$ does not satisfy conditions 2,3 of the definition of the Wiener process.

To see that the paths of two versions of a process can look very different in general, we have the following classical simple example.

Example 2.18

On $\Omega = [0, 1]$ with Lebesgue measure, put $X(t, \omega) = 0$ and take $Y(t, \omega) = \mathbf{1}_{\{t\}}(\omega)$. Of course, for each t, $Y(t)$ is zero almost surely, but the processes are different since all paths are different: for fixed ω, $Y(t, \omega) = \mathbf{1}_{\{\omega\}}(t)$.

A stronger notion of equivalence of processes is provided by a third way of describing a stochastic process: we treat X as a random variable defined on Ω, with values in the set of all paths:

$$\Omega \ni \omega \mapsto (t \mapsto X(t, \omega)) \in \mathbb{R}^{\mathbb{T}}.$$

Thus to treat two processes as the same we should demand that P-almost all their paths coincide, in other words, that the exceptional P-null sets found in the definition of versions can be adjusted to apply simultaneously to all t in $\mathbb{T}$:

Definition 2.19

We say that two processes are **indistinguishable** if $P(\{\omega : X(t, \omega) = Y(t, \omega)$ for all $t\}) = 1$.

This of course implies that Y is a version of X, but not conversely. However, if the paths of both processes are continuous, the two concepts coincide.

Exercise 2.8   Prove the last claim.

2.6 Properties of paths

Next we explore properties of the paths $t \to W(t, \omega)$ of W. Continuity of paths is one of the defining conditions, so the Wiener process is continuous by definition.

While negative results are usually not important when developing the properties of a process, here we have an intriguing property which seems relevant from the point of view of modelling financial markets, namely differentiability. The derivative of a time-dependent function represents the velocity of an object whose position is described by that function. Velocity is a phenomenon of the physical world and applies to objects with positive mass, which have some inertia in their movements. However, prices or any other economic quantities are products of human minds. As may be observed, actual stock prices appear to fluctuate abruptly and without a clear pattern. So the next fact supports the case for employing the Wiener process as a modelling vehicle in financial markets.

Proposition 2.20

For each t, almost all paths of W are not differentiable at t.

One can prove a stronger result by saying that almost all paths are nowhere differentiable, but this would require a bit of technical effort, and after all, this is just a side dish.

Proof   We fix t and show that the set

$$A = \{\omega : s \to W(s, \omega) \text{ has a derivative at } t\}$$

has probability zero (more precisely, is a subset of a set of probability zero). If a function has derivative at t, then the ratio $\frac{W(t+\varepsilon)-W(t)}{\varepsilon}$ has a limit as $\varepsilon \to 0$ so this ratio, as a function of ε, is bounded for small ε. So we have

$$A \subset \bigcup_{k=1}^{\infty} \bigcup_{n=1}^{\infty} A_n^k$$

where

$$A_n^k = \left\{ \omega : -k \le \frac{W(t+\varepsilon)-W(t)}{\varepsilon} \le k, 0 < \varepsilon < \frac{1}{n} \right\}$$
$$= \left\{ \omega : -k\sqrt{\varepsilon} \le \frac{W(t+\varepsilon)-W(t)}{\sqrt{\varepsilon}} \le k\sqrt{\varepsilon}, 0 < \varepsilon < \frac{1}{n} \right\}.$$

Fix k and estimate the probability of A_n^k employing the fact that the standard normal cumulative distribution function N is increasing and continuous:

$$P(A_n^k) = N(k\sqrt{\varepsilon}) - N(-k\sqrt{\varepsilon}) \le N\left(\frac{k}{\sqrt{n}}\right) - N\left(-\frac{k}{\sqrt{n}}\right) \to 0$$

as $n \to \infty$. Since the sets increase with n,

$$\Omega \setminus A_n^k \supset \Omega \setminus A_{n+1}^k,$$

so

$$P\left(\bigcup_{n=1}^{\infty} A_n^k\right) = P\left(\Omega \setminus \bigcap_{n=1}^{\infty}(\Omega \setminus A_n^k)\right) = 1 - \lim_n P(\Omega \setminus A_n^k) = 0.$$

Finally, by subadditivity

$$P(A) \le \sum_{k=1}^{\infty} P\left(\bigcup_{n=1}^{\infty} A_n^k\right) = 0.$$

$\square$

So the Wiener process has rather 'wild' path properties, which creates problems in developing an integral calculus based upon W. But the price is worth paying and precisely this irregularity is intimately related to the beauty of the mathematical theory.

From the point of view of financial modelling, we could even say that continuity is an unwanted feature since in reality the prices jump. However, the lack of a derivative creates a possibility of observing a 'jump' since we can only record the path's position at some discrete instants and large continuous changes over small intervals would be observed as jumps.

Further evidence of wild behaviour of Wiener paths is provided by the analysis of their variation. We extend the definition of variation given above for discrete-time processes, recalling that scaled random walks have infinite variation in the limit, but bounded quadratic variation. So we begin with the latter.

For any t, we consider a sequence of partitions $\pi_n = \{t_0, t_1, \ldots, t_n\}$ of $[0, t]$, that is $0 = t_0 < t_1 \cdots < t_n = t$ assuming that $\max_{j=1,\ldots,n-1}\{t_{j+1} - t_j\} \to 0$ as $n \to \infty$.

Definition 2.21

For any process X and $t \in [0, T]$, write

$$V^2_{[0,t]}(n) = V^2_{[0,t]}((X(t_k))_{k \le n}) = \sum_{j=0}^{n-1} (X(t_{j+1}) - X(t_j))^2.$$

If there exists a process $[X, X] = \{[X, X](t) : t \in [0, T]\}$ such that for all t, $V^2_{[0,t]}(n) \to [X, X](t)$ in probability for any sequence of partitions of $[0, t]$, we call $[X.X]$ the **quadratic variation process** of X in the interval $[0, t]$.

Note that $V^2_{[0,t]}$ coincides with the quadratic variation of scaled random walks. We can take the analogy further.

Proposition 2.22

The quadratic variation of the Wiener process is $[W, W](t) = t$.

Proof We shall prove that $\sum_{j=0}^{n-1}(W(t_{j+1}) - W(t_j))^2$ converges to t in $L^2(\Omega)$, which, as we know from [PF], implies convergence in probability. So consider

$$\sum_{j=0}^{n-1} (W(t_{j+1}) - W(t_j))^2 - t = \sum_{j=0}^{n-1} \left[(W(t_{j+1}) - W(t_j))^2 - (t_{j+1} - t_j) \right].$$

The expectation of this sum is zero since $\mathbb{E}((W(t_{j+1}) - W(t_j))^2) = t_{j+1} - t_j$, so the expectation of the square coincides with the variance. The terms are independent so

$$\text{Var}\left(\sum_{j=0}^{n-1} \left[(W(t_{j+1}) - W(t_j))^2 - (t_{j+1} - t_j) \right] \right)$$

$$= \sum_{j=0}^{n-1} \text{Var}\left[(W(t_{j+1}) - W(t_j))^2 - (t_{j+1} - t_j) \right]$$

$$= \sum_{j=0}^{n-1} \text{Var}(W(t_{j+1}) - W(t_j))^2$$

as adding a constant does not change the variance.

For any normal random variable Y with zero expectation and variance σ^2, we have $\mathbb{E}(Y^4) = 3\sigma^4$ so $\mathrm{Var}(Y^2) = \mathbb{E}(Y^4) - (\mathbb{E}(Y^2))^2 = 2\sigma^4$ (see [PF]).

Applying this to each term we obtain

$$\sum_{j=0}^{n-1} \mathrm{Var}(W(t_{j+1}) - W(t_j))^2 = 2 \sum_{j=0}^{n-1} (t_{j+1} - t_j)^2$$

$$\leq 2 \max_{j=0,\dots,n-1} \{t_{j+1} - t_j\} \sum_{j=0}^{n-1} (t_{j+1} - t_j)$$

$$= 2 \max_{j=0,\dots,n-1} \{t_{j+1} - t_j\} t \to 0$$

as $n \to \infty$. $\square$

The variation of a general continuous-time process is defined similarly:

Definition 2.23

For any process $X(t)$, $t \in [0, T]$, write

$$V_{[0,t]}(n) = V_{[0,t]}((X(t_k))_{k \leq n}) = \sum_{j=0}^{n-1} |X(t_{j+1}) - X(t_j)|$$

and the **variation** of X is defined as the limit in probability of $V_{[0,t]}(n)$ as $n \to 0$, all t.

Proposition 2.24

The variation of Wiener process is infinite.

Proof   First note that

$$\sum_{j=0}^{n-1} (W(t_{j+1}) - W(t_j))^2 \leq \max_{j=0,\dots,n-1} \{W(t_{j+1}) - W(t_j)\} \sum_{j=0}^{n-1} |W(t_{j+1}) - W(t_j)|.$$

Since the paths are continuous, they are uniformly continuous on a bounded interval so $\max_{j=0,\dots,n-1} \{W(t_{j+1}) - W(t_j)\} \to 0$ as $\max_{j=0,\dots,n-1} \{t_{j+1} - t_j\} \to 0$. Now if the variation were finite, we would have

$$\sup \sum_{j=0}^{n-1} |W(t_{j+1}) - W(t_j)| < \infty$$

(where the supremum is taken over all partitions $\{t_j\}$ of $[0, t]$) and this would imply that

$$\sum_{j=0}^{n-1} (W(t_{j+1}) - W(t_j))^2 \to 0$$

almost surely, but we know that this limit is t in probability so t is also the almost sure limit for some subsequence. The contradiction shows that the variation must be infinite. □

2.7 Martingale properties

In order to describe further properties of the process W, we begin with the continuous-time counterparts of definitions given in Chapter 1 for discrete processes. Let $X = (X(t))_{t \in \mathbb{T}}$ be a stochastic process on the probability space $(\Omega, \mathcal{F}, P)$.

Definition 2.25
A family $(\mathcal{F}_t)_{t \in \mathbb{T}}$ of sub-σ-fields of $\mathcal{F}$ is called a **filtration** if $\mathcal{F}_s \subset \mathcal{F}_t$ for $s \leq t$. The filtration $\mathcal{F}_t^X = \sigma(X(s) : s \leq t)$, $t \in \mathbb{T}$, will be called the **natural filtration** for the stochastic process X, or the **filtration generated** by X.

Definition 2.26
A stochastic process $X = (X(t))_{t \in \mathbb{T}}$ is **adapted** to the filtration $(\mathcal{F}_t)_{t \in \mathbb{T}}$ if for all $t \in \mathbb{T}$, $X(t)$ is $\mathcal{F}_t$-measurable.

Note that the natural filtration of X is the smallest filtration to which X is adapted.

Our definition of a stochastic process X demands that it should be measurable as a function of the pair (t, ω), so that the inverse image of a real Borel set must lie in the σ-field $\mathcal{B}(\mathbb{T}) \times \mathcal{F}$. On the other hand, if X is adapted to a given filtration $\mathcal{F}_t$, then for each fixed $t \in \mathbb{T}$ the inverse image of a real Borel set is in $\mathcal{F}_t$. To link the two, one may make the following definition:

Definition 2.27
Given a filtration $\mathcal{F}_t$, a stochastic process $X : \mathbb{T} \times \Omega \to \mathbb{R}$ is **progressive** (or progressively measurable) with respect to $\mathcal{F}_t$ if, for each $t \in \mathbb{T}$, the map $(s, \omega) \to X(s, \omega)$ is $\mathcal{B}([0, t]) \times \mathcal{F}_t$-measurable.

It is possible to show that any (measurable) adapted process has a progressive version. We shall not need this deep result, since we concern ourselves solely with path-continuous processes, in which case adapted processes are always progressive. This fact is useful in many applications, as we shall see.

Proposition 2.28
Let $X : \mathbb{T} \times \Omega \to \mathbb{R}$ be a path-continuous process, adapted to a filtration $\mathcal{F}_t$. Then X is progressive.

Proof   Fix t in $\mathbb{T}$. Define $X^{(n)}(t, \omega) = X(t, \omega)$, and for $s < t$, let

$$X^{(n)}(s, \omega) = X\left(\frac{(k+1)t}{2^n}, \omega\right) \text{ when } s \in \left[\frac{kt}{2^n}, \frac{(k+1)t}{2^n}\right), \ k = 0, 1, ..., 2^n - 1.$$

This defines $X^{(n)}$ as a piecewise constant map $[0, t] \times \Omega \to \mathbb{R}$, so it is $\mathcal{B}([0, t]) \times \mathcal{F}_t$-measurable. By path-continuity, $X^{(n)}(s, \omega) \to X(s, \omega)$ for almost all ω, so the limit remains $\mathcal{B}([0, t]) \times \mathcal{F}_t$-measurable and X is progressive. $\square$

Definition 2.29

A stochastic process $X = (X(t))_{t \in \mathbb{T}}$ is a **martingale** (respectively, submartingale, supermartingale) for the filtration $(\mathcal{F}_t)_{t \in \mathbb{T}}$, if X is adapted to $(\mathcal{F}_t)_{t \in \mathbb{T}}$, $X(t)$ is integrable for each t, and for $s \le t$

$$\mathbb{E}(X(t)|\mathcal{F}_s) = X(s) \text{ (respectively, } \ge, \le).$$

(The requirement that X is $\mathcal{F}_t$-adapted is not needed for a martingale since this is implied by the above condition.)

Remark 2.30

It is traditional in stochastic analysis to assume that the filtrations one works with satisfy some additional assumptions which have become known as **the usual conditions**. These are as follows: given a filtration $(\mathcal{F}_t)_{t \ge 0}$ with $\mathcal{F}_\infty = \sigma(\bigcup_{t \ge 0} \mathcal{F}_t)$:
    (i) all subsets of P-null sets in $\mathcal{F}_\infty$ are members of $\mathcal{F}_0$,
    (ii) the filtration is right-continuous, i.e. for every $t \ge 0$, $\mathcal{F}_t = \bigcap_{u > t} \mathcal{F}_u$.
    These properties are needed to avoid various technical problems, especially in relation to stopping times, which arise when one deals with general stochastic processes. We will not need them for the properties of the Wiener process we discuss, thus we will work with the natural filtration $\mathcal{F}_t^W$, despite the fact that it turns out not to satisfy the usual conditions – although it can be suitably enlarged to do so.

Proposition 2.31

For $0 < s \le t < u$, the increment $W(u) - W(t)$ is independent of the σ-field $\mathcal{F}_s^W$. In particular, $W(u) - W(t)$ is independent of $\mathcal{F}_t^W$.

Proof   The σ-field $\mathcal{F}_s^W = \sigma\{W(r) : r \le s\}$ is generated by the family of random variables $W(r)$ for $r \le s$, and for arbitrary $u > t \ge s \ge r$ the increments $W(u) - W(t)$ and $W(r) - W(0) = W(r)$ are independent. So the random variable $W(u) - W(t)$ is independent of $\mathcal{F}_s^W$ for any $s \le t$ (see [PF]). $\square$

In Exercise 2.6 it was shown that the process W_u defined for $t \geq 0$ by $W_u = W(t + u) - W(u)$ is again a Wiener process. The above proposition shows that $W_u(t)$ is independent of $\mathcal{F}_u^W$, and so is any of its increments $W_u(t) - W_u(s) = W(t + u) - W(s + u)$ for $0 \leq s \leq t$. We shall make good use of this fact in the next section.

The following properties of the Wiener process are easy consequences of its definition.

Theorem 2.32
Each of the following processes is a martingale with respect to $\mathcal{F}_t^W$:
  1. $W(t)$,
  2. $W^2(t) - t$,
  3. $\exp(\sigma W(t) - \frac{1}{2}\sigma^2 t)$.

Proof   1. Let $0 < s < t$. As $W(s)$ is $\mathcal{F}_s^W$-measurable and $W(t) - W(s)$ and $\mathcal{F}_s^W$ are independent by the above proposition, we have

$$\mathbb{E}(W(t)|\mathcal{F}_s^W) - W(s) = \mathbb{E}(W(t) - W(s)|\mathcal{F}_s^W) = \mathbb{E}(W(t) - W(s)) = 0.$$

2. Guided by Proposition 1.20 for martingales in discrete time we first show that

$$\mathbb{E}(W^2(t) - W^2(s)|\mathcal{F}_s^W) = \mathbb{E}([W(t) - W(s)]^2|\mathcal{F}_s^W). \qquad (2.1)$$

Indeed,

$$\begin{aligned}
\mathbb{E}([W(t) - W(s)]^2|\mathcal{F}_s^W) &= \mathbb{E}(W^2(t) - 2W(t)W(s) + W^2(s)|\mathcal{F}_s^W) \\
&= \mathbb{E}(W^2(t)|\mathcal{F}_s^W) - 2\mathbb{E}(W(t)W(s)|\mathcal{F}_s^W) + \mathbb{E}(W^2(s)|\mathcal{F}_s^W) \\
&= \mathbb{E}(W^2(t)|\mathcal{F}_s^W) - 2W(s)\mathbb{E}(W(t)|\mathcal{F}_s^W) + W^2(s) \\
&= \mathbb{E}(W^2(t)|\mathcal{F}_s^W) - W^2(s).
\end{aligned}$$

Due to independence of $W(t) - W(s)$ and $\mathcal{F}_s^W$, we have

$$\mathbb{E}([W(t) - W(s)]^2|\mathcal{F}_s^W) = \mathbb{E}([W(t) - W(s)]^2) = t - s,$$

which implies the claim.

3. We know that if Y has normal distribution with zero expectation and

variance σ^2, then $\mathbb{E}(e^Y) = e^{\frac{1}{2}\sigma^2}$. This immediately implies the result:

$$\mathbb{E}\left(\exp\left(\sigma W(t) - \frac{1}{2}\sigma^2 t\right)\Big|\mathcal{F}_s^W\right)$$

$$= \exp\left(\sigma W(s) - \frac{1}{2}\sigma^2 t\right)\mathbb{E}(\exp(\sigma(W(t) - W(s)))|\mathcal{F}_s^W)$$

$$= \exp\left(\sigma W(s) - \frac{1}{2}\sigma^2 t\right)\mathbb{E}(\exp(\sigma(W(t) - W(s))))$$

$$= \exp\left(\sigma W(s) - \frac{1}{2}\sigma^2 t\right)\exp\left(\frac{1}{2}\sigma^2(t - s)\right)$$

$$= \exp\left(\sigma W(s) - \frac{1}{2}\sigma^2 s\right).$$

□

We observe that the proof of (2.1) only uses the martingale property of W so we have a very useful result which holds for any martingale $M(t)$ defined abstractly on a filtered space $(\Omega, \mathcal{F}, (\mathcal{F}_t)_{t\in\mathbb{T}}, P)$:

Theorem 2.33
If $M(t)$ is a martingale with respect to $\mathcal{F}_t$, then

$$\mathbb{E}(M^2(t) - M^2(s)|\mathcal{F}_s) = \mathbb{E}([M(t) - M(s)]^2|\mathcal{F}_s).$$

In particular

$$\mathbb{E}(M^2(t) - M^2(s)) = \mathbb{E}([M(t) - M(s)]^2).$$

Exercise 2.9   Prove this theorem.

Exercise 2.10   Consider a process X on $\Omega = [0, 1]$ with Lebesgue measure, given by $X(0, \omega) = 0$, and $X(t, \omega) = \mathbf{1}_{[0,\frac{1}{t}]}(\omega)$ for $t > 0$. Find the natural filtration $\mathcal{F}_t^X$ for X.

Exercise 2.11   Find $M(t) = \mathbb{E}(Z|\mathcal{F}_t^X)$ where $\mathcal{F}_t^X$ is constructed in the previous exercise.

Exercise 2.12   Is $Y(t, \omega) = t\omega - \frac{1}{2}t$ a martingale ($\mathcal{F}_t^X$ as above)? Compute $\mathbb{E}(Y(t))$.

2.8 Doob's inequalities

To describe path properties of W relating to its behaviour as $t \longrightarrow \infty$, we first make a brief detour to derive continuous-time analogues for continuous submartingales of two inequalities due to Doob which were proved in the discrete-time setting as Theorems 1.36 and 1.37, respectively. To obtain the continuous-time results, we use approximation via dyadic rationals in $[0, T]$:

Lemma 2.34
Let $(X(t))_{t\in[0,T]}$ be a non-negative continuous submartingale and let $\lambda > 0$. Define $Z(T) = \sup_{t\in[0,T]} X(t)$. Then

$$P(Z(T) > \lambda) \le \frac{1}{\lambda}\mathbb{E}(X(T)).$$

Moreover, if $X(T) \in L^2(\Omega)$, then

$$P(Z(T) > \lambda) \le \frac{1}{\lambda^2}\mathbb{E}(X^2(T)) \tag{2.2}$$

and

$$\mathbb{E}(Z^2(T)) \le 4\mathbb{E}(X^2(T)). \tag{2.3}$$

Proof For fixed $n \in \mathbb{N}$, define the finite index set $D(n,T) = \{\frac{iT}{2^n} : 0 \le i \le 2^n\}$ of dyadic rationals in $[0, T]$ and apply Theorem 1.36 to $Y(i) = X(\frac{iT}{2^n})$ so that

$$\lambda P\left(\max_{i=1,2,4,\dots,2^n} X\left(\frac{iT}{2^n}\right) > \lambda \right) \le \mathbb{E}(X(T)).$$

Since X is path-continuous, $\lim_{n\to\infty}(\max_{j\in D(n,T)} X(j, \omega)) = Z(T, \omega)$ almost surely. So if $A_n = \{\omega : \max_{j\in D(n,T)} X(j) > \lambda\}$ and $A = \{\omega : Z(T, \omega) > \lambda\}$, then $\mathbf{1}_{A_n} \nearrow \mathbf{1}_A$ almost surely, and the monotone convergence theorem ensures that $P(\max_{j\in D(n,T)} X(j) > \lambda)$ converges to $P(Z(T) > \lambda)$, which proves the first claim.

When X is a non-negative submartingale, then so is X^2, using Jensen's inequality with $\phi(x) = x^2$. We obtain (2.2) by replacing λ, X by λ^2, X^2 in the first inequality.

For (2.3), observe first that $\mathbb{E}(X^2(t)) \le \mathbb{E}(X^2(T))$ for all $t \in [0, T]$, so that $\sup_{t\in[0,T]} \mathbb{E}(X^2(t)) = \mathbb{E}(X^2(T))$, which means that X is L^2-bounded. Now Theorem 1.37 shows that for every $n \ge 1$

$$\mathbb{E}(\max_{j\in D(n,T)} X(j))^2 \le 4\mathbb{E}(X^2(T)).$$

But $\max_{j \in D(n,T)} X(j) \to \sup_{t \in [0,T]} X(t)$ as $n \to \infty$, as the dyadic rationals are dense and X is continuous. So (2.3) follows by dominated convergence. □

Trivially, we can replace $Z(T) = \sup_{t \in [0,T]} X(t)$ by $Z(t) = \sup_{u \in [s,t]} X(u)$ in the second inequality, which then reads

$$\mathbb{E}(Z^2(t)) \le 4\mathbb{E}(X^2(t)).$$

This leads in particular to a simple proof of a 'strong law of large numbers' for the Wiener process W.

Proposition 2.35
For almost all $\omega \in \Omega$, we have $\lim_{t \to \infty} \frac{W(t,\omega)}{t} = 0$.

Proof First observe that for $s < u < t$,

$$\mathbb{E}\left(\sup_{u \in [s,t]}\left(\frac{W(u)}{u}\right)^2\right) \le \frac{1}{s^2}\mathbb{E}(\sup_{u \in [s,t]}(W^2(u)))$$

$$\le \frac{4}{s^2}\mathbb{E}(W^2(t)) \text{ (Doob inequality, } W^2 \text{ is a submartingale)}$$

$$= \frac{4t}{s^2} \text{ (variance of } W(t) \text{ equals } t\text{).}$$

Apply this with $s = 2^n$ and $t = 2^{n+1}$, so that

$$\mathbb{E}\left(\sup_{u \in [2^n, 2^{n+1}]}\left(\frac{W(u)}{u}\right)^2\right) \le 4 \times 2^{-2n}\mathbb{E}(W(2^{n+1})^2) = 8 \times 2^{-n}.$$

Now for any $\varepsilon > 0$ we have

$$\sup_{u \in [2^n, 2^{n+1}]}\left(\frac{W(u)}{u}\right)^2 > \varepsilon^2 \quad \text{iff} \quad \sup_{u \in [2^n, 2^{n+1}]}\left|\frac{W(u)}{u}\right| > \varepsilon$$

and

$$\mathbb{E}\left(\sup_{u \in [2^n, 2^{n+1}]}\left(\frac{W(u)}{u}\right)^2\right) \ge \varepsilon^2 P\left(\sup_{u \in [2^n, 2^{n+1}]}\left(\frac{W(u)}{u}\right)^2 > \varepsilon^2\right),$$

so that

$$P\left(\sup_{u \in [2^n, 2^{n+1}]}\left|\frac{W(u)}{u}\right| > \varepsilon\right) \le \left(\frac{8}{\varepsilon^2}\right) \times 2^{-n}.$$

Hence with

$$A_n = \left\{\sup_{u \in [2^n, 2^{n+1}]}\left|\frac{W(u)}{u}\right| > \varepsilon\right\}$$

we see that $\sum_{n\geq 1} P(A_n)$ converges, so by the first Borel–Cantelli lemma (see [PF]) the set

$$A = \limsup_n A_n = \bigcap_{n\geq 1}\bigcup_{k\geq n} A_k$$

is P-null. Hence, almost surely, $|\frac{W(t)}{t}|$ exceeds ε in only finitely many intervals $[2^n, 2^{n+1}]$, so $\lim_{t\to\infty} \frac{W(t)}{t} = 0$ almost surely.   □

This shows that, asymptotically, almost every path of the Wiener process 'grows more slowly' than t; mirroring the square-root scaling we used for the approximating random walks considered at the beginning of this chapter (see also Exercise 2.1). Nevertheless, almost every path reaches every point of the real line, as the next exercise will show. It makes essential use of the symmetry properties derived in Exercises 2.4 and 2.6.

Exercise 2.13 Prove that for almost all paths of the Wiener process W we have $\sup_{t\geq 0} W(t) = +\infty$ and $\inf_{t\geq 0} W(t) = -\infty$.

Finally, the strong law enables us to tidy up a loose end left in Exercise 2.6.

Exercise 2.14 Use Proposition 2.35 to complete the proof that the inversion of a Wiener process is a Wiener process, by verifying path-continuity at $t = 0$.

2.9 Stopping times

In discrete time we observed the important role played by stopping times, particularly in their interaction with martingales, and showed that the martingale property is preserved under 'stopping' and 'sampling' a process with stopping times. In the next section and in Chapter 4 we shall have need of the continuous-time analogues of these results. To describe them we must first extend the concept of stopping time to the continuous-time setting, where it is somewhat more subtle. We will restrict attention to finite-valued stopping times.

Definition 2.36
Given a filtration $(\mathcal{F}_t)_{t \leq T}$ we say that $\tau : \Omega \to [0, \infty)$ is a (finite-valued) **stopping time** for $(\mathcal{F}_t)_{t \leq T}$ if for all t

$$\{\omega : \tau(\omega) \leq t\} \in \mathcal{F}_t.$$

We say that τ is **bounded** if its range in contained in $[0, T]$ for some $T > 0$.

Note that this is identical to a description we had in discrete time, except that $t \in [0, \infty)$ replaces $n \in \mathbb{N}$, but now the definition is not equivalent to $\{\omega : \tau(\omega) = t\} \in \mathcal{F}_t$, since we have an uncountable set of indices. We note some immediate properties which follow exactly as in the discrete case.

Proposition 2.37
If τ, ν are stopping times for the filtration $(\mathcal{F}_t)_{t \geq 0}$, then so are $\tau \vee \nu = \max\{\tau, \nu\}$ and $\tau \wedge \nu = \min\{\tau, \nu\}$.

Proof   For $t \geq 0$, we have

$$\{\tau \vee \nu \leq t\} = \{\tau \leq t\} \cap \{\nu \leq t\}$$
$$\{\tau \wedge \nu \leq t\} = \{\tau \leq t\} \cup \{\nu \leq t\},$$

where both right-hand sides are in the σ-field $\mathcal{F}_t$. $\square$

Exercise 2.15   Let $(\tau_n)_{n \geq 1}$ be a sequence of stopping times. Show that $\sup_n \tau_n$ and $\inf_n \tau_n$ are stopping times.

Suppose that $\mathcal{F}_t = \mathcal{F}_t^X$, the natural filtration for X, then the above definition captures the idea of deciding to stop on the basis of the information generated by the process.

As in the discrete case, given a stopping time τ, we can combine it with X to create a new random variable $X(\tau) : \Omega \to \mathbb{R}$, defined by $\omega \to X(\tau(\omega), \omega)$. As in Definition 1.33, this produces a natural σ-field – again with the event $\{\tau = t\}$ replaced by $\{\tau \leq t\}$:

Definition 2.38
The σ-field of events **known by time** τ is defined as

$$\mathcal{F}_\tau = \{A \in \mathcal{F} : \text{ for all } t \geq 0, A \cap \{\tau \leq t\} \in \mathcal{F}_t\}.$$

Exercise 2.16   Verify that $\mathcal{F}_\tau$ is a σ-field when τ is a stopping time.

When $\tau_0(\omega) = t_0$ is constant (as in the previous exercise), then $\mathcal{F}_{\tau_0} = \mathcal{F}_{t_0}$. A stopping time τ is obviously $\mathcal{F}_\tau$-measurable because $\{\tau \le t\} \cap \{\tau \le t\} \in \mathcal{F}_t$ for all t. Comparison of the σ-fields $\mathcal{F}_\nu$ and $\mathcal{F}_\tau$ for given stopping times ν, τ is left as an exercise:

Exercise 2.17 Show that if $\nu \le \tau$, then $\mathcal{F}_\nu \subset \mathcal{F}_\tau$, and that $\mathcal{F}_{\nu \wedge \tau} = \mathcal{F}_\nu \cap \mathcal{F}_\tau$.

Exercise 2.18 Let W be a Wiener process. Show that the natural filtration is left-continuous: for each $t \ge 0$ we have $\mathcal{F}_t = \sigma(\bigcup_{s<t} \mathcal{F}_s)$. Deduce that if $\nu_n \nearrow \nu$, where ν_n, ν are $\mathcal{F}_t^W$-stopping times, then $\sigma(\bigcup_{n \ge 1} \mathcal{F}_{\nu_n}^W) = \mathcal{F}_{\nu.}^W$.

When X is a continuous adapted process, the random variable $X(\tau)$ is also $\mathcal{F}_\tau$-measurable – to prove this claim we make a small detour, which will also provide an analogue of Theorem 1.31 as well as introducing the natural concept of the 'stopped process', which will play a significant role in 'localisation' arguments we shall need in Chapter 4.

We define a new process on $[0, \infty) \times \Omega$, given by the random variables $\omega \to X(t \wedge \tau(\omega))$. We record this formally for processes X adapted to the filtered space $(\Omega, \mathcal{F}, (\mathcal{F})_{t \ge 0}, P)$.

Definition 2.39
If X is an adapted process and $\tau : \Omega \to [0, \infty)$ is a stopping time, the **stopped process** X_τ is defined on $[0, \infty) \times \Omega$ by the formula

$$X_\tau(t, \omega) = X(t \wedge \tau(\omega), \omega).$$

For each ω, X_τ 'freezes' the path $t \to X(t, \omega)$ at the level $X(\tau(\omega))$. We now show that when X is continuous and adapted, then X_τ is adapted. Note that we cannot use the argument used in discrete time, since now the range of τ may be uncountable. It is here that the requirement that X should be progressive (see Definition 2.27) becomes essential.

Proposition 2.40
If X is a continuous, adapted process, then so is the stopped process X_τ.

Proof We need to show that for any Borel set B of real numbers and any $t \ge 0$, the set $\{X_\tau \in B\} \cap (\tau \le t)$ is in $\mathcal{F}_t$. We observe that for fixed t, the map $(s, \omega) \to X(s \wedge \tau(\omega), \omega)$ from $[0, t] \times \Omega$ into $\mathbb{R}$ is the composition of two maps. First, we have $\alpha : (s, \omega) \rightarrow (s \wedge \tau(\omega), \omega)$ as a map from $[0, t] \times \Omega$ into itself. Since $t \wedge \tau$ is a stopping time, it is $\mathcal{F}_{t \wedge \tau}$-measurable, hence also $\mathcal{F}_t$-measurable by Exercise 2.17. This means that the map α is measurable with respect to the product σ-field $\mathcal{B}([0, t]) \times \mathcal{F}_t$. Now compose α with X: we have

$$(s, \omega) \rightarrow X(s \wedge \tau(\omega), \omega) = X \circ \alpha(s, \omega),$$

so it only remains to show that X is also measurable with respect to this product σ-field. But this follows from Proposition 2.28, which shows that X is progressive, so that for any $t \geq 0$, its restriction to $[0, t] \times \Omega$ is $\mathcal{B}([0, t]) \times \mathcal{F}_t$-measurable.   □

Corollary 2.41
If X is continuous and adapted and τ is a stopping time, the random variable $X(\tau)$ is $\mathcal{F}_\tau$-measurable.

Proof   We have to show that for real Borel subsets B and $t \geq 0$, $\{X(\tau) \in B\} \cap (\tau \leq t) \in \mathcal{F}_\tau$. But this set is $\{X(t \wedge \tau) \in B\} \cap \{\tau \leq t\}$ and both sets in this intersection are in $\mathcal{F}_\tau$, as X_τ is adapted and τ is a stopping time.   □

We are ready to apply the above to continuous L^2-bounded martingales – note that when the time set is $[0, T]$, this class includes the Wiener process W, since $\mathbb{E}(W^2(s)) = s \leq T$ for all s in $[0, T]$.

For the remainder of this section, we assume that we are given a filtered space $(\Omega, \mathcal{F}, \mathcal{F}_t, P)$.

Theorem 2.42 (Optional stopping)
Let $M = (M(t))_{t \geq 0}$ be a continuous L^2-bounded martingale and τ be a finite-valued stopping time for the filtration $\mathcal{F}_t$. Then the stopped process defined by $X(t) = M(t \wedge \tau)$ is also an $\mathcal{F}_t$-martingale.

Proof   The claim is that $X(t)$ is integrable and that $\mathbb{E}(X(t)|\mathcal{F}_s) = X_s$ for $s \leq t$. We introduce a sequence of discrete stopping times approximating τ from above: for fixed $n \geq 1$ we multiply each of the dyadic rationals $\frac{k}{2^n}$, $k \in \mathbb{Z}$, by $(t - s)$ and add s. The range of τ_n is contained in the sequence $U_n = \{s + \frac{k}{2^n}(t - s) : k \in \mathbb{Z}\}$ and we set $\tau_n(\omega) = \min\{u \in U_n : u \geq \tau(\omega)\}$. Since the dyadic rationals are dense in $\mathbb{R}$, it follows that $\tau_n(\omega) \searrow \tau(\omega)$ as $n \rightarrow \infty$, for each ω in Ω. Each τ_n is a stopping time, since if $u = s + \frac{k}{2^n}(t - s)$ and $v = s + \frac{(k-1)}{2^n}(t - s)$, then

$$\{\tau_n = u\} = \{v < \tau \leq u\} = \{\tau \leq u\} \backslash \{\tau \leq v\} \in \mathcal{F}_u.$$

We apply optional stopping (Theorem 1.31) to the discrete martingale $\{M(u), \mathcal{F}_u : u \in U_n\}$ to conclude that for each $n \geq 1$ the stopped process $X_n(u) = M(u \wedge \tau_n)$, $u \in U_n$, is a martingale. But for all n we have s and t in U_n ($k = 0$ gives s and $k = 2^n$ yields t) so that for each $n \geq 1$

$$\mathbb{E}(M(t \wedge \tau_n)|\mathcal{F}_s) = M(s \wedge \tau_n).$$

We show that this identity is preserved in the limit as $n \to \infty$.

On the right we have $M(s \wedge \tau_n) \to M(s \wedge \tau)$ for each ω, by the path-continuity of M, while, on the left, similarly, $M(t \wedge \tau_n) \to M(t \wedge \tau)$ for each ω. This ensures that $X(t)$ is integrable for each t : since $\{|M(t \wedge \tau_n)| : n \geq 1\}$ is a (discrete) submartingale, so its expectations increase to that of $|M(t)|$, which is finite by hypothesis.

We apply dominated convergence to the sequence $|M(t \wedge \tau_n)|$ to see that $M(t \wedge \tau)$ is integrable. Next, as $\{M(u) : u \in U_n\}$ is L^2-bounded, Theorem 1.39 ensures the convergence of $M(t \wedge \tau_n)$ in L^2-norm to its almost sure limit $M(t \wedge \tau)$. Since conditional expectation does not increase the L^2-norm, the same applies to their $\mathcal{F}_s$-conditional expectations, so that, finally,

$$\mathbb{E}(M(t \wedge \tau)|\mathcal{F}_s) = M(s \wedge \tau).$$

□

In discrete time the martingale property is preserved under stopping times for L^2-bounded martingales: given stopping times $v \leq \tau$ we showed in Theorem 1.40 that $\mathbb{E}(M(\tau)|\mathcal{F}_v) = M(v)$. The continuous-time version can be deduced from this result, but it needs quite careful preparation, since the proof proceeds by approximating stopping times from above by countably valued stopping times, and requires analysis of the behaviour of the associated σ-fields. This analysis and the proof of the theorem are deferred to the end of this chapter. We will not be using the next result in this volume; however, it is important for many applications to be discussed later in this series.

Theorem 2.43 (Optional sampling)
Let $M = (M(t))_{t \geq 0}$ be a continuous L^2-bounded martingale and let v, τ be finite-valued stopping times for $\mathcal{F}_t$, with $v \leq \tau$. Then

$$\mathbb{E}(M(\tau)|\mathcal{F}_v) = M(v).$$

Proof See page 74. □

2.10   Markov property

We extend the notion of Markov process presented in Chapter 1 in discrete time to processes $(X(t))_{t \in [0,T]}$ defined on a filtered probability space.

Definition 2.44
An adapted process $X(t)$ is **Markov** if for all bounded Borel functions $f :$ $\mathbb{R} \to \mathbb{R}$, for all $0 \le s \le t \le T$

$$\mathbb{E}(f(X(t))|\mathcal{F}_s) = \mathbb{E}(f(X(t))|\mathcal{F}_{X(s)}). \tag{2.4}$$

The right-hand side of (2.4) as an $\mathcal{F}_{X(s)}$-measurable random variable can be written as a Borel function of $X(s)$ (see [PF]). This function is defined on the range of $X(s)$ and it is extended to the whole $\mathbb{R}$ by putting zero where needed and the result is denoted by $T_{s,t}f :$

$$(T_{s,t}f)(X(s)) = \mathbb{E}(f(X(t))|\mathcal{F}_{X(s)}).$$

In most situations of interest, and certainly in the examples we will consider, one can obtain $T_{s,t}f$ as a measurable function of x, as well as giving 'transition probabilities' for the process X by taking $f = \mathbf{1}_A$, so that $\mu(x, A) = (T_{s,t}\mathbf{1}_A)(x)$ represents the probability that $X(t) \in A$, conditioned on $X(s) = x$.

A classical example of a Markov process is the Wiener process considered with its natural filtration. This fact follows from the next proposition, since the Wiener process clearly satisfies the hypothesis.

Proposition 2.45
A process with independent increments is a Markov process with respect to the filtration generated.

Proof   We argue in the spirit of Example 1.42. If X has independent increments, then $X(t) - X(s)$ is independent of $\mathcal{F}_s^X$. For any bounded Borel function f, write $f(X(t)) = f(X(s) + X(t) - X(s)) = F(X(s), X(t) - X(s))$ with $F(x, y) = f(x + y)$ and by Lemma 1.43

$$\mathbb{E}(f(X(t))|\mathcal{F}_s^X) = G(X(s)),$$

where $G(x) = \mathbb{E}(F(x, X(t) - X(s)))$. Similarly,

$$\mathbb{E}(f(X(t))|\mathcal{F}_{X(s)}) = G(X(s)),$$

which completes the proof.   □

The above proof shows that for the Wiener process

$$(T_{s,t}f)(x) = \mathbb{E}(f(x + W(t) - W(s)))$$

$$= \frac{1}{\sqrt{2\pi(t - s)}} \int_{\mathbb{R}} f(x + y)e^{-\frac{y^2}{2(t-s)}} dy$$

$$= \frac{1}{\sqrt{2\pi(t - s)}} \int_{\mathbb{R}} f(u)e^{-\frac{(u-x)^2}{2(t-s)}} dy.$$

On the other hand, $(T_{0,t-s}f)(x) = \mathbb{E}(f(x + W(t - s)))$ is exactly the same, so we have an example of the following class of Markov processes.

Definition 2.46
A Markov process is **homogeneous** if

$$T_{s,t}f = T_{s+a,t+a}f \tag{2.5}$$

for any real a such that $s + a, t + a \in [0, T]$,

The above condition is equivalent to

$$T_{s,t}f = T_{0,t-s}f$$

for all s, t, since taking $a = -s$ in (2.5) gives the above equality, and conversely, the above line implies that both sides of (2.5) are the same. For homogeneous processes, the family of operations $T_{s,t}$ can be parametrised by single letter with $T_u = T_{0,u}$. Intuitively, considering a time interval, its length is all that matters.

Going back to the Wiener process, take $f = \mathbf{1}_B$ for a Borel set B and then

$$(T_u\mathbf{1}_B)(x) = \mathbb{E}(\mathbf{1}_B(x + W(u))) = P(x + W(u) \in B)$$

or considering this for $W(t + u) - W(t)$, which is a Wiener process for $u \geq 0$, for fixed t, assuming $W(t) = x$ the above has an obvious meaning as a transition probability; informally, the probability of being in position x at time t and in the set B at time $t + u$.

Exercise 2.19 Show that if $X(t)$ is Markov, then for any $0 \leq t_0 < t_1 < \cdots < t_N \leq T$ the sequence $(X(t_n))_{n=0,\ldots,N}$ is a discrete-time Markov process.

We turn finally to a significant strengthening of the Markov property for the Wiener process. As we have observed, for fixed $u > 0$ the shifted process $W^u(t) = W(u+t) - W(u)$ is again a Wiener process. The question arises:

does this remain true if we replace the fixed time $u > 0$ by a 'random time'? If so, then one may 're-start' a Wiener process once its paths have reached a pre-assigned level, and this flexibility is often needed in applications.

The following simple fact will be used in the proof.

Exercise 2.20 Let W be a Wiener process. Show that for $x \in \mathbb{R}$, $t \geq 0$, $M(t) = \exp\{ixW(t) + \frac{1}{2}x^2 t\}$ defines a martingale with respect to the natural filtration of W. (Recall from [PF] that expectations of complex-valued random variables are defined via taking the expectations of their real and imaginary parts separately.)

Theorem 2.47

Let W be a Wiener process and let τ be a finite-valued stopping time. Then the process W^τ defined by $W^\tau(t) = W(\tau + t) - W(\tau)$ is a Wiener process for the filtration $(\mathcal{F}^W_{\tau+t})_{t \geq 0}$, and its increments are independent of the σ-field $\mathcal{F}^W_\tau$.

Proof Fix $t \geq 0$. We need to show that for any partition $0 = t_0 < t_1 \leq \cdots \leq t_n$ of $[0, t]$, the increments $W^\tau(t_j) - W^\tau(t_{j-1})$, $j = 1, \ldots, n$, are independent random variables with normal distribution, mean zero and variance $(t_j - t_{j-1})$ and that they are independent of the σ-field $\mathcal{F}^W_\tau$.

Write $Y_j = W^\tau(t_j) - W^\tau(t_{j-1}) = W(\tau + t_j) - W(\tau + t_{j-1})$ for the increments of W^τ and $s_j = t_j - t_{j-1}$ for the lengths of the partition intervals, $j = 1, 2, \ldots, n$. We claim that it will suffice to show that for all real numbers $x_1, \ldots, x_n$ and every bounded $\mathcal{F}^W_\tau$-measurable random variable Z we have

$$\mathbb{E}\left(Z \exp\left\{i \sum_{j=1}^n x_j Y_j\right\}\right) = \mathbb{E}(Z) \prod_{j=1}^n \exp\left\{-\frac{1}{2}x_j^2 s_j\right\}. \tag{2.6}$$

Assume for the moment that this has been done.

First, with $Z = 1$, the identity shows that we obtain the characteristic function of the random vector

$$\mathbf{Y} = (Y_j)_{j \leq n} = (W^\tau(t_1) - W^\tau(t_0), W^\tau(t_2) - W^\tau(t_1), \ldots, W^\tau(t_n) - W^\tau(t_{n-1}))$$

as

$$\mathbb{E}\left(\exp\left\{\sum_{j=1}^n ix_j(W^\tau(t_j) - W^\tau(t_{j-1}))\right\}\right) = \prod_{j=1}^n \exp\left\{-\frac{1}{2}x_j^2(t_j - t_{j-1})\right\}.$$

This shows that the vector of these increments of the process W^τ is centred and Gaussian, and has a diagonal covariance matrix with diagonal entries $s_j = (t_j - t_{j-1})$. Therefore the increments are independent and have the required distribution. The other two conditions for W^τ to be a Wiener process are trivially satisfied: path-continuity follows from that of W, and $W^\tau(0) = 0$.

The independence of the increments from $\mathcal{F}_\tau^W$ follows on taking $Z = \exp\{ix_0Y_0\}$ for an arbitrary $\mathcal{F}_\tau^W$-measurable random variable Y_0 : the identity (2.6) then reads

$$\mathbb{E}\left(\exp\{ix_0Y_0\}\exp\left\{i\sum_{j=1}^n x_jY_j\right\}\right)$$

$$= \mathbb{E}\left(\exp\left\{i\sum_{j=0}^n x_jY_j\right\}\right)$$

$$= \mathbb{E}(\exp\{ix_0Y_0\})\prod_{J=1}^n \exp\left\{-\frac{1}{2}x_j^2s_j\right\}$$

$$= \mathbb{E}(\exp\{ix_0Y_0\})\mathbb{E}\left(\exp\left\{i\sum_{j=1}^n x_jY_j\right\}\right),$$

since $\prod_{J=1}^n \exp\{-\frac{1}{2}x_j^2s_j\} = \mathbb{E}(\exp\{i\sum_{j=1}^n x_jY_j\})$, as already noted. The identity

$$\mathbb{E}\left(\exp\left\{i\sum_{j=0}^n x_jY_j\right\}\right) = \mathbb{E}(\exp\{ix_0Y_0\})\mathbb{E}\left(\exp\left\{i\sum_{j=1}^n x_jY_j\right\}\right)$$

shows that the characteristic function of the pair $(Y_0, \mathbf{Y})$ splits into the product of their respective characteristic functions, and by a monotone class argument (see [PF] for details) this suffices to prove that Y_0 and $\mathbf{Y}$ are independent. Since Y_0 is an arbitrary $\mathcal{F}_\tau^W$-measurable random variable, we have shown that for any partition $(t_j)_{j\le n}, n \ge 1$, the vector of increments of W^τ is independent of $\mathcal{F}_\tau^W$.

We now turn to deriving (2.6). Fix $N > 0$. We wish to apply the optional sampling theorem to an L^2-bounded martingale and arbitrary stopping time ν. Since the martingale $M(t) = \exp\{ixW(t) + \frac{1}{2}x^2t\}$ is L^2-bounded on $[0, N]$, we first take the stopping time $\nu_N = \nu \wedge N$ to obtain

$$\mathbb{E}(M(\nu_N + t)|\mathcal{F}_{\nu_N}^W) = M(\nu_N).$$

In other words,

$$\exp\left\{\frac{1}{2}x^2(\nu_N + t)\right\}\mathbb{E}(\exp\{ixW(\nu_N + t)\}|\mathcal{F}_{\nu_N}^W) = \exp\left\{\frac{1}{2}x^2\nu_N\right\}\exp\{ixW(\nu_N)\}$$

so that

$$\mathbb{E}(\exp\{ix[W(v_N + t) - W(v_N)] + \frac{1}{2}x^2t\}|\mathcal{F}_{v_N}) = 1. \qquad (2.7)$$

Now let $N \to \infty$, then (2.7) becomes

$$\mathbb{E}(\exp\{ix[W(v + t) - W(v)] + \frac{1}{2}x^2t\}|\mathcal{F}_v^W) = 1, \qquad (2.8)$$

since W is path-continuous and $v_N \nearrow v$.

As indicated above, we take any partition $0 = t_0 < t_1 \leq \cdots \leq t_n$ of $[0, t]$, real numbers $x_1, \ldots, x_n$, and a bounded $\mathcal{F}_\tau^W$-measurable real-valued function Z. With Y_j and s_j $(1 \leq j \leq n)$ defined as above, using the $\mathcal{F}_\tau^W$-measurability of Z and conditioning on $\mathcal{F}_{\tau+t_{n-1}}^W$ inside the expectation, we obtain

$$\mathbb{E}\left(Z \exp\left\{\sum_{j=1}^n ix_j Y_j + \frac{1}{2}x_j^2 s_j\right\}\right) = \mathbb{E}\left(Z\mathbb{E}\left(\exp\left\{\sum_{j=1}^n ix_j Y_j + \frac{1}{2}x_j^2 s_j\right\}\bigg|\mathcal{F}_{\tau+t_{n-1}}^W\right)\right).$$

The inner conditional expectation is that of a product of exponentials, all but the last being $\mathcal{F}_{\tau+t_{n-1}}^W$-measurable, so we can take them outside the conditioning. With $v = \tau + t_{n-1}$ and $t = s_n = t_n - t_{n-1}$, the final term becomes

$$\mathbb{E}(\exp\{ix_n(W(\tau + t_n) - W(\tau + t_{n-1})) + \frac{1}{2}x_n^2 s_n\}|\mathcal{F}_{\tau+t_{n-1}}^W)$$

$$= \mathbb{E}(\exp\{ix_n(W(v + t) - W(v)) + \frac{1}{2}x_n^2 t\}|\mathcal{F}_v^W)$$

$$= 1,$$

where we have used (2.8). We have therefore shown that

$$\mathbb{E}\left(Z \exp\left\{\sum_{j=1}^n ix_j Y_j + \frac{1}{2}x_j^2 s_j\right\}\right) = \mathbb{E}\left(Z \exp\left\{\sum_{j=1}^{n-1} ix_j Y_j + \frac{1}{2}x_j^2 s_j\right\}\right),$$

and continuing in this fashion, we can remove the terms in the sum on the right one by one, by conditioning successively on $\mathcal{F}_{\tau+t_j}^W$ with $j = n - 2, \ldots, 2, 1, 0$. This proves that for every bounded $\mathcal{F}_\tau^W$-measurable Z we have

$$\mathbb{E}\left(Z \exp\left\{\sum_{j=1}^n ix_j Y_j + \frac{1}{2}x_j^2 s_j\right\}\right) = \mathbb{E}(Z),$$

which proves our claim and hence the theorem.   □

2.11 Proofs

Theorem 2.7
The process $(W(t))_{t\in[0,1]}$ defined by

$$W(t,\omega) = \sum_{n=0}^{\infty} a_n \psi_n(t) G_n(\omega)$$

is a Wiener process.

Proof   We prove this result in five steps.
Step 1. Auxiliary general estimate.
   We claim that there exists a random variable C such that

$$|G_n(\omega)| \le C(\omega) \sqrt{\log n} \quad \text{for } n \ge 2, \text{ where } C < \infty \text{ almost surely.}$$

To see this take $x \ge 0$ and using the symmetry of the standard normal density we have

$$P(|G_n| \ge x) = \frac{2}{\sqrt{2\pi}} \int_x^{\infty} e^{-\frac{y^2}{2}} dy.$$

Let $x_n \ge 1$, $n \ge 2$ so that $e^{-\frac{y^2}{2}} \le y e^{-\frac{y^2}{2}}$ for $y \in [x_n, \infty)$ and consequently

$$P(|G_n| \ge x_n) \le \frac{2}{\sqrt{2\pi}} \int_{x_n}^{\infty} y e^{-\frac{y^2}{2}} dy = \frac{-2}{\sqrt{2\pi}} e^{-\frac{y^2}{2}} \Big|_{x_n}^{\infty} = \frac{2}{\sqrt{2\pi}} e^{-\frac{x_n^2}{2}}.$$

If $\sum_{n=2}^{\infty} e^{-\frac{x_n^2}{2}} < \infty$, then we will be able to apply the first Borel–Cantelli Lemma. This will be possible if

$$e^{-\frac{x_n^2}{2}} = \frac{1}{n^\alpha} \quad \text{for } \alpha > 1.$$

Solving for x_n we get $x_n = \sqrt{2\alpha \log n}$ for $n \ge 2$ so

$$\sum_{n=2}^{\infty} P(|G_n| \ge \sqrt{2\alpha \log n}) \le \sqrt{\frac{2}{\pi}} \sum_{n=2}^{\infty} \frac{1}{n^\alpha} < \infty.$$

By the Borel–Cantelli Lemma, for $A_n = \{|G_n| \ge \sqrt{2\alpha \log n}\}$

$$P(A_\infty) = P(\limsup_{n\to\infty} A_n) = 0, \quad \text{where } A_\infty = \bigcap_{n=1}^{\infty} \bigcup_{m=n}^{\infty} A_m.$$

If $A'_\infty = \Omega \backslash A_\infty$, then $P(A'_\infty) = 1$ and for every $\omega \in A'_\infty = \bigcup_{n=1}^{\infty} \bigcap_{m=n}^{\infty} (\Omega \backslash A_m)$ there exists $n_0 = n_0(\omega)$ such that $\omega \notin A_m$ for $m \ge n_0$ which means $|G_m(\omega)| \le \sqrt{2\alpha} \sqrt{\log m}$ for $m \ge n_0$.

Defining

$$C(\omega) = \max \left\{ \frac{|G_k(\omega)|}{\sqrt{\log k}} : 2 \leq k \leq n_0(\omega) \right\} \vee \sqrt{2\alpha}$$

for $\omega \in A'_\infty$ we obtain the required inequality.

Step 2. Series convergence and path-continuity.

Denote $\tilde{\psi}(t, \omega) = \psi_0(t)G_0(\omega) + a_1 G_1(\omega)$. Using the estimate from Step 1 we have

$$W(t, \omega) = \tilde{\psi}(t, \omega) + \sum_{n=2}^{\infty} a_n \psi_n(t) G_n(\omega)$$

$$\leq \tilde{\psi}(t, \omega) + C_n(\omega) \sum_{n=2}^{\infty} a_n \psi_n(t) \sqrt{\log n}.$$

It is convenient to split the sum into segments according to the form of the coefficients a_n

$$\sum_{n=2}^{\infty} a_n \psi_n(t) \sqrt{\log n} = \sum_{j=1}^{\infty} \sum_{k=0}^{2^j - 1} 2^{-(\frac{j}{2}+1)} \psi_{2^j + k}(t) \sqrt{\log(2^j + k)}.$$

For fixed $j \geq 1$, given arbitrary t, only one of the numbers $\psi_{2^j}(t), \ldots, \psi_{2^{j+1}-1}(t)$ is non-zero. Since $|\psi_n| \leq 1$, the sum over k for fixed j can be estimated as follows

$$\sum_{k=0}^{2^j - 1} 2^{-(\frac{j}{2}+1)} \psi_{2^j + k}(t) \sqrt{\log(2^j + k)} \leq 2^{-(\frac{j}{2}+1)} \sqrt{\log(2^j + 2^j - 1)}$$

$$\leq \frac{\sqrt{\log 2}}{2} \frac{\sqrt{j}}{(\sqrt{2})^j}.$$

Going back to the main estimation

$$\sum_{n=2}^{\infty} a_n \psi_n(t) |G_n(\omega)| \leq C(\omega) \sum_{j=1}^{\infty} \frac{\sqrt{j}}{(\sqrt{2})^j}.$$

The series is uniformly convergent, so the paths $t \mapsto W(t, \omega)$ are continuous functions on $[0, 1]$ for $\omega \in A'_\infty$.

Step 3. Normal distribution

We shall show that for any $t_1 < t_2 < \cdots < t_n$ the random vector $(W(t_1), \ldots, W(t_n))$ has normal distribution with zero mean and covariance matrix $c_{ij} = \min\{t_i, t_j\}$. To this end, it is sufficient to show that its characteristic function ϕ is of the form

$$\phi(x_1, \ldots, x_n) = \exp\left\{-\frac{1}{2}\sum x_i x_j \min\{t_i, t_j\}\right\}.$$

We begin with the definition of the characteristic function ϕ

$$\phi(x_1, \ldots, x_n) = \mathbb{E}\exp\left(i\sum_{i=1}^{n} x_i W(t_i)\right)$$

$$= \mathbb{E}\exp\left(i\sum_{i=1}^{n} x_i \sum_{n=0}^{\infty} a_n \psi_n(t_i) G_n\right)$$

$$= \prod_{n=0}^{\infty} \mathbb{E}\exp\left(ia_n G_n \sum_{i=1}^{n} x_i \psi_n(t_i)\right) \quad \text{(because } G_n \text{ are independent)}$$

$$= \prod_{n=0}^{\infty} \mathbb{E}\exp\left(-\frac{1}{2}a_n^2\left(\sum_{i=1}^{n} x_i \psi_n(t_i)\right)^2\right) \quad \left(\text{since } \mathbb{E}(\exp(iG_n y)) = \exp\left(-\frac{1}{2}y^2\right)\right)$$

$$= \mathbb{E}\exp\left(-\frac{1}{2}\sum_{n=0}^{\infty} a_n^2 \sum_{i=1}^{n}\sum_{j=1}^{n} x_i \psi_n(t_i) x_j \psi_n(t_j)\right)$$

$$= \exp\left(-\frac{1}{2}\sum_{i,j=1}^{n} x_i x_j \min\{t_i, t_j\}\right) \quad \text{(by Lemma 2.6)}.$$

Step 4. Normal increments For simplicity of notation, we may take $t_1 < t_2$. From Step 3 we have

$$\mathbb{E}[\exp(i(x_1 W(t_1) + x_2 W(t_2)))] = \exp\left(-\frac{1}{2}\sum_{i,j=1}^{2} x_i x_j \min\{t_i, t_j\}\right)$$

$$= \exp\left(-\frac{1}{2}(x_1^2 t_1 + 2x_1 x_2 t_1 + x_2^2 t_2)\right).$$

Next take $x_2 = x$, $x_1 = -x$

$$\mathbb{E}[\exp(ix(W(t_2) - W(t_1)))] = \exp\left(-\frac{1}{2}x^2(t_2 - t_1)\right)$$

and we can see that the increment has normal distribution with expectation zero and variance $t_2 - t_1$. In the same way, we can show that the vector of increments $(W(t_n) - W(t_{n-1}), \ldots, W(t_2) - W(t_1))$ has multivariate normal distribution.

Step 5. Independent increments. We already know that to show the independence of a normal vector it is sufficient to show that the covariance matrix is diagonal. For simplicity of notation, we restrict ourselves to proving that $\mathbb{E}((W(t_2) - W(t_1))(W(t_4) - W(t_3))) = 0$ when $0 \le t_1 < t_2 \le t_3 < t_4$:

$$\mathbb{E}((W(t_2) - W(t_1))(W(t_4) - W(t_3)))$$
$$= \mathbb{E}(W(t_2)W(t_4)) + \mathbb{E}(W(t_1)W(t_3)) - \mathbb{E}(W(t_1)W(t_4)) - \mathbb{E}(W(t_2)W(t_3))$$
$$= c_{24} + c_{13} - c_{14} - c_{23} = t_2 + t_1 - t_1 - t_2 \text{ (by Step 3)}$$
$$= 0.$$

It is routine to prove that the increments $W(t_2) - W(t_1), \ldots, W(t_n) - W(t_{n-1})$ where $0 \le t_1 < t_2 < \ldots < t_n \le 1$, are independent. This confirms that W is a Wiener process on $[0, 1]$. $\square$

Theorem 2.43 (Optional Sampling)
Let $M = (M(t))_{t \ge 0}$ be a continuous L^2-bounded martingale and let v, τ be finite-valued stopping times on the filtered space $(\Omega, \mathcal{F}, \mathcal{F}_t, P)$, with $v \le \tau$. Then

$$\mathbb{E}(M(\tau)|\mathcal{F}_v) = M(v).$$

Before proving this we need to discuss the relation of the filtration $(\mathcal{F}_t)_{t \ge 0}$ to its right-continuous extension $(\mathcal{G}_t)_{t \ge 0}$ where by definition $\mathcal{G}_t = \bigcap_{s > t} \mathcal{F}_s$. As $\mathcal{F}_u \subset \mathcal{F}_v$ for $u < v$, it is obvious that $\mathcal{F}_t \subset \mathcal{G}_t$, and these filtrations coincide under the 'usual conditions' since then $\mathcal{F}_t = \bigcap_{s > t} \mathcal{F}_s$ is given by the right-continuity assumption. In the literature, $\mathcal{G}_t$ is often denoted by $\mathcal{F}_{t+}$. Note that it is automatically right-continuous. We first consider stopping times for the filtration $(\mathcal{G}_t)_{t \ge 0}$.

Lemma 2.48
τ is a $\mathcal{G}_t$-stopping time if and only if for all $t > 0$, $\{\tau < t\} \in \mathcal{F}_t$.

Proof of the Lemma   Suppose $\{\tau < t\} \in \mathcal{F}_t$ for all $t > 0$. Then $\{\tau \le t\} = \bigcap_{s > t}\{\tau < s\}$ for all $s > t$, so $\{\tau \le t\} \in \mathcal{G}_t$, so τ is a $\mathcal{G}_t$-stopping time. Conversely, suppose τ is a $\mathcal{G}_t$-stopping time, so that for all $u \ge 0$, $\{\tau \le u\} \in \bigcap_{s > u} \mathcal{F}_s$. Now for any $t > 0$,

$$\{\tau < t\} = \cup_{n \ge 1}\left\{\tau \le t - \frac{1}{n}\right\} \in \bigcup_{n \ge 1} \mathcal{G}_{t - \frac{1}{n}}.$$

But $\mathcal{G}_{t - \frac{1}{n}} \subset \mathcal{F}_t$ by construction, as $(\mathcal{F}_u)_{u \ge 0}$ increases with u. $\square$

Recall that for any filtration $\mathcal{H}_t$ on $(\Omega, \mathcal{F}, P)$ a stopping time v defines the σ-field $\mathcal{H}_v = \{A \in \mathcal{F} : \text{for all } t \ge 0, A \cap \{v \le t\} \in \mathcal{H}_t\}$. We apply this to a $\mathcal{G}_t$-stopping time τ, so that by the previous Lemma,

$$\mathcal{G}_\tau = \{A \in \mathcal{F} : \text{for all } t > 0, A \cap \{\tau < t\} \in \mathcal{F}_t\}.$$

In proving the Optional Sampling Theorem, we wish to approximate the given $\mathcal{F}_t$-stopping times from above by stopping times that take values at dyadic rationals. For this, we need the following lemma.

Lemma 2.49

Suppose that $(\xi_n)_{n\geq 1}$ is a sequence of $\mathcal{F}_t$-stopping times and $\xi_n \searrow \xi$. Then ξ is a $\mathcal{G}_t$-stopping time and $\mathcal{G}_\xi = \bigcap_{n\geq 1}\mathcal{G}_{\xi_n}$. If, moreover, the ξ_n are finite-valued and $\xi_n > \xi$ for each n, then $\mathcal{G}_\xi = \bigcap_{n\geq 1}\mathcal{F}_{\xi_n}$.

Proof of the Lemma Since for each ω, $\xi_n(\omega) \searrow \xi(\omega)$, we have $\{\xi < t\} = \bigcup_{n\geq 1}\{\xi_n < t\}$, and the sets on the right have the form

$$\{\xi_n < t\} = \bigcup_{m\geq 1}\left\{\xi_n \leq t - \frac{1}{m}\right\},$$

so they belong to $\mathcal{F}_t$, hence so does $\{\xi < t\}$. So ξ is a $\mathcal{G}_t$-stopping time by Lemma 2.48.

The σ-fields $\mathcal{G}_{\xi_n}$ and $\mathcal{G}_\xi$ are well defined, as the ξ_n and ξ are $\mathcal{G}_t$-stopping times, and trivially $\mathcal{G}_\xi \subset \mathcal{G}_{\xi_n}$ for each $n \geq 1$, so that $\mathcal{G}_\xi \subseteq \bigcap_{n\geq 1}\mathcal{G}_{\xi_n}$.

For the opposite inclusion, fix A such that for all $t > 0$ and all $n \geq 1$, $A \cap \{\xi_n < t\} \in \mathcal{F}_t$. Then, as above,

$$A \cap \{\xi < t\} = \bigcup_{n\geq 1}(A \cap \{\xi_n < t\})$$

also belongs to $\mathcal{F}_t$, so $A \in \mathcal{G}_\xi$.

For the final claim, we need to show that $\mathcal{G}_\xi \subset \mathcal{F}_{\xi_n}$ for all $n \geq 1$. But since $\xi < \xi_n$, $A \in \mathcal{G}_\xi$ can be written as

$$A = \bigcup_{r\in\mathbb{Q}}(A \cap \{\xi < r < \xi_n\})$$

and a typical set in this union is $A \cap \{\xi < r\} \cap \{\xi_n > r\}$. Consider

$$B = A \cap \{\xi < r\} \cap \{\xi_n > r\} \cap \{\xi_n \leq t\}$$

for $t \geq 0$. Since $A \in \mathcal{G}_\xi$, we have $A \cap \{\xi < r\} \in \mathcal{F}_r \subset \mathcal{F}_t$, while $\{\xi_n > r\} \in \mathcal{F}_r \subset \mathcal{F}_t$ and obviously $\{\xi_n \leq t\} \in \mathcal{F}_t$. This shows that $B \in \mathcal{F}_t$, so that $A \in \mathcal{F}_{\xi_n}$. □

We now apply these considerations to our continuous L^2-bounded martingale M.

Proof of the Optional Sampling Theorem For any given finite-valued $\mathcal{F}_t$-stopping time ξ, fix $n \geq 1$, and for $\omega \in \Omega$ let $\xi_n(\omega) = \frac{k}{2^n}$ when $\frac{k-1}{2^n} \leq \xi(\omega) < \frac{k}{2^n}$. These are (countably valued) $\mathcal{F}_t$-stopping times, since

$$\left\{\xi_n = \frac{k}{2^n}\right\} = \left\{\xi < \frac{k}{2^n}\right\}\bigg\backslash\left\{\xi < \frac{k-1}{2^n}\right\} \in \mathcal{F}_{k/2^n}.$$

They clearly decrease with n and their limit is ξ, since for every ω we have $|\xi_n(\omega) - \xi(\omega)| \leq \frac{1}{2^n}$, which goes to zero as $n \to \infty$. Finally, recall that $\mathcal{G}_t = \bigcap_{s>t} \mathcal{F}_s$ and note that for $A \in \mathcal{G}_t$ we have

$$A \cap \left\{ \xi_n = \frac{k}{2^n} \right\} = \left(A \cap \left\{ \xi < \frac{k}{2^n} \right\} \right) \setminus \left(A \cap \left\{ \xi < \frac{k}{2^n} \right\} \right) \in \mathcal{F}_{k/2^n}.$$

Apply this to each of the stopping times ν, τ in the statement of the theorem. We then have a sequence of countably valued (at dyadic rationals) stopping times ν_n, τ_n with $\nu_n \leq \tau_n$ for each n, and since M is L^2-bounded we can employ Theorem 1.40 to conclude that for each n and every $A \in \mathcal{F}_{\nu_n}$ we have

$$\int_A M(\tau_n)dP = \int_A M(\nu_n)dP. \tag{2.9}$$

This relation therefore holds for A in $\mathcal{G}_\nu$ by the above Lemma, and hence for all A in $\mathcal{F}_\nu$. To complete the proof we need to show that (2.9) holds for ν and τ, so we need a limit argument. Path-continuity of M ensures that $M(\nu_n(\omega), \omega) \to M(\nu(\omega), \omega)$ and $M(\tau_n(\omega), \omega) \to M(\tau(\omega), \omega)$ almost surely, but we need convergence in L^1-norm.

So, with $\xi = \tau$ or $\xi = \nu$, we have, for almost all $\omega \in \Omega$,

$$M(\xi_n(\omega), \omega) \to M(\xi(\omega), \omega).$$

Using the discrete optional sampling theorem for the (finite!) index set $\{\frac{k}{2^{n+1}} : k \geq 0\} \cap [0, t+1]$, we have from the optional sampling theorem in discrete time that $M(\xi_n)$ is integrable for each $n \geq 1$, and, since $\mathcal{F}_{\xi_{n+1}} \subset \mathcal{F}_{\xi_n}$,

$$\mathbb{E}(M(\xi_n)|\mathcal{F}_{\xi_{n+1}}) = M(\xi_{n+1}). \tag{2.10}$$

So we write $Y_n = M(\xi_n)$ and $\mathcal{H}_n = \mathcal{F}_{\xi_n}$ for each n. Then $(Y_n, \mathcal{H}_n)_{n \geq 1}$ is a **reverse martingale**, by which we mean that for $n \geq 1$, $\mathcal{H}_{n+1} \subset \mathcal{H}_n \subset \mathcal{F}$, Y_n is integrable and $\mathbb{E}(Y_n|\mathcal{H}_{n+1}) = Y_{n+1}$.

Recall from [PF] that a family $\mathcal{K} \subset L^1(\Omega, \mathcal{F}, P)$ is **uniformly integrable** if

$$\sup_{X \in \mathcal{K}} \int_{\{|X| > K\}} |X| \, dP \to 0 \text{ as } K \to \infty,$$

and that for any sequence (X_n) and X in L^1 we have $X_n \to X$ in L^1-norm (i.e. $\mathbb{E}(|X_n - X|) \to 0$ as $n \to \infty$) if and only if the following two conditions are satisfied:

   (i) (X_n) is uniformly integrable.
   (ii) $X_n \to X$ in probability.

We already know that, almost surely, and hence in probability,

$$M(\xi_n(\omega), \omega) \to M(\xi(\omega), \omega) \text{ as } n \to \infty.$$

To conclude that the convergence is also in L^1-norm, we now only need the following result. □

Lemma 2.50

A reverse martingale $(Y_n)_{n \geq 1}$ is uniformly integrable.

Proof of the Lemma We have

$$Y_2 = \mathbb{E}(Y_1 | \mathcal{H}_2),$$
$$Y_3 = \mathbb{E}(Y_2 | \mathcal{H}_3) = \mathbb{E}(\mathbb{E}(Y_1 | \mathcal{H}_2 | \mathcal{H}_3) = \mathbb{E}(Y_1 | \mathcal{H}_3),$$

and so, generally, $Y_n = \mathbb{E}(Y_1 | \mathcal{H}_n)$. We know from [PF] that for any integrable Y, the family $\{\mathbb{E}(Y | \mathcal{G}) : \mathcal{G} \text{ a sub-}\sigma\text{-field of} \mathcal{F}\}$ is uniformly integrable, so the result follows. Hence

$$M(\xi_n(\omega), \omega) \to M(\xi(\omega), \omega) \text{ in } L^1\text{-norm}$$

and the limit is integrable, since it is the conditional expectation of Y_1 relative to $\bigcap_{n \geq 1} \mathcal{H}_{\xi_n} = \mathcal{G}_\xi$.

Now apply this convergence result separately for $\xi_n = \nu_n, \xi = \nu$ and $\xi_n = \tau_n, \xi = \tau$. For any $A \in \mathcal{F}_\nu$, we have, as $n \to \infty$,

$$\mathbb{E}(1_A(M(\nu_n) - M(\nu))) \to 0,$$
$$\mathbb{E}(1_A(M(\tau_n) - M(\tau))) \to 0.$$

Thus (2.9) holds in the limit as $n \to \infty$, and for all $A \in \mathcal{F}_\nu$ we have

$$\int_A M(\tau) dP = \int_A M(\nu) dP.$$

□

3

Stochastic integrals

3.1   Motivation

We motivated the definition of the Wiener process by considering the limit behaviour of scaled random walks. Here we extend this informal approach to the stock prices given by binomial trees. The notation is as at the beginning of Chapter 2.

Fix $t > 0$ and let $h = \frac{t}{N}$ be the length of a single time step, and consider the corresponding scaled random walk $Z_h(t) = \sqrt{h} \sum_{n=1}^{N} L(n)$. The binomial tree has the form

$$S_h(nh) = S_N((n-1)h)(1 + K(n))$$

with independent returns

$$K(n) = \begin{cases} U & \text{with probability } \frac{1}{2}, \\ D & \text{with probability } \frac{1}{2}. \end{cases}$$

Let $k(n)$ be the corresponding logarithmic rate of return,

$$k(n) = \log(1 + K(n))$$

and assume

$$k(n) = \begin{cases} mh + \sigma \sqrt{h}, \\ mh - \sigma \sqrt{h}, \end{cases}$$

for some constants m, σ, which can always be found given D, U, and have the obvious meaning:

$$\mathbb{E}(k(n)) = mh,$$
$$\text{Var}(k(n)) = \sigma^2 h.$$

Now

$$S_h(t) = S_h(0) e^{k(1)+\ldots+k(N)}$$
$$= S_h(0) \exp \left\{ mt + \sigma \sqrt{h} \sum_{n=1}^{N} L(n) \right\}$$
$$= S_h(0) \exp\{mt + \sigma Z_h(t)\}.$$

This motivates the form of continuous-time stock prices, which are assumed to be given for each $t \geq 0$ by

$$S(t) = S(0) e^{mt + \sigma W(t)}.$$

We wish to find an equation which captures the dynamics of S, so we consider the next value on the tree

$$S_h(t + h) = S(0) \exp\{m(t + h) + \sigma Z_h(t + h)\}$$
$$= S_h(t) \exp\{mh + \sigma \sqrt{h} L(n + 1)\}.$$

Using the Taylor formula for the exponential,

$$e^x = 1 + x + \frac{1}{2} x^2 + \cdots,$$

we obtain

$$S_h(t + h) = S_h(t)[1 + mh + \sigma \sqrt{h} L(n + 1) + \frac{1}{2} \left(mh + \sigma \sqrt{h} L(n + 1) \right)^2 + \cdots]$$

$$= S_h(t)[1 + mh + \sigma \sqrt{h} L(n + 1) + \frac{1}{2} m^2 h^2 + mh^{3/2} L(n + 1)$$

$$+ \frac{1}{2} \sigma^2 h + \cdots]$$

$$= S_h(t) \left[1 + \left(m + \frac{1}{2} \sigma^2 \right) h + \sigma \sqrt{h} L(n + 1) + O(h^{3/2}) \right]$$

$$= S_h(t) \left[1 + \left(m + \frac{1}{2} \sigma^2 \right) h + \sigma \left(Z_h(t + h) - Z_h(t) \right) + O(h^{3/2}) \right],$$

where $O(h^{3/2})$ denotes all terms containing h raised to the power $3/2$ or higher.

Let $\mu = m + \frac{1}{2}\sigma^2$ and after rearranging we have

$$\frac{S_h(t+h) - S_h(t)}{h} = \mu S_h(t) + \sigma \frac{Z_h(t+h) - Z_h(t)}{h} S_h(t) + O(h^{1/2}),$$

where $O(h^{1/2})$ stands for the terms containing h to the power $1/2$ or higher.

In the limit, we are tempted to write

$$\frac{dS(t)}{dt} = \mu S(t) + \sigma S(t) \frac{dW(t)}{dt}, \qquad (3.1)$$

but this is impossible as the derivative of W does not exist. However, in the theory of differential equations the problem

$$x'(t) = f(x(t)), \quad x(0) = x_0,$$

is equivalent to the integral equation

$$x(t) = x_0 + \int_0^t f(x(u))du.$$

The way around the irregularity of the paths of the Wiener process is to give meaning to the integral form of (3.1), that is to consider the integral equation

$$S(t) = S(0) + \int_0^t \mu S(u)du + \int_0^t \sigma S(u)dW(u).$$

and give some meaning to the integral involving W, called a **stochastic integral**.

As we shall see later, the above informal computations make some deeper sense since at heart they involve the key fact of stochastic analysis, the Itô formula, so the scope of the above motivation is much broader than it might seem at first sight.

3.2   Definition of the Itô integral

A natural idea would be to define $\int_a^b f(t)dW(t)$ as the Stieltjes integral for each ω separately, integrating $f(t, \omega)$ with respect to $W(t, \omega)$. This cannot be pursued directly since the classical construction works only for functions of finite variation, and the paths of W do not have this property. We can define the Stieltjes-type integral for simple (step) processes but the further extension of the integral to a larger class of processes f, which is the crucial requirement, cannot be achieved individually for each ω.

The space $\mathcal{M}^2$ of integrands

We begin with identifying the class of stochastic processes that we wish to allow as integrands.

Definition 3.1
Write

$$\mathcal{M}^2 = \left\{ f : [0, T] \times \Omega \to \mathbb{R} : f \text{ is adapted, } \mathbb{E}\left(\int_0^T f^2(t)dt \right) < \infty \right\}.$$

The next proposition describes a simple class of processes belonging to this space. The result is obvious and we highlight it only because it is used frequently. The fact that we restrict our attention to a finite time interval is crucial here.

Proposition 3.2
If f is adapted and bounded, so that for some $C \in \mathbb{R}$, $|f(t, \omega)| \le C$ for all t, ω, then $f \in \mathcal{M}^2$.

Proof In general, the integral of a bounded function can be estimated by the bound multiplied by the measure of the whole space. The first inequality below uses monotonicity of the integral. The integral with respect to time is computed first, providing a deterministic bound, so the final steps are trivial:

$$\mathbb{E}\left(\int_0^T f^2(t)dt \right) \le \mathbb{E}\left(\int_0^T C^2 dt \right) = \mathbb{E}(TC^2) = TC^2.$$

$\square$

Exercise 3.1 Prove that W and W^2 are in $\mathcal{M}^2$.

Next, we introduce a class of processes which forms the basis of all that follows.

Definition 3.3
We say that $f \in \mathcal{M}^2$ is **simple**, writing $f \in \mathcal{S}^2$, if we can find a partition $0 = t_0 < t_1 < \cdots < t_n = T$, and $\mathcal{F}_{t_k}$-measurable random variables ξ_k with $\mathbb{E}(\xi_k^2) < \infty$, $k = 0, 1, 2, \ldots, n-1$, such that

$$f(t, \omega) = \xi_0 \mathbf{1}_{\{0\}} + \sum_{k=0}^{n-1} \xi_k(\omega) \mathbf{1}_{(t_k, t_{k+1}]}(t). \tag{3.2}$$

It should be no surprise that the space $\mathcal{S}^2$ of simple processes is dense in $\mathcal{M}^2$, which, after all, is a vector subspace of the space of square-integrable functions defined on $[0, T] \times \Omega$. However, the important requirement of adaptedness, which also dictates the form of the simple processes we use, complicates the proof of the result.

Theorem 3.4

For every process $f \in \mathcal{M}^2$ there exists a sequence $(f_n)_{n \geq 1}$ of simple processes $f_n \in \mathcal{S}^2$ such that

$$\lim_{n \to \infty} \mathbb{E} \int_0^T (f(t) - f_n(t))^2 dt = 0.$$

Proof   First, we show that we may assume without loss that f is bounded. Let $f \in \mathcal{M}^2$ and for $n \geq 1$ define a sequence of bounded processes

$$g_n(t, \omega) = \begin{cases} f(t, \omega) \text{ if } |f(t, \omega)| \leq n, \\ 0 \text{ otherwise.} \end{cases}$$

They are clearly adapted, so belong to $\mathcal{M}^2$. Assume that each of them can be approximated by simple processes. To conclude that the same holds for f, it remains to observe that $g_n \to f$ in $\mathcal{M}^2$. Since $g_n(t, \omega) \to f(t, \omega)$ for all (t, ω) and $|f(t, \omega) - g_n(t, \omega)|^2 \leq 4|f(t, \omega)|^2$, we have the desired convergence by the dominated convergence theorem, applied to the Lebesgue measure first, and expectation next:

$$\mathbb{E} \int_a^b (f(t) - g_n(t))^2 dt \to 0.$$

If f is bounded and has continuous paths, approximation by simple functions is straightforward: take any system of partitions $\{t_k^n\}$ of $[0, T]$ with $\max_k |t_{k+1}^n - t_k^n| \to 0$ as $n \to \infty$ and put $\xi_k^n = f(t_k^n)$ thus defining f_n by

$$f_n(t) = f(0)\mathbf{1}_{\{0\}} + \sum_{i=0}^{n-1} f(t_i^n)\mathbf{1}_{(t_i^n, t_{i+1}^n]}(t).$$

We wish to show that

$$\int_0^T (f(t) - f_n(t))^2 dt \to 0 \quad \text{almost surely.} \tag{3.3}$$

Fix ω and take any $\varepsilon > 0$. The path $t \mapsto f(t, \omega)$ is uniformly continuous (we are working on a bounded interval $[0, T]$), so there is a $\delta > 0$ such that $|t - s| < \delta$ implies $|f(s, \omega) - f(t, \omega)| < \varepsilon$. Take N so large that $\max_k |t_{k+1}^n - t_k^n| < \delta$ for $n \geq N$, hence $|f(t, \omega) - f_n(t, \omega)| < \varepsilon$ for $t \in [0, T]$. As a consequence,

$\int_0^T (f(t,\omega) - f_n(t,\omega))^2 dt < T\varepsilon^2$ and the convergence (3.3) is established. Since f is bounded and the same is true for f_n, this convergence of random variables is dominated (by a constant, so integrable over Ω) and we have proved our claim.

For bounded but not necessarily continuous f we can try using integral averages instead of values of f to define the coefficients of the approximating simple processes:

$$\xi_k^n = f(0)\mathbf{1}_{\{0\}} + \frac{1}{t_k^n - t_{k-1}^n} \int_{t_{k-1}^n}^{t_k^n} f(t)dt,$$

which works, but requires a good deal of effort – establishing adaptedness is tricky. For our applications we only need processes with continuous paths, so we shall leave the full proof as an option for the reader to explore; see page 99. □

Integrals of simple processes

The integral of a real function defined on an interval is a number, while a process is a function with random variables as values, so it is quite natural that the integral of a process will be defined as a random variable.

Definition 3.5
The **stochastic (Itô) integral** of a simple process $f \in \mathcal{S}^2$ is given by

$$I(f) = \sum_{k=0}^{n-1} \xi_k(W(t_{k+1}) - W(t_k)).$$

For any subinterval $[a, b] \subset [0, T]$, observing that $\mathbf{1}_{[a,b]}f \in \mathcal{S}^2$ (expand the partition $\{t_k\}$ by adding a, b if necessary) we write

$$\int_a^b f(t)dW(t) = I(\mathbf{1}_{[a,b]}f).$$

Remark 3.6
Note that a simple process can be written in many ways, as the following example illustrates: $\xi_1 \mathbf{1}_{(1,3]} = \xi_1 \mathbf{1}_{(1,2]} + \xi_1 \mathbf{1}_{(2,3]}$. Here the stochastic integral does not depend on such a modification, since $\xi_1(W(2) - W(1)) + \xi_1(W(3) - W(2)) = \xi_1(W(3) - W(1))$. This idea is exploited in the next exercise.

> **Exercise 3.2** Prove that in general $I(f)$ does not depend on a particular representation of f.

We begin with two elementary algebraic properties:

Proposition 3.7 (Linearity)

Given f, g in $\mathcal{S}^2$ and real numbers α, β, let $h = \alpha f + \beta g$. Then $h \in \mathcal{S}^2$ and $I(h) = \alpha I(f) + \beta I(g)$. Hence for $[a, b] \subset [0, T]$,

$$\int_a^b h(t)dW(t) = \alpha \int_a^b f(t)dW(t) + \beta \int_a^b g(t)dW(t).$$

Proof To see that h is simple, note that $h(0) = \alpha f(0) + \beta g(0)$ and that h is constant on the intervals of the common refinement of the two partitions defining f and g respectively. For example, for $t > 0$ let

$$f(t) = \xi_0 \mathbf{1}_{\{0\}} + \xi_1 \mathbf{1}_{(0,1]} + \xi_2 \mathbf{1}_{(1,3]},$$
$$g(t) = \eta_0 \mathbf{1}_{\{0\}} + \eta_1 \mathbf{1}_{(0,2]} + \eta_2 \mathbf{1}_{(2,3]},$$

and then

$$h(t) = (\alpha\xi_0 + \beta\eta_0)\mathbf{1}_{\{0\}} + (\alpha\xi_1 + \beta\eta_1)\mathbf{1}_{(0,1]} + (\alpha\xi_2 + \beta\eta_1)\mathbf{1}_{(1,2]} + (\alpha\xi_2 + \beta\eta_2)\mathbf{1}_{(2,3]}.$$

Now some simple algebra gives the desired relation

$$
\begin{aligned}
I(h) &= (\alpha\xi_1 + \beta\eta_1)(W(1) - W(0)) + (\alpha\xi_2 + \beta\eta_1)(W(2) - W(1)) \\
&\quad + (\alpha\xi_2 + \beta\eta_2)(W(3) - W(2)) \\
&= \alpha\left[\xi_1(W(1) - W(0)) + \xi_2(W(2) - W(1)) + \xi_2(W(3) - W(2))\right] \\
&\quad + \beta\left[\eta_1(W(1) - W(0)) + \eta_1(W(2) - W(1)) + \eta_2(W(3) - W(2))\right] \\
&= \alpha I(f) + \beta I(g).
\end{aligned}
$$

The extension of this argument to a general case is routine but notationally complex, hence we have just illustrated the main point. The final claim follows because $h\mathbf{1}_{[a,b]} = \alpha f\mathbf{1}_{[a,b]} + \beta g\mathbf{1}_{[a,b]}$. $\square$

Exercise 3.3   Give a proof for the general case.

Proposition 3.8

If $f \in \mathcal{S}^2$ and $0 \le a < c < b \le T$, then

$$\int_a^c f(t)dW(t) + \int_c^b f(t)dW(t) = \int_a^b f(t)dW(t).$$

Proof Add c to the partition $(t_k)_{k \le n}$ defining f, $t_k < c \le t_{k+1}$, say. This does not alter the integral, since the value ξ_k of f on the subinterval $(t_k, t_{k+1}]$ is fixed, while with the extended partition the contribution to the integral is

$$\xi_k(W(t_{k+1}) - W(c)) + \xi_k(W(c) - W(t_k)) = \xi_k(W(t_{k+1}) - W(t_k)).$$

So splitting the sum at c yields the desired result. □

The expectation of the increments of the Wiener process is zero and the same feature of the integral follows from an application of the tower property of the conditional expectation, used to handle multiplication by ξ_k. Note that since W is a martingale and the integrands have the right measurability, the stochastic integral we have defined can be regarded as a discrete-time martingale transform, as in Theorem 1.15. Hence the next result is no surprise.

Theorem 3.9
For $f \in S^2$, we have $\mathbb{E} \int_0^T f(t)dW(t) = 0$.

Proof The first step is straightforward: by linearity of the expectation

$$\mathbb{E}\left(\sum_{k=0}^{n-1} \xi_k(W(t_{k+1}) - W(t_k))\right) = \sum_{k=0}^{n-1} \mathbb{E}[\xi_k(W(t_{k+1}) - W(t_k))],$$

and we are done if each term on the right is zero. It would be nice to pull out ξ_k but these are random variables, so the tower property comes into play with carefully chosen σ-fields:

$$\mathbb{E}[\xi_k(W(t_{k+1}) - W(t_k))] = \mathbb{E}[\mathbb{E}(\xi_k(W(t_{k+1}) - W(t_k))|\mathcal{F}_{t_k})]$$
$$= \mathbb{E}[\xi_k\mathbb{E}(W(t_{k+1}) - W(t_k)|\mathcal{F}_{t_k})]$$

by taking out what is known. Next, by the independence of $W(t_{k+1}) - W(t_k)$ and $\mathcal{F}_{t_k}$, the conditional expectation becomes the expectation and we arrive at the result:

$$\mathbb{E}[\xi_k\mathbb{E}(W(t_{k+1}) - W(t_k)|\mathcal{F}_{t_k})] = \mathbb{E}(\xi_k\mathbb{E}(W(t_{k+1}) - W(t_k))) = 0.$$

□

The variance of the increment of the Wiener process is the length of the time interval and this enables us to compute the variance of the stochastic integral. The result is our first look at the important Itô isometry, which will play a crucial role in what follows. For integrals of simple processes, the proof is a straightforward calculation.

Theorem 3.10
For $f \in S^2$, we have

$$\mathbb{E}\left(\left[\int_0^T f(t)dW(t)\right]^2\right) = \mathbb{E}\left(\int_0^T f^2(t)dt\right). \qquad (3.4)$$

Proof The left-hand side is the natural starting point – we can insert the definition of stochastic integral:

$$\text{LHS} = \mathbb{E}\left(\left[\sum_{k=0}^{n-1} \xi_k(W(t_{k+1}) - W(t_k))\right]^2\right)$$

$$= \mathbb{E}\left(\sum_{i,k=0}^{n-1} \xi_i\xi_k(W(t_{i+1}) - W(t_i))(W(t_{k+1}) - W(t_k))\right)$$

$$= \sum_{k=0}^{n-1} \mathbb{E}(\xi_k^2(W(t_{k+1}) - W(t_k))^2)$$

$$+ 2\sum_{i<k} \mathbb{E}(\xi_i\xi_k(W(t_{i+1}) - W(t_i))(W(t_{k+1}) - W(t_k))) = A + 2B, \quad \text{say.}$$

We shall show that $A = \mathbb{E}\int_a^b f^2(t)dt$, and $B = 0$. We tackle A first using the technique we have already used

$$A = \sum_{k=0}^{n-1} \mathbb{E}(\xi_k^2(W(t_{k+1}) - W(t_k))^2)$$

$$= \sum_{k=0}^{n-1} \mathbb{E}(\mathbb{E}(\xi_k^2(W(t_{k+1}) - W(t_k))^2|\mathcal{F}_{t_k})) \quad \text{(tower property)}$$

$$= \sum_{k=0}^{n-1} \mathbb{E}(\xi_k^2\mathbb{E}((W(t_{k+1}) - W(t_k))^2|\mathcal{F}_{t_k})) \quad \text{(taking out the known)}$$

$$= \sum_{k=0}^{n-1} \mathbb{E}(\xi_k^2\mathbb{E}((W(t_{k+1}) - W(t_k))^2)) \quad \text{(independence)}$$

$$= \mathbb{E}\left(\sum_{k=0}^{n-1} \xi_k^2(t_{k+1} - t_k)\right) \quad \text{(definition of } W)$$

$$= \mathbb{E}\left(\int_a^b f^2(t)dt\right)$$

as claimed.

The second term is dealt with similarly, with extra care needed when we choose the σ-field – it must correspond to the later instant to pull out all factors except one increment of Wiener process. Consider just one term with $i < k$,

$$\mathbb{E}[\xi_i \xi_k (W(t_{i+1}) - W(t_i))(W(t_{k+1}) - W(t_k))]$$
$$= \mathbb{E}[\mathbb{E}(\xi_i \xi_k (W(t_{i+1}) - W(t_i))(W(t_{k+1}) - W(t_k))|\mathcal{F}_k)]$$
$$= \mathbb{E}[\xi_i \xi_k (W(t_{i+1}) - W(t_i))\mathbb{E}(W(t_{k+1}) - W(t_k)|\mathcal{F}_{t_k})] = 0,$$

since by independence $\mathbb{E}((W(t_{k+1}) - W(t_k))|\mathcal{F}_{t_k}) = \mathbb{E}(W(t_{k+1}) - W(t_k)) = 0$ and so $B = 0$. □

Exercise 3.4 Prove the last two properties for $\int_a^b f(t)dW(t)$, $[a, b] \subset [0, T]$.

General definition of the integral

To define the stochastic integral for any $f \in \mathcal{M}^2$, we take a sequence $f_n \in \mathcal{S}^2$ with $\mathbb{E} \int_0^T (f - f_n)^2(t)dt \to 0$, as provided by Theorem 3.4. The stochastic integral of each f_n is defined and we wish to show that the sequence $I(f_n)$ converges. To get convergence in $L^2(\Omega)$ it is sufficient to note that the sequence $I(f_n)$ is Cauchy in this space. This follows from the isometry (3.4) since f_n is Cauchy in $L^2([0, T] \times \Omega)$: we have for $m, n \geq 0$,

$$\mathbb{E}\left(\int_0^T (f_n(t) - f_m(t))dW(t)\right)^2 = \mathbb{E} \int_0^T (f_n(t) - f_m(t))^2 dt$$

and the right-hand side goes to zero as $m, n \to \infty$. By linearity of the integral,

$$\int_0^T (f_n(t) - f_m(t))dW(t) = \int_0^T f_n(t)dW(t) - \int_0^T f_m(t)dW(t)$$

so we have shown that $I(f_n) = \int_0^T f_n(t)dW(t)$ is Cauchy in $L^2(\Omega)$, and as such it converges.

Definition 3.11

We write

$$I(f) = \int_0^T f(t)dW(t) = \lim_{n \to \infty} I(f_n)$$

and call this random variable the **stochastic (Itô) integral** of f.

The next exercise guarantees that this limit is well defined.

Exercise 3.5   Prove that the stochastic integral does not depend on the choice of the sequence f_n approximating f.

Exercise 3.6   Show that

$$\int_0^t s\,dW(s) = tW(t) - \int_0^t W(s)\,ds.$$

Remark 3.12

The above construction can be cast nicely in a general functional-analytic framework. The set $\mathcal{S}^2$ is dense in $\mathcal{M}^2$ with respect to the norm

$$\|f\|^2_{L^2([0,T]\times\Omega)} = \mathbb{E}\int_0^T f^2(t)\,dt.$$

The notation means that we consider the function f as defined on the product space $[0,T] \times \Omega$, measurable with respect to the product σ-field $\mathcal{B}([0,T]) \times \mathcal{F}$, and the integral of f^2 on the right is taken with respect to the product measure $m \times P$, where $\mathcal{B}([0,T])$ denotes the Borel σ-field and m the Lebesgue measure on $[0,T]$ (see [PF] for details). By Theorem 3.4 the mapping $I : \mathcal{S}^2 \to L^2(\Omega)$ is an isometry: $\|f\|_{L^2([0,T]\times\Omega)} = \|I(f)\|_{L^2(\Omega)}$, so it can be uniquely extended on the whole of $\mathcal{M}^2$ with the isometry property preserved.

3.3   Properties

The general stochastic integral has the same basic properties as the integral of simple functions. It is convenient to begin with the isometry.

Theorem 3.13

For $f \in \mathcal{M}^2$,

$$\mathbb{E}\left(\left[\int_0^T f(t)\,dW(t)\right]^2\right) = \mathbb{E}\left(\int_0^T f^2(t)\,dt\right).$$

Proof   Any norm $\|\cdot\|$ on a vector space V is a continuous function, since for x, y in V we have $|\,\|x\| - \|y\|\,| \leq \|x - y\|$. We apply this in $L^2([0,T] \times \Omega)$ for processes (integrands) and in $L^2(\Omega)$ for our stochastic integrals. Take

$f_n \in \mathcal{S}^2$ such that $\|f - f_n\|_{L^2([0,T]\times\Omega)} \to 0$ as $n \to \infty$. In other words, $\mathbb{E}(\int_0^T (f - f_n)^2(t)dt) \to 0$, so

$$\mathbb{E}\left(\int_0^T f_n^2(t)dt\right) \to \mathbb{E}\left(\int_0^T f^2(t)dt\right).$$

Similarly, the definition of the integral implies

$$\mathbb{E}\left(\left[\int_0^T f_n(t)dW(t)\right]^2\right) \to \mathbb{E}\left(\left[\int_0^T f(t)dW(t)\right]^2\right).$$

As f_n is simple, $\mathbb{E}([\int_0^T f_n(t)dW(t)]^2) = \mathbb{E}(\int_0^T f_n^2(t)dt)$ by (3.4), so the two limits coincide, and the isometry is preserved in the limit. □

Exercise 3.7 Compute the variance of the random variable $\int_0^T (W(t) - t)dW(t)$.

Theorem 3.14
$\mathbb{E}\left(\int_0^T f(t)dW(t)\right) = 0$ *for* $f \in \mathcal{M}^2$.

Proof It is convenient to use the I notation here: for $f_n \in \mathcal{S}^2$ approximating f, we have

$$\begin{aligned}
[\mathbb{E}(I(f))]^2 &= [\mathbb{E}(I(f - f_n))]^2 \quad \text{(since } \mathbb{E}(I(f_n)) = 0) \\
&\le \mathbb{E}[I(f - f_n)]^2 \quad \text{(by Jensen's inequality)} \\
&= \mathbb{E}\left[\int_0^T (f - f_n)^2(t)dt\right] \quad \text{(previous theorem)} \\
&\to 0 \quad \text{as } n \to \infty.
\end{aligned}$$

□

By the same token, the algebraic properties we have proved should be preserved in the limit and we leave the details to the reader.

Exercise 3.8 Prove that if $f, g \in \mathcal{M}^2$ and α, β are real numbers, then

$$I(\alpha f + \beta g) = \alpha I(f) + \beta I(g).$$

Exercise 3.9 Prove that for $f \in \mathcal{M}^2$, $a < c < b$,

$$\int_a^b f(s)dW(s) = \int_a^c f(s)dW(s) + \int_c^b f(s)dW(s).$$

The stochastic integral as a process

We have defined the stochastic integral $\int_a^b f(s)dW(s)$ over any interval $[a, b]$. Now consider $[a, b] = [0, t]$ for any $t \in [0, T]$. We wish to construct a process

$$t \mapsto \int_0^t f(s)dW(s) = \int_0^T f(s)\mathbf{1}_{[0,t]}(s)dW(s) \text{ for given } f \text{ in } \mathcal{M}^2. \quad (3.5)$$

However, this requires some work. One would think that all that is needed is to take the integral over $[0, t]$ for each t separately and form the required process by arranging these integrals into a time-indexed family of random variables. This is not so simple. The problem is that the random variable $\int_0^t f(s)dW(s)$ is only defined almost surely, being the limit of a sequence of random variables, so it makes sense outside a set A_t with $P(A_t) = 0$. If we work with a countable family of time instants (a sequence), this would be acceptable since the exceptional set would still have zero probability, so the whole process would be meaningful on a set of full probability. For an uncountable family of times t, the exceptional set can be large and the common set on which all random variables have a meaning can be even empty. In applications, the definition of a function for a countable family of times is often sufficient to determine the values for all instants, but continuity is needed for the extension. We shall see that the process we are going to build will be continuous but at this stage we do not even know if it exists.

We tackle this by building a continuous martingale M which will be a version of the process (3.5) and then we will use the natural notation

$$M(t) = \int_0^t f(s)dW(s).$$

Since the proof is lengthy and somewhat involved, we state the existence result and defer the proof to the end of the chapter.

Theorem 3.15

If $f \in \mathcal{M}^2$, then there exists a continuous martingale M such that for all t

$$P\left(M(t) = \int_0^T (\mathbf{1}_{[0,t]}f)(s)dW(s)\right) = 1.$$

Proof The idea is to approximate f by simple processes g_n, observe that the stochastic integrals of $\mathbf{1}_{[0,t]}g_n$ are martingales with continuous paths and prove that they converge uniformly to obtain the desired martingale. For details, see page 101. □

Exercise 3.10 Show that the process $M(t) = \int_0^t \sin(W(t))dW(t)$ is a martingale.

We do not distinguish between different versions of a process. For any f in $\mathcal{M}^2$, the above theorem therefore identifies the stochastic process $(t, \omega) \to \int_0^T (\mathbf{1}_{[0,t]}f)(s, \omega)dW(s, \omega)$ with the martingale $M(t)$. We may ask whether this idea can be applied with $f = W$; in particular, what the integrals $\int_0^t W(s)dW(s)$ might be. The next two exercises explore this question.

Exercise 3.11 For each t in $[0, T]$, compare the mean and variance of the Itô integral $\int_0^t W(s)dW(s)$ with those of the random variable $\frac{1}{2}(W(t)^2 - t)$.

Exercise 3.12 Use the identity $2a(b - a) = (b^2 - a^2) - (b - a)^2$ and appropriate approximating partitions to show from first principles that $\int_0^T W(s)dW(s) = \frac{1}{2}(W(T)^2 - T)$.

3.4 Itô processes

Our goal is to study more general processes that in addition to a stochastic integral include a Lebesgue type integral in their definition.

Let $a : \Omega \times [0, T] \to \mathbb{R}$ satisfy

$$P\left(\left\{\omega : \int_0^T |a(s, \omega)|ds < \infty\right\}\right) = 1$$

and fix a process $b \in \mathcal{M}^2$.

Definition 3.16
A process of the form

$$X(t) = X(0) + \int_0^t a(s)ds + \int_0^t b(s)dW(s) \qquad \text{for } t \in [0, T]$$

is called an **Itô process** and a, b are called the **characteristics** of X (a is often called the **drift**).

A commonly accepted practice is to use the following differential notation

$$dX(t) = a(t)dt + b(t)dW(t)$$

and accordingly to say that X has a **stochastic differential**. It will be often convenient to manipulate the differential symbols but one has to remember that they have no mathematical meaning, being just an abbreviated notation of the integral formulation.

We begin with some basic properties of Itô processes.

Proposition 3.17
Almost all paths of X are continuous.

Proof This follows from the facts that the first integral, defined path by path, is continuous as the function of t and the second integral has continuous paths almost surely as a result of Theorem 3.15.   □

Proposition 3.18
If a = 0, then X is a martingale.

Proof The martingale property is just a consequence of Theorem 3.15.
                                                                        □

Proposition 3.19
If $\mathbb{E} \int_0^t |a(s)|ds < \infty$, then $\mathbb{E}(X(t)) = X(0) + \int_0^t \mathbb{E}(a(s))ds$.

Proof The expectation of the stochastic integral is zero and the claim follows, since by Fubini's theorem we can write $\mathbb{E} \int_0^t a(s)ds = \int_0^t \mathbb{E}(a(s))ds$.
                                                                        □

Next we generalise the isometry property of the integral, replacing the expectation by conditional expectations.

Theorem 3.20 (Conditional Itô isometry)

If $f \in \mathcal{M}^2$, $[a,b] \subset [0,T]$, then

$$\mathbb{E}\left(\left[\int_a^b f(s)dW(s)\right]^2 |\mathcal{F}_a\right) = \mathbb{E}\left(\int_a^b f^2(s)ds|\mathcal{F}_a\right).$$

Proof This can be proved by arguments similar to those for the unconditional isometry but we will give a different proof. By the definition of conditional expectation we have to show that for each $A \in \mathcal{F}_a$

$$\int_A \left(\int_a^b f(s)dW(s)\right)^2 dP = \int_A \mathbb{E}\left(\int_a^b f^2(s)ds|\mathcal{F}_a\right)dP.$$

The integral over A can be written as the expectation, so the goal takes the form

$$\mathbb{E}\left[\mathbf{1}_A\left(\int_a^b f(s)dW(s)\right)^2\right] = \mathbb{E}\left[\mathbf{1}_A \mathbb{E}\left(\int_a^b f^2(s)ds|\mathcal{F}_a\right)\right]. \qquad (3.6)$$

The right-hand side is easier to handle. The random variable $\mathbf{1}_A$ is $\mathcal{F}_a$-measurable so

$$\mathbf{1}_A \mathbb{E}\left(\int_a^b f^2(s)ds|\mathcal{F}_a\right) = \mathbb{E}\left(\mathbf{1}_A \int_a^b f^2(s)ds|\mathcal{F}_a\right)$$

$$= \mathbb{E}\left(\int_a^b \mathbf{1}_A f^2(s)ds|\mathcal{F}_a\right)$$

so by the tower property and the obvious fact $\mathbf{1}_A^2 = \mathbf{1}_A$

$$\text{RHS of } (3.6) = \mathbb{E}\left(\int_a^b (\mathbf{1}_A f(s))^2 ds\right).$$

By the unconditional Itô isometry

$$\text{RHS of } (3.6) = \mathbb{E}\left[\left(\int_a^b \mathbf{1}_A f(s)dW(s)\right)^2\right].$$

Comparing this with the left-hand side, all that is needed is to move $\mathbf{1}_A$ inside the stochastic integral. We have the linearity property of the integral, but this is a random variable, not a constant. However, being $\mathcal{F}_a$-measurable, it can be treated as a constant. This fact, formulated more generally, is given below, so the proof is complete. $\qquad\square$

Lemma 3.21

If X is $\mathcal{F}_a$-measurable and bounded, $f \in \mathcal{M}^2$, then

$$X \int_a^b f(s)dW(s) = \int_a^b X f(s)dW(s).$$

Proof   See page 105.   □

Exercise 3.13   Give a direct proof of Theorem 3.20 following the
method used for proving the unconditional Itô isometry.

One of the basic properties of the Wiener process is that $W^2(t) - t$ is
a martingale. The function t acts as a 'compensator', which must be sub-
tracted from the submartingale $W^2(t)$ in order to recover the martingale
property. This is intuitively clear: the mass (expectation) of a submartingale increases, so to make it a martingale one has to subtract something to
make the expectation constant. Our next goal is to extend this construction
to stochastic integrals. We know that the stochastic integral is a martingale,
its square is a submartingale, and we identify the compensator.

Theorem 3.22
If $f \in \mathcal{M}^2$, $M(t) = \int_0^t f(s)dW(s)$, then $M^2(t) - \int_0^t f^2(s)ds$ is a martingale.

Proof   Assume $s < t$. We begin with exploiting Theorem 2.33 and then
the conditional isometry to find

$$\mathbb{E}(M^2(t) - M^2(s)|\mathcal{F}_s) = \mathbb{E}((M(t) - M(s))^2|\mathcal{F}_s)$$

$$= \mathbb{E}\left(\left(\int_s^t f(u)dW(u)\right)^2 |\mathcal{F}_s\right)$$

$$= \mathbb{E}\left(\int_s^t f^2(u)du|\mathcal{F}_s\right).$$

Now subtract $\mathbb{E}(\int_0^t f^2(u)du|\mathcal{F}_s)$ on both sides and use linearity of condi-
tional expectation to obtain

$$\mathbb{E}\left(M^2(t) - \int_0^t f^2(u)du|\mathcal{F}_s\right) = \mathbb{E}\left(M^2(s) + \int_s^t f^2(u)du - \int_0^t f^2(u)du|\mathcal{F}_s\right).$$

On the right

$$\int_s^t f^2(u)du - \int_0^t f^2(u)du = -\int_0^s f^2(u)du,$$

which brings the right-hand side to the form

$$\mathbb{E}\left(M^2(s) - \int_0^s f^2(u)du|\mathcal{F}_s\right) = M^2(s) - \int_0^s f^2(u)du$$

completing the proof.   □

Quadratic variation of an Itô process

Our main goal now is to show that the compensator of the process given by a stochastic integral is equal to the quadratic variation. The first step is a technical lemma valid for arbitrary bounded continuous martingales.

Lemma 3.23
If $M(t)$ is a martingale with continuous paths and $|M(t, \omega)| \leq C < \infty$, then $\mathbb{E} \sum_{i=0}^{n-1} (M(t_{i+1}) - M(t_i))^4 \to 0$ as $\max(t_{i+1} - t_i) \to 0$, $0 = t_0 < t_1 < \cdots < t_n = t$.

Proof   See page 105. □

Theorem 3.24
Suppose $f \in \mathcal{M}^2$ is such that for some positive numbers C, D, $\int_0^T f^2(s)ds \leq C$ and $M(t) = \int_0^t f(s)dW(s)$ satisfies $|M(t)| \leq D$. Then

$$[M, M](t) = \int_0^t f^2(s)ds.$$

Proof   Fix $t \in [0, T]$ and take any partition $0 = t_0 < t_1 < \cdots < t_n = t$. We wish to show that

$$X_n = \sum_{i=0}^{n-1} (M(t_{i+1}) - M(t_i))^2 - \int_0^t f^2(s)ds \to 0$$

as the mesh of the partition $\max(t_{i+1} - t_i)$ converges to zero. Splitting the integral into a sum of integrals over smaller intervals we have

$$X_n = \sum_{i=0}^{n-1} \left((M(t_{i+1}) - M(t_i))^2 - \int_{t_i}^{t_{i+1}} f^2(s)ds \right) = \sum_{i=0}^{n-1} Y_i \quad \text{say.}$$

We prove that $X_n \to 0$ in L^2, which implies convergence in probability. To this end, we estimate the expectation of the square of X_n

$$\mathbb{E}(X_n^2) = \mathbb{E}\left(\sum_{i<n} Y_i \right)^2 = \sum_{i<n} \mathbb{E}(Y_i^2) + 2 \sum_{i<j<n} \mathbb{E}(Y_i Y_j).$$

The second term is zero: note that

$$\mathbb{E}(Y_i Y_j) = \mathbb{E}(\mathbb{E}(Y_i Y_j | \mathcal{F}_{t_j})) = \mathbb{E}(Y_i \mathbb{E}(Y_j | \mathcal{F}_{t_j}))$$

and that

$$\mathbb{E}(Y_j|\mathcal{F}_{t_j}) = \mathbb{E}((M(t_{j+1}) - M(t_j))^2 - \int_{t_j}^{t_{j+1}} f^2(s)ds|\mathcal{F}_{t_j})$$

$$= \mathbb{E}(M^2(t_{j+1}) - M^2(t_j) - \int_{t_j}^{t_{j+1}} f^2(s)ds|\mathcal{F}_{t_j})$$

$$= \mathbb{E}(M^2(t_{j+1}) - \int_0^{t_{j+1}} f^2(s)ds|\mathcal{F}_{t_j}) - [M^2(t_j) - \int_0^{t_j} f^2(s)] = 0$$

because, as we have just seen, $M^2(t) - \int_0^t f^2(s)ds$ is a martingale. We are left to deal with $\sum_{i<n} \mathbb{E}(Y_i^2)$:

$$\sum_{i<n} \mathbb{E}(Y_i^2) \le 2 \sum_{i<n} \mathbb{E}((M(t_{i+1}) - M(t_i))^4) + 2 \sum_{i<n} \mathbb{E}\left(\int_{t_i}^{t_{i+1}} f^2(s)ds\right)^2$$

using the elementary inequality $(a - b)^2 \le 2a^2 + 2b^2$ with $a = (M(t_{i+1}) - M(t_i))^2$, $b = \int_{t_i}^{t_{i+1}} f^2(s)ds$.

The first term on the right converges to zero by Lemma 3.23, so we are just left with the second term. Fix $\omega \in \Omega$. We know from real analysis that the function $g(t, \omega) = \int_0^t f^2(s, \omega)ds$, $t \in [0, T]$ is continuous on the closed interval $[0, T]$ because $f^2(t, \omega)$ is integrable. Therefore $t \mapsto g(t, \omega)$ is uniformly continuous on $[0, T]$. Hence for every sequence $\varepsilon_n \to 0$, $\varepsilon_n > 0$ there exists a sequence $\delta_n \to 0$ such that $\max_i(t_{i+1} - t_i) < \delta_n$ implies $\int_{t_i}^{t_{i+1}} f^2(s, \omega)ds < \varepsilon_n$. Using this fact we obtain

$$\sum_{i<n} \left(\int_{t_i}^{t_{i+1}} f^2(s)ds\right)^2 \le \left(\max_{i<n} \int_{t_i}^{t_{i+1}} f^2(s)ds\right) \sum_{i<n} \int_{t_i}^{t_{i+1}} f^2(s)ds$$

$$\le \varepsilon_n \int_0^t f^2(s)ds \le \varepsilon_n C \to 0,$$

using our assumption that $\int_0^t f^2(s)ds \le C$. This proves that the sequence on the left converges to zero almost surely. This convergence is dominated, so the expectation converges to zero as well. $\square$

Theorem 3.25
If $X(t) = X(0) + \int_0^t a(s)ds$, then $[X, X](t) = 0$ for $t \in [0, T]$.

Proof Reasoning similarly for $X(t, \omega)$ as for $g(t, \omega)$ in the last part of the proof of Theorem 3.24 we establish that, if a sequence $\varepsilon_n \to 0$, $\varepsilon_n > 0$, then

$$\sum_{i<n}(X(t_{i+1},\omega) - X(t_i,\omega))^2$$

$$\leq \max_{i<n}|X(t_{i+1},\omega) - X(t_i,\omega)| \sum_{i<n}|X(t_{i+1},\omega) - X(t_i,\omega)|$$

$$\leq \varepsilon_n \int_0^T |a(s,\omega)|ds \to 0, \quad \text{as } \max_{i<n}(t_{i+1} - t_i) \to 0.$$

(Note that this uses the assumption made on a at the beginning of this section, namely that the integral is finite for almost all ω.) The inequality implies that the sequence $\sum(X(t_{i+1}) - X(t_i))^2$ converges to zero almost surely, which completes the proof. □

Theorem 3.26
For an Itô process $dX(t) = a(t)dt + b(t)dW(t)$, with $\int_0^T b(s)dW(s)$ bounded, $[X,X](t) = \int_0^t b^2(s)ds$.

Proof Write $Y(t) = X(0) + \int_0^t a(s)ds$, $Z(t) = \int_0^t b(s)dW(s)$ and then

$$\sum_{i<n}(X(t_{i+1}) - X(t_i))^2 = \sum_{i<n}(Y(t_{i+1}) - Y(t_i) + Z(t_{i+1}) - Z(t_i))^2$$

$$= \sum_{i<n}(Y(t_{i+1}) - Y(t_i))^2 + \sum_{i<n}(Z(t_{i+1}) - Z(t_i))^2$$

$$+2\sum_{i<n}(Y(t_{i+1}) - Y(t_i))(Z(t_{i+1}) - Z(t_i)).$$

The first term converges to zero almost everywhere, the second to $\int_0^t b^2(s)ds$ in probability by Theorem 3.24. The result follows from the fact that the third also converges to zero since by the Schwarz inequality

$$\sum_{i<n}(Y(t_{i+1}) - Y(t_i))(Z(t_{i+1}) - Z(t_i))$$

$$\leq \sqrt{\sum_{i<n}(Y(t_{i+1}) - Y(t_i))^2} \sqrt{\sum_{i<n}(Z(t_{i+1}) - Z(t_i))^2}$$

and the upper bound converges to zero as a product of two sequences, with one converging to zero and the other bounded. □

With the experience gathered so far we can conclude with a very important result, with consequences in the theory of derivative pricing in particular.

Theorem 3.27

The representation of an Itô process in the form adt + bdW is unique. That is, suppose

$$dX_1(t) = a_1(t)dt + b_1(t)dW(t),$$
$$dX_2(t) = a_2(t)dt + b_2(t)dW(t),$$

with $\int_0^T b_i(s)dW(s)$, $i = 1, 2$, *bounded, and assume* $X_1(t) = X_2(t)$. *Then* $a_1(t) = a_2(t)$, $b_1(t) = b_2(t)$ *for almost all t, almost surely.*

Proof   The process $Y = X_1 - X_2$ is an Itô process since

$$Y(t) = X_1(t) - X_2(t) = \int_0^t (a_1 - a_2)(s)ds + \int_0^t (b_1 - b_2)(s)dW(s).$$

But $Y = 0$ almost everywhere so for almost all $\omega \in \Omega$

$$\int_0^t (a_1 - a_2)(s)ds = -\int_0^t (b_1 - b_2)(s)dW(s) = Z(t).$$

The quadratic variation of the process on the left is zero so the same is true for the process on the right. But we know that

$$[Z, Z](t) = \int_0^t (b_1(s) - b_2(s))^2 ds$$

so for this to be zero we must have $b_1 = b_2$ for almost all ω. Hence $Z(t) = 0$ for almost all $\omega \in \Omega$, which in turn gives for every t in $[0, T]$ that

$$\int_0^t (a_1(s) - a_2(s))ds = 0,$$

so that $a_1(t) = a_2(t)$ for almost all $t \in [0, T]$. Intuitively, this is clear since the integral of $a_1 - a_2$ over each interval is zero and we leave the details as an exercise.   □

Exercise 3.14   Show $\int_0^t g(s)ds = 0$ for all $t \in [0, T]$ implies $g = 0$ almost surely on $[0, T]$.

Remark 3.28

We made convenient but very restrictive assumptions to ensure that certain processes are bounded by deterministic constants. For instance, the assumption that $\int_0^T b(t)dW(t)$ is bounded excludes constant b since $W(T)$ is not bounded, so such an assumption requires very special behaviour of the integrand, and this cannot be expected in applications. The good news is that in the next chapter we will learn a technique which will enable us to relax this assumption.

3.5 Proofs

Theorem 3.4

For every process $f \in M^2$, there exists a sequence $(f_n)_{n\geq 1}$ of simple processes $f_n \in S^2$ such that

$$\lim_{n\to\infty} \mathbb{E} \int_0^T (f(t) - f_n(t))^2 dt = 0.$$

Proof We need prove the theorem only for bounded processes. Assume that $|g(t, \omega)| \leq c$ for all $(t, \omega) \in [0, T] \times \Omega$ and $g(t, \omega) = 0$ for $t \notin [0, T]$. On $\mathbb{R}$, define the sequence of functions $(h_n)_{n\geq 1}$,

$$h_n(t) = \frac{i}{n} \mathbf{1}_{(\frac{i}{n}, \frac{i+1}{n}]}(t), \text{ where } i \in \mathbb{Z}, \ n = 1, 2, \dots. \tag{3.7}$$

Our aim is to use the functions h_n to construct simple processes approximating g. Note that for each t the difference between $h_n(t)$ and t is less than $\frac{1}{n}$. Applying the Fubini theorem to the bounded function g we see that $g(\cdot, \omega)$ is square-integrable for each $\omega \in \Omega$. Hence the functions $(t, s) \to g(t + s, \omega), t \in \mathbb{R}, s \in [0, 1], \omega \in \Omega$ are also square-integrable and we shall prove below (Lemma 3.29) that

$$\lim_{h\to 0} \int_0^1 (g(t + s + h, \omega) - g(t + s, \omega))^2 ds = 0$$

for all $t \in \mathbb{R}, \omega \in \Omega$. Assuming this result, it follows in particular that we can write, for all $t \in \mathbb{R}, \omega \in \Omega$

$$\lim_{n\to\infty} \int_0^1 (g(h_n(t) + s, \omega) - g(t + s, \omega))^2 ds = 0, \tag{3.8}$$

since for each $t \in \mathbb{R}$ the sequence $h_n(t) - t \to 0$ as $n \to \infty$. Now consider the functions

$$q_n(t, s, \omega) = g(h_n(t) + s, \omega) - g(t + s, \omega), \quad t \in \mathbb{R}, \quad s \in [0, 1], \quad \omega \in \Omega, \tag{3.9}$$

for $n \geq 1$. They are $B(\mathbb{R} \times [0, 1]) \times \mathcal{F}$ measurable and bounded by an integrable function on $\mathbb{R} \times [0, 1] \times \Omega$. Indeed, we have $|q_n(t, s, \omega)| \leq 2c\mathbf{1}_{[-1, T+1]}(t)$

because g is bounded by c. These properties and the Fubini theorem provide measurable, bounded functions $\bar{q}_n$ on $\mathbb{R} \times \Omega$, if we define

$$\bar{q}_n(t, \omega) = \int_0^1 (q_n(t, s, \omega))^2 ds \le 4c^2 \mathbf{1}_{[-1, T+1]}(t).$$

Thus the convergence obtained in (3.8) is dominated, and we obtain

$$\lim_{n \to \infty} \int_\Omega \int_\mathbb{R} \int_0^1 (q_n(t, s, \omega))^2 ds dt P(d\omega) = \lim_{n \to \infty} \int_\Omega \int_\mathbb{R} \bar{q}_n(t, \omega) dt P(d\omega) = 0.$$

This means that the sequence $(q_n)_{n \ge 1}$ converges to zero in the norm of $L^2(\mathbb{R} \times [0, 1] \times \Omega)$, where the first two factors in the bracket have Lebesgue measure and the final one has the measure P. This implies that there exists a subsequence $(q_{k(n)})_n$ of $(q_n)_n$ converging to zero almost surely with respect to the product measure on $\mathbb{R} \times [0, 1] \times \Omega$. As a consequence, we obtain that for almost all $s \in [0, 1]$ the subsequence $(q_{k(n)})_n$ converges to zero almost surely on $\mathbb{R} \times \Omega$. Choose one such $\tilde{s} \in [0, 1]$. Again using the dominated convergence theorem and changing the variable $(t \to \tau = t + \tilde{s})$ we conclude that

$$\lim_{n \to \infty} \int_\Omega \int_\mathbb{R} (g(h_{k(n)}(\tau - \tilde{s}) + \tilde{s}, \omega) - g(\tau, \omega))^2 d\tau P(d\omega)$$

$$= \lim_{n \to \infty} \int_\Omega \int_\mathbb{R} q_{k(n)}(\tau - \tilde{s}, \tilde{s}, \omega) d\tau P(d\omega) = 0.$$

Putting $\tilde{f}_n(t, \omega) = g(h_n(t - \tilde{s}) + \tilde{s}, \omega)$ for $t \in [0, T]$, $\omega \in \Omega$, we obtain, finally

$$\lim_{n \to \infty} \mathbb{E} \int_0^T (g(t, \cdot) - \tilde{f}_{k(n)}(t, \cdot))^2 dt = 0. \tag{3.10}$$

Let us now look more closely at the definition of $\tilde{f}_n$. Let

$$i_n = \max\{i \in \mathbb{Z} : \frac{i}{n} + \tilde{s} \le a\}$$

$$m_n = \max\{m \in \mathbb{Z} : \frac{i_n + m}{n} + \tilde{s} < b\}.$$

Since $g(t, \omega) = 0$ for $t \notin [0, T]$, according to the definition of h_n we obtain

$$\tilde{f}_n(t, \omega) = \begin{cases} g(0) & \text{for } t \in (0, \frac{i_n+1}{n} + \tilde{s}] \\ g(\frac{i_n+1}{n} + \tilde{s}, \omega) & \text{for } t \in (\frac{i_n+1}{n} + \tilde{s}, \frac{i_n+2}{n} + \tilde{s}] \\ \dots & \dots \\ g(\frac{i_n+m_n}{n} + \tilde{s}, \omega) & \text{for } t \in (\frac{i_n+m_n}{n} + \tilde{s}, 1]. \end{cases}$$

From this exact formula for $\tilde{f}_n$, we see that $\tilde{f}_n$ are simple bounded functions,

$\tilde{f}_n(t)$ are $\mathcal{F}_t$-measurable for all $t \in [0, T]$ and $\tilde{f}_n \in L^2[0, T]$. The following Lemma, applied to $g(t + s, \omega)$ for each $t \in \mathbb{R}, \omega \in \Omega$ in the above, now completes the proof. □

Lemma 3.29
For any square-integrable real function $f(s)$, we have

$$\lim_{h \to 0} \int_0^1 (f(s + h) - f(s))^2 ds = 0.$$

In particular, with g as in the proof of Theorem 3.4 we obtain

$$\lim_{h \to 0} \int_0^1 (g(t + s + h, \omega) - g(t + s, \omega))^2 ds = 0$$

for all $t \in \mathbb{R}, \omega \in \Omega$.

Proof See [PF]. □

Theorem 3.15
If $f \in \mathcal{M}^2$, then there exists a continuous martingale M such that for all t

$$P\left(M(t) = \int_0^T (1_{[0,t]} f)(s) dW(s)\right) = 1.$$

Proof We know that there exists a sequence of simple process $g_n \in \mathcal{S}^2$, $n \geq 1$ such that

$$\mathbb{E} \int_0^T (g_n(s) - f(s))^2 ds \to 0.$$

Clearly, $1_{[0,t]} g_n \in \mathcal{S}^2$ ($\mathbb{E} \int_0^T 1_{[0,t]} g_n^2 ds \leq \mathbb{E} \int_0^T g_n^2 ds < \infty$) and so the following integrals are well defined

$$M_n(t) = \int_0^T (1_{[0,t]} g_n)(s) dW(s) \qquad \text{for } t \in [0, T].$$

Let the processes g_n be of the form

$$g_n(s) = \xi_0 1_{\{0\}} + \sum_{i=0}^{N-1} 1_{(t_i, t_{i+1}]} \xi_i,$$

where $0 = t_0 < t_1 < \cdots < t_N = T$, $\xi_i \in L^2(\Omega)$ and ξ_i are $\mathcal{F}_{t_i}$-measurable. (Here both sequences t_i, ξ_i depend on n.) Fix t, which must belong to one of the intervals, $t \in (t_m, t_{m+1}]$ for some m, so

$$(\mathbf{1}_{[0,t]}g_n)(s) = \xi_0 \mathbf{1}_{\{0\}} + \sum_{i=0}^{N-1} \mathbf{1}_{[0,t]}(s)\mathbf{1}_{(t_i,t_{i+1}]}(s)\xi_i$$

$$= \xi_0 \mathbf{1}_{\{0\}} + \sum_{i=0}^{m-1} \mathbf{1}_{(t_i,t_{i+1}]}(s)\xi_i + \mathbf{1}_{(t_m,t]}(s)\xi_m.$$

The stochastic integral of a simple function can be computed directly

$$M_n(t) = \int_0^T (\mathbf{1}_{[0,t]}g_n)(s)dW(s) = \sum_{i=0}^{m-1} \xi_i(W(t_{i+1}) - W(t_i)) + \xi_m(W(t) - W(t_m)),$$

and this is continuous in t (in the sense that almost all paths are continuous) since the only place t appears is in the last term and W has continuous paths. We will find the desired $M(t)$ as the limit of $M_n(t)$. To have $M(t)$ with continuous paths we need to establish the uniform convergence of the paths of $M_n(t)$.

Let $s < t$, $s \in (t_j, t_{j+1}]$, say ($t \in (t_m, t_{m+1}]$ so $j \leq m$),

$$\mathbb{E}(M_n(t)|\mathcal{F}_s) = \mathbb{E}\left(\sum_{i=0}^{m-1} \xi_i(W(t_{i+1}) - W(t_i)) + \xi_m(W(t) - W(t_m))|\mathcal{F}_s\right)$$

$$= \mathbb{E}\left(\sum_{i=0}^{j-1} \xi_i(W(t_{i+1}) - W(t_i))|\mathcal{F}_s\right) + \mathbb{E}(\xi_j(W(t_{j+1}) - W(t_j))|\mathcal{F}_s)$$

$$+ \mathbb{E}\left(\sum_{i=j+1}^{m-1} \xi_i(W(t_{i+1}) - W(t_i))|\mathcal{F}_s\right) + \mathbb{E}(\xi_m(W(t) - W(t_m))|\mathcal{F}_s)$$

$$= \sum_{i=0}^{j-1} \xi_i(W(t_{i+1}) - W(t_i)) + \xi_j(W(s) - W(t_j)) \quad \text{(measurability)}$$

$$+ \mathbb{E}\left(\sum_{i=j+1}^{m-1} \xi_i(W(t_{i+1}) - W(t_i))\right) + \mathbb{E}(\xi_m(W(t) - W(t_m)))$$

$$\text{(independence)}$$

$$= M_n(s) \quad \text{(expectations vanish as before)}$$

so M_n is a martingale. The same is true for M_k and also for $M_n - M_k$, any n, k.

Recall the Doob inequality, proved in Lemma 2.34: if $M \in \mathcal{M}^2$ is a martingale, then

$$P(\sup_{t\in[0,T]} |M(t)| > \lambda) \le \frac{1}{\lambda^2} \mathbb{E}(M(T)^2). \tag{3.11}$$

This applied to the difference $M_n - M_k$ gives

$$P(\sup_{t\in[0,T]} |M_n(t) - M_k(t)| > \lambda) \le \frac{1}{\lambda^2} \mathbb{E}((M_n(T) - M_k(T))^2). \tag{3.12}$$

We compute the expectation on the right inserting the definitions and employing linearity

$$\mathbb{E}((M_n(T) - M_k(T))^2) = \mathbb{E}\left(\int_0^T g_n(s)dW(s) - \int_0^T g_k(s)dW(s)\right)^2$$

$$= \mathbb{E}\left(\int_0^T (g_n(s) - g_k(s))dW(s)\right)^2$$

$$= \mathbb{E}\int_0^T (g_n(s) - g_k(s))^2 ds,$$

where the final step uses the isometry property.

Since $\mathbb{E}(\int_0^T (g_n(s) - f(s))^2 ds) \to 0$, there is n_1 such that for $k \ge n_1$

$$\mathbb{E}\left(\int_0^T (g_{n_1}(s) - g_k(s))^2 ds\right) < 2^{-3}.$$

Next, there is $n_2 > n_1$ such that for all $k \ge n_2$

$$\mathbb{E}\left(\int_0^T (g_{n_2}(s) - g_k(s))^2 ds\right) < 2^{-3\times 2}.$$

In general, there is $n_j > n_{j-1}$ such that for all $k \ge n_j$

$$\mathbb{E}\left(\int_0^T (g_{n_j}(s) - g_k(s))^2 ds\right) < 2^{-3j}.$$

This gives the estimate for all j, for all $k \ge n_j$

$$\mathbb{E}((M_{n_j}(T) - M_k(T))^2) < 2^{-3j}. \tag{3.13}$$

Now we use (3.11) to get for each j the following estimate holding for any λ

$$P(\sup_{t\in[0,T]} |M_{n_j}(t) - M_{n_{j+1}}(t)| > \lambda) \le \frac{1}{\lambda^2} 2^{-3j}.$$

Let $\lambda = 2^{-j}$ and so

$$P\left(\sup_{t\in[0,T]} |M_{n_j}(t) - M_{n_{j+1}}(t)| > \frac{1}{2^j}\right) \le 2^{-2j}.$$

Since the series on the right converges, $\sum 2^{-2j} < \infty$, by the Borel–Cantelli lemma there is a set Ω' with $P(\Omega') = 1$ so that on Ω'

$$\sup_{t\in[0,T]} |M_{n_j}(t,\omega) - M_{n_{j+1}}(t,\omega)| \le \frac{1}{2^j} \quad \text{for } j \ge L.$$

Note that the index L depends on ω.

This gives uniform convergence of $M_{n_j}(t,\omega)$ with respect to $t \in [0,T]$ for all $\omega \in \Omega'$ since $M_{n_j}(t,\omega)$ is Cauchy in $C([0,T])$ with the supremum norm. The limit is denoted by $M(t)$.

The above estimates also show that for each t the sequence of random variables $M_{n_j}(t)$ converges on Ω'. This property and (3.13) give the convergence in L^2. The martingale property holds for each M_{n_j}, so to show that M is a martingale it is sufficient to note that the equality $\mathbb{E}(M_{n_j}(t)|\mathcal{F}_s) = M_{n_j}(s)$ is preserved in the limit. $M_{n_j}(s)$ converges on Ω', so almost surely on Ω and in the limit we have $M(s)$ on the right. On the left, we note first that if a sequence of random variables converges in L^2, their conditional expectations relative to a fixed sub-σ-field also converge in L^2. We can now argue as on the right.

Finally, we show that the constructed process fulfills the promise, that is $M(t)$ is almost surely the same as $\int_0^T (\mathbf{1}_{[0,t]}f)(s)dW(s)$. First,

$$\mathbb{E}\int_0^T (\mathbf{1}_{[0,t]}(s)g_{n_j}(s) - \mathbf{1}_{[0,t]}(s)f(s))^2 ds \le \mathbb{E}\int_0^T (g_{n_j}(s) - f(s))^2 ds \to 0$$

so

$$\mathbb{E}\left(\int_0^T (\mathbf{1}_{[0,t]}(s)g_{n_j}(s) - \mathbf{1}_{[0,t]}(s)f(s))dW(s)\right)^2 \to 0.$$

We know that

$$\mathbb{E}\left(\int_0^T (\mathbf{1}_{[0,t]}(s)g_{n_j}(s)dW(s) - M(t)\right)^2 \to 0$$

and the limit of a sequence is determined uniquely, so

$$\int_0^T \mathbf{1}_{[0,t]}(s)f(s)dW(s) = M(t)$$

for almost all ω. $\square$

Lemma 3.21

If X is F_a-measurable and bounded, $f \in \mathcal{M}^2$, then

$$X \int_a^b f(s)dW(s) = \int_a^b Xf(s)dW(s).$$

Proof First note that $Xf \in \mathcal{M}^2$ so that the right-hand side makes sense. This is obvious because $|X| \leq C$ implies $X^2 f^2 \leq C^2 f^2$ and the integrability follows immediately. Adaptedness of f is of course not destroyed by multiplying by X.

If f is simple, so is Xf, and the claim boils down to elementary algebra. The problem reduces to passing to the limit in

$$X \int_a^b f_n(s)dW(s) = \int_a^b Xf_n(s)dW(s),$$

where f_n converge to f in $\mathcal{M}^2$. Boundedness of X makes this task easy:

$$\mathbb{E}\left(X \int_a^b f(s)dW(s) - X \int_a^b f_n(s)dW(s)\right)^2$$

$$\leq C^2 \mathbb{E}\left(\int_a^b f(s)dW(s) - \int_a^b f_n(s)dW(s)\right)^2 \to 0,$$

$$\mathbb{E}\int_0^T (Xf_n(s) - Xf(s))^2\, ds \leq C^2 \mathbb{E}\int_0^T (f_n(s) - f(s))^2\, ds \to 0,$$

which gives the claim $\qquad\qquad\square$

Lemma 3.23

If $M(t)$ is a martingale with continuous paths and $|M(t, \omega)| \leq C < \infty$, then

$$\mathbb{E}\sum (M(t_{i+1}) - M(t_i))^4 \to 0$$

as $\max(t_{i+1} - t_i) \to 0$, $0 = t_0 < t_1 < \cdots < t_n = t$.

Proof We analyse the sum under the expectation; the first step is the estimate

$$\sum_{i=0}^{n-1}(M(t_{i+1}) - M(t_i))^4 \leq \max_{i=0,\ldots,n-1}(M(t_{i+1}) - M(t_i))^2 \sum_{i=0}^{n-1}(M(t_{i+1}) - M(t_i))^2.$$

$$(3.14)$$

The paths of M are uniformly continuous since we consider a bounded time interval, so for each $\varepsilon > 0$ there exists $\delta > 0$ such that, if $\max(t_{i+1} - t_i) \leq \delta$, then

$$\max(M(t_{i+1}) - M(t_i))^2 \leq \varepsilon^2,$$

which proves that the sequence on the left converges to zero almost surely. We seem to be close to our target: a bounded M allows us to apply dominated convergence and the only problem is the second factor, which only needs to be shown to be bounded (in some sense). The difficulty, however, is that the number of its components grows with n. A nice trick is to force cancellations using Theorem 2.33:

$$\mathbb{E}\left(\sum(M(t_{i+1}) - M(t_i))^2\right) = \mathbb{E}\left(\sum \mathbb{E}((M(t_{i+1}) - M(t_i))^2|\mathcal{F}_{t_i})\right)$$
$$= \mathbb{E}\left(\sum \mathbb{E}((M^2(t_{i+1}) - M^2(t_i))|\mathcal{F}_{t_i})\right)$$
$$= \mathbb{E}\left(\sum(M^2(t_{i+1}) - M^2(t_i))\right)$$
$$= \mathbb{E}(M^2(t) - M^2(0)) \leq 2C^2.$$

This is not straightforward since the expectation in (3.14) concerns a product, so we cannot use the above computation directly. Expectation of the product can be however estimated by the expectations of the factors by using the Schwartz inequality – a price has to be paid, in that the powers involved increase:

$$\mathbb{E}\sum(M(t_{i+1}) - M(t_i))^4$$
$$\leq \mathbb{E}\left(\max(M(t_{i+1}) - M(t_i))^2 \sum(M(t_{i+1}) - M(t_i))^2\right)$$
$$\leq \sqrt{\mathbb{E}(\max(M(t_{i+1}) - M(t_i))^2)^2} \sqrt{\mathbb{E}\left(\sum(M(t_{i+1}) - M(t_i))^2\right)^2}.$$

The higher power does no harm to the first factor: $\max(M(t_{i+1}) - M(t_i))^2$ goes to zero, hence so does its square, even faster. Boundedness allows use of the dominated convergence theorem and

$$\mathbb{E}\left(\max(M(t_{i+1}) - M(t_i))^2\right)^2 \to 0.$$

The proof thus reduces to showing that $\mathbb{E}\left(\sum(M(t_{i+1}) - M(t_i))^2\right)^2$ is bounded by a constant independent of the choice of the partition $\{t_i\}$. For the expression under the expectation, simple algebra gives

$$\left(\sum (M(t_{i+1}) - M(t_i))^2\right)^2$$

$$\leq \sum (M(t_{i+1}) - M(t_i))^4 + 2\sum_{i<j} (M(t_{i+1}) - M(t_i))^2 (M(t_{j+1}) - M(t_j))^2$$

$$\leq 4C^2 \sum (M(t_{i+1}) - M(t_i))^2$$

$$+ 2\sum_{i=1}^{n-1} (M(t_{i+1}) - M(t_i))^2 \sum_{j=i+1}^{n-1} (M(t_{j+1}) - M(t_j))^2.$$

In the last step we used the boundedness of M but only selectively (in the first sum) – cunningly we are going to exploit the trick mentioned before and we like the squares. The second term has to be handled in a subtle way. The problem here is that the number of terms in the sum varies and we estimate the square leaving some terms which will later cancel out, which requires a meticulous approach.

After applying the expectation, we know that the first sum poses no difficulties, as observed above

$$\mathbb{E}\left(\sum (M(t_{i+1}) - M(t_i))^2\right) \leq 2C^2.$$

The same method is useful in the second sum. Introducing appropriate conditional expectations (a familiar method by now) and using Theorem 2.33 we find

$$\mathbb{E}\left(\sum_{i=1}^{n-1} (M(t_{i+1}) - M(t_i))^2 \sum_{j=i+1}^{n-1} (M(t_{j+1}) - M(t_j))^2\right)$$

$$= \mathbb{E}\left(\sum_{i=1}^{n-1} (M(t_{i+1}) - M(t_i))^2 \mathbb{E}\left(\sum_{j=i+1}^{n-1} (M(t_{j+1}) - M(t_j))^2 | \mathcal{F}_{t_{j+1}}\right)\right)$$

$$= \mathbb{E}\left(\sum_{i=1}^{n-1} (M(t_{i+1}) - M(t_i))^2 \mathbb{E}\left(\sum_{j=i+1}^{n-1} (M^2(t_{j+1}) - M^2(t_j)) | \mathcal{F}_{t_{j+1}}\right)\right)$$

$$= \mathbb{E}\left(\sum_{i=1}^{n-1} (M(t_{i+1}) - M(t_i))^2 \mathbb{E}(M^2(t) - M^2(t_{i+1}))\right)$$

$$\leq C^2 \mathbb{E}\left(\sum_{i=1}^{n-1} (M(t_{i+1}) - M(t_i))^2\right).$$

We have reduced the problem to an estimate we have already used a number of times:

$$\mathbb{E}\left(\sum_{i=1}^{n-1}(M(t_{i+1}) - M(t_i))^2\right) \leq C^2,$$

and this completes the story.   □

4

Itô formula

4.1   A heuristic derivation

The theory of stochastic integration, and, as a consequence, much of modern mathematical finance, is based on solving the following problem: if X is an Itô process, and $F(t, x)$ is a smooth function of two variables, is $Y(t) = F(t, X(t))$ again an Itô process and, if so, what are its characteristics a_Y, b_Y? We begin with a heuristic attempt to guess the answer.

For this, let us assume that F depends on x only, and that X is the simplest Itô process. So let $a = 0$, $b = 1$, $X(0) = 0$, giving $X(t) = W(t)$. Our objective is to represent $Y(t) = F(W(t))$ as

$$F(W(t)) = F(W(0)) + \int_0^t a_Y(s)ds + \int_0^t b_Y(s)dW(s)$$

and to identify the processes a_Y and b_y. We employ approximation over a

109

short time interval. The additivity of the integral over intervals means that it would be sufficient to determine, for some $h > 0$, the ingredients of

$$F(W(t + h)) = F(W(t)) + \int_t^{t+h} a_Y(s)ds + \int_t^{t+h} b_Y(s)dW(s).$$

Use the Taylor formula:

$$F(x + y) = F(x) + F'(x)y + \frac{1}{2}F''(x)y^2 + \frac{1}{6}F'''(\theta)y^3$$

for some $\theta \in [x, x + y]$, with $x = W(t)$, $y = W(t + h) - W(t)$ to obtain

$$F(W(t + h)) = F(W(t)) + F'(W(t))[W(t + h) - W(t)]$$
$$+ \frac{1}{2}F''(W(t))[W(t + h) - W(t)]^2$$
$$+ \frac{1}{6}F'''(\theta)[W(t + h) - W(t)]^3.$$

The second term on the right looks close to the stochastic integral of $F'(W(s))$ over $[t, t+h]$, since the integrand $F'(W(t))$ is continuous in t. This ensures that the simple process $F'(W(t))\mathbf{1}_{(t,t+h]}(s)$ has stochastic integral $F'(W(t))[W(t + h) - W(t)]$, which, for small h, is close to the integral of $F'(W(s))\mathbf{1}_{(t,t+h]}(s)$, by Theorem 3.4.

The expectation of the random variable $[W(t + h) - W(t)]^2$ is h, so the second term looks like the ordinary integral of $\frac{1}{2}F''(W(s))$ with respect to s from t to $t + h$.

Similarly, $[W(t + h) - W(t)]^3$ is of order $h^{3/2}$ (let $X = W(t + h) - W(t)$ and by Cauchy–Schwarz, $\mathbb{E}|X|^3 \le \sqrt{\mathbb{E}(X^4)}\sqrt{\mathbb{E}(X^2)} = \sqrt{3}h^{3/2}$), which is small compared to h, so the last term may be discarded provided F''' is bounded, which we immediately assume. Note that it will remain small even if we work with a general interval $[0, t]$ which we split into N pieces of length $h = \frac{t}{N}$, since after adding N terms we obtain a quantity of magnitude $CN(t/N)^{3/2} = C(t/N)^{1/2} \to 0$ if $N \to \infty$.

Our educated guess, after employing additivity over intervals, is therefore a special case of the **Itô formula**:

$$F(W(t)) = F(W(0)) + \int_0^t F'(W(s))dW(s) + \frac{1}{2}\int_0^t F''(W(s))ds.$$

Hence $Y(t) = F(W(t))$ is an Itô process

$$dY(t) = a_Y(t)dt + b_Y(t)dW(t)$$

with

$$a_Y(t) = \frac{1}{2}F''(W(t)),$$
$$b_Y(t) = F'(W(t)).$$

In shorthand notation, this Itô formula reads

$$dF(W(t)) = \frac{1}{2}F''(W(t))dt + F'(W(t))dW(t).$$

Recall that the differentials here make no sense and one has to remember that whenever we write this we have in mind the integral formulation.

If $Z(t)$ is differentiable, then the differentials do make sense and

$$dF(Z(t)) = F'(Z(t))dZ(t).$$

Recall however that the Wiener process is not differentiable. Comparing these two differentials we can see that they differ by the term involving the second derivative of F. This term is called the **Itô correction.** Its presence follows from the fact that the variance of an increment of the Wiener process is the length of the incremental time step.

Example 4.1
Let $F(x) = x^2$, $Y(t) = W^2(t)$, $F'(x) = 2x$, $F''(x) = 2$ and then (compare with Exercise 3.12)

$$dW^2(t) = dt + 2W(t)dW(t).$$

Our pricipal objective in this chapter is to justify our claim and generalise it to suitable functions F of both t and x. There are few textbooks where the proof of the Itô formula is given completely, and practically all of these are quite advanced, often covering very general situations. Since this result lies at the heart of the theory of modern mathematical finance, we believe that the task of giving a complete proof is worth the effort. It will give the reader confidence and a competitive advantage over non-mathematicans, for whom an act of faith is the only way to fill the gap between intuitive arguments and a fully rigorous proof – a gap that can frequently prove to be rather treacherous.

4.2 Functions of the Wiener process

For notational simplicity, we first prove the Itô formula for a function F independent of t. We impose a technical restriction on F requiring that it vanishes outside a finite interval and, as a consequence, if F is continuous, it is also bounded. The formula holds for a wider class of functions F, but this will require additional work and will be addressed later.

We begin with a simple L^2-convergence result.

Proposition 4.2
If $f \in M^2$ has continuous paths, then for each $t \in [0, T]$, and any sequence $(t_k^n)_{k \geq 0}$ of partitions of $[0, t]$ with mesh $\max_k |t_{k+1}^n - t_k^n| \to 0$ as $n \to \infty$, we have

$$\mathbb{E}\left(\int_0^t f(s)dW(s) - \sum_{i=0}^{n-1} f(t_i^n)[W(t_{i+1}^n) - W(t_i^n)]\right)^2 \to 0 \quad as\ n \to \infty.$$

Proof In the proof of Theorem 3.4, we showed that for any fixed $t > 0$ the path-continuous bounded process f can be approximated on $[0, t]$ in the norm of M^2 by simple processes f_n of a special type: take any system of partitions $\{t_k^n\}$ of $[0, t]$ with $\max_k |t_{k+1}^n - t_k^n| \to 0$ as $n \to \infty$ and define f_n for $s \in [0, t]$ by

$$f_n(s) = f(0)\mathbf{1}_{\{0\}} + \sum_{k=0}^{n-1} f(t_i^n)\mathbf{1}_{(t_k^n, t_{k+1}^n]}(s).$$

In other words, we showed that these f_n satisfy

$$\lim_{n \to \infty} \mathbb{E} \int_0^t (f(s) - f_n(s))^2 ds = 0.$$

By the Itô isometry and linearity of the integral we obtain

$$\mathbb{E}\left(\int_0^t f(s)dW(s) - \int_0^t f_n(s)dW(s)\right)^2 \to 0$$

but by definition

$$\int_0^t f_n(s)dW(s) = \sum_{k=0}^{n-1} f(t_k^n)[W(t_{k+1}^n) - W(t_k^n)]$$

so we are done. $\qquad\square$

Remark 4.3
The proof of the Itô formula (in all its manifestations) makes essential use of the fact that the stochastic integral is constructed in two steps: first for

simple functions as a sum, then extended to functions in $\mathcal{M}^2$ by means of the Itô isometry. In defining the integral of $f \in \mathcal{M}^2$ as the limit in L^2-norm of integrals of approximating simple functions, we define the latter, as above, using, for $t \in [0, T]$, an appropriate sequence $(t_k^n)_{k \geq 0}$, $n \geq 1$, of partitions of $[0, t]$ whose mesh $\max_k |t_{k+1}^n - t_k^n| \to 0$ as $n \to \infty$. To avoid overburdening the notation, we shall write $0 = t_0 < t_1 < \cdots < t_n = t$ for a typical partition, which we treat as representing the above sequence of partitions when we let $n \to \infty$.

Corollary 4.4
Assume $G : \mathbb{R} \to \mathbb{R}$ is continuous and $G(x) = 0$ for $x \notin [-M, M]$. Then

$$\mathbb{E}\left(\int_0^t G(W(s))dW(s) - \sum_{i=0}^{n-1} G(W(t_i))[W(t_{i+1}) - W(t_i)] \right)^2 \to 0 \quad as\ n \to \infty.$$

Proof First note that G is bounded so that $G(W(t)) \in \mathcal{M}^2$. The integral $\int_0^T G(W(t))dW(t)$ is well defined and we can apply the previous proposition to $f(t) = G(W(t))$. □

The above results, while elementary, allow us the freedom to choose a very convenient sequence of partitions in defining our approximating sequences of simple functions. This is exploited in proving our first version of the Itô formula.

Theorem 4.5 (Itô formula)
Assume that $F : \mathbb{R} \to \mathbb{R}$ is twice continuously differentiable and $F(x) = 0$ for $x \notin [-M, M]$ for some M. Then the Itô formula holds in the form:

$$F(W(t)) - F(0) = \int_0^t F'(W(s))dW(s) + \frac{1}{2} \int_0^t F''(W(s))ds.$$

Proof **Step 1 – Taylor approximation.** Fix t. We use the partition $(t_i)_{i \leq n}$ with $t_i = i\frac{t}{n}$, $i = 0, 1, \ldots, n$ (whose mesh goes to zero as $n \to \infty$) and split the left-hand side into a telescoping sum

$$F(W(t)) - F(0) = \sum_{i=0}^{n-1} [F(W(t_{i+1})) - F(W(t_i))]. \tag{4.1}$$

By the Taylor formula, for $x < y$, there exists $z \in [x, y]$

$$F(y) - F(x) = F'(x)[y - x] + \frac{1}{2}F''(z)[y - x]^2$$

so, with $y = W(t_{i+1})$ and $x = W(t_i)$ we have

$$F(W(t_{i+1})) - F(W(t_i)) = F'(W(t_i))[W(t_{i+1}) - W(t_i)] + \frac{1}{2}F''(z_i)[W(t_{i+1}) - W(t_i)]^2$$
(4.2)

for some z_i between $W(t_i)$ and $W(t_{i+1})$. Next we insert (4.2) in (4.1) to get

$$F(W(t)) - F(0)$$
$$= \sum_{i=0}^{n-1} F'(W(t_i))[W(t_{i+1}) - W(t_i)] + \frac{1}{2}\sum_{i=0}^{n-1} F''(z_i)[W(t_{i+1}) - W(t_i)]^2.$$

Step 2 – Terms with F'. The approximation found in Corollary 4.4, applied to F', provides the following convergence in $L^2(\Omega)$-norm:

$$\sum_{i=0}^{n-1} F'(W(t_i))[W(t_{i+1}) - W(t_i)] \to \int_0^t F'(W(s))dW(s)$$

and so we obtain almost sure convergence along a subsequence.

Step 3 – Terms with F''. We have to show that, as $n \to \infty$,

$$\frac{1}{2}\sum_{i=0}^{n-1} F''(z_i)[W(t_{i+1}) - W(t_i)]^2 \to \frac{1}{2}\int_0^t F''(W(s))ds.$$

Step 3a – Disposing of z_i. We want to replace z_i by $W(t_i)$ so we first prove that

$$\sum_{i=0}^{n-1} [F''(z_i) - F''(W(t_i))][W(t_{i+1}) - W(t_i)]^2 \to 0$$

almost surely. This follows from the uniform continuity of F and of the paths of the Wiener process. Specifically,

- given $\varepsilon > 0$ we can find $\delta > 0$ such that, whenever $x, y, |x - y| < \delta$, we have $|F''(x) - F''(y)| < \varepsilon$,
- for almost all ω, given $\delta > 0$ we can find $\eta(\omega) > 0$ such that for all s, u, $|s - u| < \eta(\omega)$ implies $|W(s, \omega) - W(u, \omega)| < \delta$.

Fix $\omega \in \Omega$ and an arbitrary $\varepsilon > 0$, choose δ from the condition on F and for this δ find $\eta = \eta(\omega)$ from the condition for the path of W. Let $N = N(\omega)$ be such that $\frac{t}{N} < \eta$.

For $n \geq N$, $|W(t_i) - z_i| < \delta$, $|F''(W(t_i)) - F''(z_i)| < \varepsilon$ for all $i \leq n$, so for almost all $\omega \in \Omega$ we have shown that

$$\sum_{i=0}^{n-1} [F''(W(t_i)) - F''(z_i)][W(t_{i+1}) - W(t_i)]^2 \leq \varepsilon \sum_{i=0}^{n-1} [W(t_{i+1}) - W(t_i)]^2.$$

We know that the increment $W(t_{i+1}) - W(t_i)$ is centred and has variance $t_{i+1} - t_i$, so

$$\mathbb{E}\left[\sum_{i=0}^{n-1}(W(t_{i+1}) - W(t_i))^2\right] = \sum_{i=0}^{n-1}\mathbb{E}[(W(t_{i+1}) - W(t_i))^2] = \sum_{i=0}^{n-1}(t_{i+1} - t_i) = t.$$

Therefore $\sum_{i=0}^{n-1}[W(t_{i+1}) - W(t_i)]^2$ is finite for almost all ω. As $\varepsilon > 0$ is arbitrary our claim follows.

As a result of this step, it remains to show that, as $n \to \infty$,

$$\frac{1}{2}\sum_{i=0}^{n-1}F''(W(t_i))[W(t_{i+1}) - W(t_i)]^2 \to \frac{1}{2}\int_0^t F''(W(s))ds.$$

Step 3b – Links. The link between the sum and the integral is provided by the sums approximating the latter, that is

$$\frac{1}{2}\sum_{i=0}^{n-1}F''(W(t_i))[t_{i+1} - t_i].$$

By the continuity of $t \mapsto F''(W(t))$, we have almost sure convergence of approximating sums to an ordinary integral

$$\sum_{i=0}^{n-1}F''(W(t_i))[t_{i+1} - t_i] \to \int_0^t F''(W(s))ds.$$

As a result, we have reduced the task to showing that, as $n \to \infty$,

$$\sum_{i=0}^{n-1}F''(W(t_i))[W(t_{i+1}) - W(t_i)]^2 - \sum_{i=0}^{n-1}F''(W(t_i))[t_{i+1} - t_i] \to 0.$$

Step 3c – The final hurdles. It remains to show

$$\sum_{i=0}^{n-1}F''(W(t_i))X_i \to 0,$$

where $X_i = [W(t_{i+1}) - W(t_i)]^2 - [t_{i+1} - t_i]$. To obtain convergence in $L^2(\Omega)$

the first step is natural:

$$\mathbb{E}\left(\sum_{i=0}^{n-1} F''(W(t_i))X_i\right)^2$$

$$= \mathbb{E}\sum_{i=0}^{n-1}(F''(W(t_i)))^2 X_i^2 \quad \text{(diagonal)}$$

$$+2\mathbb{E}\sum_{i<j} F''(W(t_i))F''(W(t_j))X_iX_j \quad \text{(cross-terms)}.$$

Hurdle 1 – Cross-terms. The second term is zero, which follows because for $i < j$, the increment $W(t_{j+1}) - W(t_j)$ is independent of the σ-field $\mathcal{F}_{t_j}$ (see Proposition 2.31), while X_i, $F''(W(t_i))$, $F''(W(t_j))$ are $\mathcal{F}_{t_j}$-measurable. Therefore we introduce the conditional expectation with respect to $\mathcal{F}_{t_j}$: $\mathbb{E}(\cdot) = \mathbb{E}(\mathbb{E}(\cdot|\mathcal{F}_{t_j}))$, to find

$$\mathbb{E}(F''(W(t_i))F''(W(t_j))X_iX_j)$$

$$= \mathbb{E}(\mathbb{E}(F''(W(t_i))F''(W(t_j))X_iX_j|\mathcal{F}_{t_j})) \text{ (tower property)}$$

$$= \mathbb{E}(F''(W(t_i))F''(W(t_j))X_i\mathbb{E}(X_j|\mathcal{F}_{t_j})) \text{ (taking out the known)}$$

$$= \mathbb{E}(F''(W(t_i))F''(W(t_j))X_i\mathbb{E}(X_j)) \text{ (independence)}$$

$$= \mathbb{E}(X_j)\mathbb{E}(F''(W(t_i))F''(W(t_j))X_i),$$

and now we observe that $\mathbb{E}(X_j) = 0$, as the increment $W(t_{j+1}) - W(t_j)$ has variance $t_{j+1} - t_j$ by the definition of the Wiener process W.

Hurdle 2 – Diagonal. The first term contains F'', which is bounded, so set $\sup_{x\in[-M,M]}[F''(x)]^2 = C$. Now

$$\mathbb{E}\sum_{i=0}^{n-1}(F''(W(t_i)))^2 X_i^2 \le C\mathbb{E}\left(\sum_{i=0}^{n-1} X_i^2\right)$$

$$= C\sum_{i=0}^{n-1}\mathbb{E}(\{[W(t_{i+1}) - W(t_i)]^2 - [t_{i+1} - t_i]\}^2)$$

after inserting the expression for X_i. We have to show that the last sum converges to zero. We will employ the fact that the increments of W are normally distributed.

First, obviously,

$$\{[W(t_{i+1}) - W(t_i)]^2 - [t_{i+1} - t_i]\}^2$$
$$= [W(t_{i+1}) - W(t_i)]^4 - 2[W(t_{i+1}) - W(t_i)]^2[t_{i+1} - t_i] + [t_{i+1} - t_i]^2.$$

Taking expectations we find

$$\mathbb{E}(\{[W(t_{i+1}) - W(t_i)]^2 - [t_{i+1} - t_i]\}^2)$$
$$= \mathbb{E}([W(t_{i+1}) - W(t_i)]^4) - 2\mathbb{E}[W(t_{i+1}) - W(t_i)]^2[t_{i+1} - t_i] + [t_{i+1} - t_i]^2$$
$$= \mathbb{E}([W(t_{i+1}) - W(t_i)]^4) - \left(\frac{t}{n}\right)^2,$$

since $\mathbb{E}([W(t_{i+1}) - W(t_i)]^2) = t_{i+1} - t_i = \frac{t}{n}$ by our choice of the partition (t_i) with $t_i = i\frac{t}{n}$.

The increment $W(t_{i+1}) - W(t_i)$ has normal distribution with zero expectation so using the general fact that for such a random variable X, $\mathbb{E}(X^4) = 3(\text{Var}(X))^2$ (see [PF])

$$\mathbb{E}([W(t_{i+1}) - W(t_i)]^4) = 3\{\mathbb{E}([W(t_{i+1}) - W(t_i)]^2)\}^2$$
$$= 3[t_{i+1} - t_i]^2 = 3\left(\frac{t}{n}\right)^2.$$

Putting the above pieces together we get

$$\sum_{i=0}^{n-1} \mathbb{E}(\{[W(t_{i+1}) - W(t_i)]^2 - [t_{i+1} - t_i]\}^2) = n2\left(\frac{t}{n}\right)^2 = \frac{2t^2}{n} \to 0 \quad (4.3)$$

and again we have convergence almost surely for a subsequence. This completes the proof, taking a common subsequence for different cases, by selecting them consecutively – taking a subsequence of a subsequence in each case. □

It is very instructive to see alternative arguments which employ some general properties of W and so provide the experience needed in a general case.

Exercise 4.1 Show that for cross-terms all we need is the fact that $W^2(t) - t$ is a martingale.

Exercise 4.2 Verify the convergence claimed in (4.3), using the fact that quadratic variation of W is t.

4.3 Functions of Itô processes

We will generalise the Itô formula in two directions:

- allowing more general processes to replace W,
- allowing more general functions F.

First, we discuss the version of the formula for $F(X(t))$ with F independent of t and with W replaced by a bounded Itô process X. We formalise some notation.

Definition 4.6

For $k \geq 1$, we denote by $C^k(\mathbb{R})$, shortened to C^k when the context is clear, the collection of all real functions F with continuous derivatives of all orders up to k.

Theorem 4.7 (Itô formula)

Assume that $F : \mathbb{R} \to \mathbb{R}$ is twice differentiable with continuous F'' (often written as $F \in C^2$) and $F(x) = 0$ for $x \notin [-M, M]$ for some M. Assume that X is an Itô process

$$dX = a(t)dt + b(t)dW(t),$$

where $b \in \mathcal{M}^2$ and both a and b have continuous paths, and where X and b are bounded by a deterministic constant. Then the process $F(X(t))$ is an Itô process and the Itô formula holds in the form:

$$F(X(t)) - F(0) = \int_0^t F'(X(s))a(s)ds + \int_0^t F'(X(s))b(s)dW(s)$$
$$+ \frac{1}{2} \int_0^t F''(X(s))b^2(s)ds.$$

This can be written concisely in differential form as

$$dF(X(t)) = \left(F'(X(s))a(s) + \frac{1}{2} F''(X(s))b^2(s) \right) ds$$
$$+ F'(X(s))b(s)dW(s).$$

Remark 4.8

The assumption that X is bounded is brutally restrictive: since W is involved, it means in particular that the integral $\int_0^t b(s)dW(s)$ is bounded, so that our condition excludes constant b. It is clear that we will eventually need to find ways of relaxing this condition.

Remark 4.9

The proof of Theorem 4.7 follows the same lines as that of Theorem 4.5. Having done Exercises 4.1 and 4.2, the reader will see that the heart of the argument lies in the fact that the quadratic variation of X is $\int_0^t b^2(s)ds$, and that this process also acts as the compensator of the square of the stochastic integral.

Proof of Theorem 4.7 The steps of the proof mirror those given above, where $X = W$.

Step 1 – Taylor expansion. Fix t, let $t_i = i\frac{t}{n}$, $i = 0, 1, \ldots, n$. We begin as before by decomposing the left-hand side

$$F(X(t)) - F(0) = \sum_{i=0}^{n-1} [F(X(t_{i+1})) - F(X(t_i))]$$

and using the Taylor formula

$$F(X(t_{i+1})) - F(X(t_i)) = F'(X(t_i))[X(t_{i+1}) - X(t_i)] + \frac{1}{2} F''(z_i)[X(t_{i+1}) - X(t_i)]^2$$

for some z_i between $X(t_i)$ and $X(t_{i+1})$ to obtain

$$F(X(t)) - F(0)$$
$$= \sum_{i=0}^{n-1} F'(X(t_i))[X(t_{i+1}) - X(t_i)] + \frac{1}{2} \sum_{i=0}^{n-1} F''(z_i)[X(t_{i+1}) - X(t_i)]^2. \quad (4.4)$$

Step 2 – Terms with F'. This step is more complicated than in the special case of $X = W$. First, inserting the increments of X to the first component on the right of (4.4) we have

$$\sum_{i=0}^{n-1} F'(X(t_i))[X(t_{i+1}) - X(t_i)] = \sum_{i=0}^{n-1} F'(X(t_i))[\int_{t_i}^{t_{i+1}} a(s)ds + \int_{t_i}^{t_{i+1}} b(s)dW(s)]$$

and we have to prove

$$\sum_{i=0}^{n-1} F'(X(t_i)) \int_{t_i}^{t_{i+1}} a(s)ds \to \int_0^t F'(X(s))a(s)ds, \quad (4.5)$$

$$\sum_{i=0}^{n-1} F'(X(t_i)) \int_{t_i}^{t_{i+1}} b(s)dW(s) \to \int_0^t F'(X(s))b(s)dW(s). \quad (4.6)$$

For (4.5) note that $F'(X(t))$ is uniformly continuous, so for each $\varepsilon > 0$, we have $\delta > 0$ such that $|t - s| < \delta$ gives $|F'(X(t)) - F'(X(s))| < \varepsilon$. Consider $n \geq N$, with $\frac{1}{N} < \delta$, so that

$$|\sum_{i=0}^{n-1} F'(X(t_i)) \int_{t_i}^{t_{i+1}} a(s)ds - \int_0^t F'(X(s))a(s)ds|$$

$$\leq \sum_{i=0}^{n-1} \int_{t_i}^{t_{i+1}} |a(s)||F'(X(t_i)) - F'(X(s))|ds \leq \varepsilon \int_0^t |a(s)|ds.$$

For (4.6) to use Proposition 4.2 applied to the process $F'(X(t))b(t)$ it is sufficient to show that in $L^2(\Omega)$

$$\sum_{i=0}^{n-1} F'(X(t_i))b(t_i)(W(t_{i+1}) - W(t_i)) - \sum_{i=0}^{n-1} F'(X(t_i)) \int_{t_i}^{t_{i+1}} b(s)dW(s) \to 0.$$

We introduce $b_n(t) = \sum_{i=0}^{n-1} b(t_i)\mathbf{1}_{[t_i,t_{i+1})}(t)$ and so

$$\mathbb{E}\left(\sum_{i=0}^{n-1} F'(X(t_i))b(t_i)(W(t_{i+1}) - W(t_i)) - \sum_{i=0}^{n-1} F'(X(t_i)) \int_{t_i}^{t_{i+1}} b(s)dW(s) \right)^2$$

$$= \mathbb{E}\left(\sum_{i=0}^{n-1} F'(X(t_i))^2 Y_i^2 \right) + 2\mathbb{E}\left(\sum_{k<j} F'(X(t_k))Y_k F'(X(t_j))Y_j \right)$$

where

$$Y_i = \int_{t_i}^{t_{i+1}} (b_n(s) - b(s))dW(s).$$

The first term converges to zero since it is estimated by

$$\sup |F'(X(t))|^2 \sum_{i=0}^{n-1} \mathbb{E}\left(\int_{t_i}^{t_{i+1}} (b_n(s) - b(s))dW(s) \right)^2$$

and now can we use the Itô isometry and $\mathbb{E}\int_0^t [b_n(s) - b(s)]^2 ds \to 0$.

Each component of the second sum is zero: To see this let $k < j$ and perform a routine computation

$$\mathbb{E}(F'(X(t_k))Y_k F'(X(t_j))Y_j) = \mathbb{E}(\mathbb{E}(F'(X(t_k))Y_k F'(X(t_j))Y_j | \mathcal{F}_{t_j}))$$

$$= \mathbb{E}(F'(X(t_k))Y_k F'(X(t_j))\mathbb{E}(Y_j | \mathcal{F}_{t_j})) = 0$$

since $\mathbb{E}(Y_j | \mathcal{F}_{t_j}) = 0$ by the martingale property of the stochastic integral.
Step 3 – Terms with F''. We have to show

$$\sum_{i=0}^{n-1} F''(z_i)[X(t_{i+1}) - X(t_i)]^2 \to \int_0^t F''(X(s))b^2(s)ds.$$

Step 3a – Disposing of z_i. We prove that z_i can be replaced by $X(t_i)$ so we prove that, in L^2,

$$\sum_{i=0}^{n-1} [F''(z_i) - F''(X(t_i))][X(t_{i+1}) - X(t_i)]^2 \to 0. \tag{4.7}$$

This follows from the uniform continuity of F and of the paths of an Itô process. Specifically,

- given $\varepsilon > 0$, we can find $\delta > 0$ such that whenever x, y, $|x - y| < \delta$, we have $|F''(x) - F''(y)| < \varepsilon$,
- for almost all ω, given $\delta > 0$ we can find $\eta(\omega) > 0$ such that for all s, u, $|s - u| < \eta(\omega)$ implies $|X(s, \omega) - X(u, \omega)| < \delta$.

Fix an arbitrary $\varepsilon > 0$, choose δ from the condition on F and for this δ find η from the condition for the path of X. Let N be such that $\frac{t}{N} < \eta$. (Here N, η depend on ω.)

For $n \geq N$, $|X(t_i) - z_i| < \delta$, $|F''(X(t_i)) - F''(z_i)| < \varepsilon$ for all i so

$$\sum_{i=0}^{n-1} [F''(X(t_i)) - F''(z_i)][X(t_{i+1}) - X(t_i)]^2 \leq \varepsilon \sum_{i=0}^{n-1} [X(t_{i+1}) - X(t_i)]^2.$$

We know from the proof of Theorem 3.24 that

$$\sum_{i=0}^{n-1} [X(t_{i+1}) - X(t_i)]^2 \rightarrow \int_0^t b^2(s)ds \quad \text{in } L^2(\Omega),$$

so a subsequence converges almost surely, and it is bounded. Letting $\varepsilon \rightarrow 0$ shows that there is a subsequence of the original sequence of partitions where (4.7) holds with almost sure convergence.

The task is thus reduced to showing that, in L^2-norm (and hence almost surely along a subsequence) we have

$$\sum_{i=0}^{n-1} F''(X(t_i))[X(t_{i+1}) - X(t_i)]^2 \rightarrow \int_0^t F''(X(s))b^2(s)ds.$$

Step 3b – Links. The best link between the sum and the integral is provided by the mixed-form sums

$$\sum_{i=0}^{n-1} F''(X(t_i)) \int_{t_i}^{t_{i+1}} b^2(s)ds$$

(this is motivated by the fact that the increments of X are integrals, multiplied by the values of $F''(X(t))$ at fixed times). This costs little since the paths of b are continuous, F'' is bounded (by C, say), so

$$\left| \sum_{i=0}^{n-1} F''(X(t_i)) \left\{ \int_{t_i}^{t_{i+1}} b^2(s)ds - b^2(t_i)[t_{i+1} - t_i] \right\} \right|$$

$$\leq C \sum_{i=0}^{n-1} \int_{t_i}^{t_{i+1}} |b^2(s) - b^2(t_i)|ds$$

$$\leq C \sum_{i=0}^{n-1} \sup_{|s-u|\leq\frac{t}{n}} |b^2(s) - b^2(u)|[t_{i+1} - t_i]$$

$$\leq Ct \sup_{|s-u|\leq\frac{t}{n}} |b^2(s) - b^2(u)| \to 0.$$

We have reduced the problem to showing that

$$\sum_{i=0}^{n-1} F''(X(t_i))[X(t_{i+1}) - X(t_i)]^2 - \sum_{i=0}^{n-1} F''(X(t_i)) \int_{t_i}^{t_{i+1}} b^2(s)ds \to 0.$$

Step 3c – Disposing of the drift. The process X has two components. The first is the drift, the second is a martingale (the stochastic integral), and we show that the first is irrelevant here. (In the case $X = W$, this step was of course not needed.) Insert

$$X(t_{i+1}) - X(t_i) = \int_{t_i}^{t_{i+1}} a(s)ds + \int_{t_i}^{t_{i+1}} b(s)dW(s)$$

and do some simple algebra

$$\sum_{i=0}^{n-1} F''(X(t_i))[X(t_{i+1}) - X(t_i)]^2$$

$$= \sum_{i=0}^{n-1} F''(X(t_i)) \left(\int_{t_i}^{t_{i+1}} a(s)ds + \int_{t_i}^{t_{i+1}} b(s)dW(s) \right)^2$$

$$= \sum_{i=0}^{n-1} F''(X(t_i)) \left(\int_{t_i}^{t_{i+1}} a(s)ds \right)^2$$

$$+ 2 \sum_{i=0}^{n-1} F''(X(t_i)) \int_{t_i}^{t_{i+1}} a(s)ds \int_{t_i}^{t_{i+1}} b(s)dW(s)$$

$$+ \sum_{i=0}^{n-1} F''(X(t_i)) \left(\int_{t_i}^{t_{i+1}} b(s)dW(s) \right)^2.$$

We shall show that the first two sums converge to zero almost surely.

They are dealt with in similar fashion: first note that $\int_0^t |a(s)|ds$ is finite almost surely. Now

$$\sum_{i=0}^{n-1} F''(X(t_i)) \left(\int_{t_i}^{t_{i+1}} a(s)ds \right)^2$$

$$\leq \sup_{x \in [-M,M]} |F''(x)| \max_i \left| \int_{t_i}^{t_{i+1}} a(s)ds \right| \sum_{i=0}^{n-1} \int_{t_i}^{t_{i+1}} |a(s)|ds,$$

$$\left| \sum_{i=0}^{n-1} F''(X(t_i)) \int_{t_i}^{t_{i+1}} a(s)ds \int_{t_i}^{t_{i+1}} b(s)dW(s) \right|$$

$$\leq \sup_{x \in [-M,M]} |F''(x)| \max_i \left| \int_{t_i}^{t_{i+1}} b(s)dW(s) \right| \sum_{i=0}^{n-1} \int_{t_i}^{t_{i+1}} |a(s)|ds.$$

The upper bounds converge to zero almost surely since the functions $t \mapsto \int_0^t a(s)ds$, $t \mapsto \int_0^t b(s)dW(s)$ are continuous, hence uniformly continuous on the interval $[0, T]$, and $\sum_{i=0}^{n-1} \int_{t_i}^{t_{i+1}} |a(s)|ds$ is bounded by a deterministic constant.

So the task boils down to showing that

$$\sum_{i=0}^{n-1} F''(X(t_i)) \left(\int_{t_i}^{t_{i+1}} b(s)dW(s) \right)^2 - \sum_{i=0}^{n-1} F''(X(t_i)) \int_{t_i}^{t_{i+1}} b^2(s)ds \to 0.$$

Step 3d – The final hurdles. It remains to show

$$\sum_{i=0}^{n-1} F''(X(t_i)) \left([Y(t_{i+1}) - Y(t_i)]^2 - \int_{t_i}^{t_{i+1}} b^2(s)ds \right) \to 0,$$

where

$$Y(t) = \int_0^t b(s)dW(s).$$

We will show that we have convergence in $L^2(\Omega)$-norm. We again have to tackle the expectation of the square of the sum, namely

$$\mathbb{E}\left(\sum_{i=0}^{n-1} F''(X(t_i))\{[Y(t_{i+1}) - Y(t_i)]^2 - \int_{t_i}^{t_{i+1}} b^2(s)ds\}\right)^2$$

$$= \mathbb{E}\sum_{i=0}^{n-1} [F''(X(t_i))]^2 \left([Y(t_{i+1}) - Y(t_i)]^2 - \int_{t_i}^{t_{i+1}} b^2(s)ds\right)^2 \text{ (diagonal)}$$

$$+2\mathbb{E}\sum_{i<j} F''(X(t_i))\left([Y(t_{i+1}) - Y(t_i)]^2 - \int_{t_i}^{t_{i+1}} b^2(s)ds\right) \times$$

$$\times F''(X(t_j))\left([Y(t_{j+1}) - Y(t_j)]^2 - \int_{t_j}^{t_{j+1}} b^2(s)ds\right) \text{ (cross-terms)}.$$

Hurdle 1 – Cross-terms. They again vanish: we show that each term in the second sum is equal to zero. Fix $i < j$ and again introduce conditional expectation with respect to $\mathcal{F}_{t_j}$: $\mathbb{E}(...) = \mathbb{E}(\mathbb{E}(...|\mathcal{F}_{t_j}))$, take out of the conditional expectation everything except $[Y(t_{j+1}) - Y(t_j)]^2 - \int_{t_j}^{t_{j+1}} b^2(s)ds$. The problem reduces to showing that the following conditional expectations are zero: $\mathbb{E}([Y(t_{j+1}) - Y(t_j)]^2 - \int_{t_j}^{t_{j+1}} b^2(s)ds|\mathcal{F}_{t_j})$.

By the property of martingales proved in Theorem 2.33,

$$\mathbb{E}((M(t) - M(s))^2|\mathcal{F}_s) = \mathbb{E}(M^2(t) - M^2(s)|\mathcal{F}_s), \quad s < t,$$

we have

$$\mathbb{E}([Y(t_{j+1}) - Y(t_j)]^2 - \int_{t_j}^{t_{j+1}} b^2(s)ds|\mathcal{F}_{t_j})$$

$$= \mathbb{E}(Y(t_{j+1})^2 - Y(t_j)^2|\mathcal{F}_{t_j}) - \mathbb{E}\left(\int_{t_j}^{t_{j+1}} b^2(s)ds|\mathcal{F}_{t_j}\right)$$

and by linearity this equals

$$= \mathbb{E}(Y(t_{j+1})^2 - \int_0^{t_{j+1}} b^2(s)ds|\mathcal{F}_{t_j}) - Y(t_j)^2 + \int_0^{t_j} b^2(s)ds = 0$$

since $Y^2(t) - \int_0^t b^2(s)ds$ is a martingale, as shown in Theorem 3.22.

Hurdle 2 – Diagonal. The argument below looks simpler than the special case, but it is not. It is shorter, but Lemma 3.23 provides a general property of martingales to handle the terms where we could perform explicit computations for W. First, F'' is bounded by C, so

$$\mathbb{E}\sum_{i=0}^{n-1}[F''(X(t_i))]^2\left((Y(t_{i+1})-Y(t_i))^2-\int_{t_i}^{t_{i+1}}b^2(s)ds\right)^2$$

$$\leq 2C\mathbb{E}\sum_{i=0}^{n-1}\left((Y(t_{i+1})-Y(t_i))^4+\left(\int_{t_i}^{t_{i+1}}b^2(s)ds\right)^2\right)$$

employing the elementary estimate $(a+b)^2 \leq 2a^2 + 2b^2$. The process Y is a bounded continuous martingale and Lemma 3.23 shows that

$$\mathbb{E}\sum_{i=0}^{n-1}(Y(t_{i+1})-Y(t_i))^4\to 0,$$

while

$$\sum_{i=0}^{n-1}\left(\int_{t_i}^{t_{i+1}}b^2(s)ds\right)^2\leq\max\left|\int_{t_i}^{t_{i+1}}b^2(s)ds\right|\sum_{i=0}^{n-1}\int_{t_i}^{t_{i+1}}b^2(s)ds$$

$$\leq\max\left|\int_{t_i}^{t_{i+1}}b^2(s)ds\right|\int_0^t b^2(s)ds$$

goes to zero since the function $t\mapsto\int_0^t b^2(s)ds$ is continuous, hence uniformly continuous, $\int_0^t b^2(s)ds$ is bounded by a deterministic constant, so the upper bound converges almost surely to zero, and the convergence is dominated.

The proof is again completed by choosing subsequences (where needed) successively along which we have almost sure convergence. □

Remark 4.10

The passage from continuous to more general functions a, b is routine and we only sketch it in outline. For each $\omega \in \Omega$, $a(\cdot, \omega) \in L^1([0, T])$ and $b(\cdot, \omega) \in L^2(0, T)$ can be approximated by a sequence of continuous functions $a_n(\cdot, \omega)$, $b_n(\cdot, \omega)$, $b_n \in \mathcal{M}^2$, with $a_n \to a$ in $L^1([0, T])$ a.s., $b_n \to b$ in $\mathcal{M}^2$. We have proved the Itô formula for each a_n, b_n

$$F(X(t))-F(0)=\int_0^t F'(X(s))a_n(s)ds+\int_0^t F'(X(s))b_n(s)dW(s)$$

$$+\frac{1}{2}\int_0^t F''(X(s))b_n^2(s)ds.$$

We can pass to the limit in all terms in the formula,. We have pointwise convergence in each case

$$F'(X(s))a_n(s) \to F'(X(s))a(s),$$
$$F''(X(s))b_n^2(s) \to F''(X(s))b^2(s),$$

and the convergence is dominated (since F' and F'' are bounded) so the integrals converge. Finally, $b_n \to b$ in $\mathcal{M}^2$, hence $F'(X(s))b_n(s) \to F'(X(s))b(s)$ in $\mathcal{M}^2$ since $F'(X(s))$ is bounded:

$$\mathbb{E} \int_0^T [F'(X(s))b_n(s) - F'(X(s))b(s)]^2 ds$$

$$\leq \sup |F'(x)| \mathbb{E} \int_0^T [b_n(s) - b(s)]^2 ds \to 0$$

so

$$\int_0^t F'(X(s))b_n(s)dW(s) \to \int_0^t F'(X(s))b(s)dW(s)$$

in L^2-norm, hence almost surely along a subsequence.

4.4   Extension to general F

The first extension is relatively easy and allows F to depend on both t and x. We employ the following notation:

Definition 4.11
Given a function $F : [0,T] \times \mathbb{R} \to \mathbb{R}$, we denote partial derivatives of $F(t,x)$ as follows:

$$F_t = \frac{\partial F}{\partial t},$$

$$F_x = \frac{\partial F}{\partial x},$$

$$F_{xx} = \frac{\partial^2 F}{\partial x^2}.$$

We denote by $C^{1,2}([0,T] \times \mathbb{R})$ the collection of functions $F(t,x)$ which have continuous derivatives F_t, F_x, F_{xx}. Again, we shorten this $C^{1,2}$ when the context is clear.

Theorem 4.12 (Itô formula)
Suppose $F(t,x)$ is in $C^{1,2}$ and $F(t,x) = 0$ for $x \notin [-M, M]$ and that

$$dX(t) = a(t)dt + b(t)dW(t),$$

where $b \in \mathcal{M}^2$, *a and b have continuous paths, and X is bounded by a deterministic constant. Then the process* $F(t, X(t))$ *is an Itô process and the Itô formula holds:*

$$F(t, X(t)) - F(0, 0) = \int_0^t F_t(s, X(s))ds + \int_0^t F_x(s, X(s))a(s)ds$$

$$+ \int_0^t F_x(s, X(s))b(s)dW(s)$$

$$+ \frac{1}{2} \int_0^t F_{xx}(s, X(s))b^2(s)ds.$$

Proof The only new argument appears at the very beginning. Fix t, let $t_i = i\frac{t}{n}$, $i = 0, 1, \ldots, n$ and use the Taylor formula

$$F(t_{i+1}, X(t_{i+1})) - F(t_i, X(t_i)) = F_t(\theta_i, X(t_i))[t_{i+1} - t_i]$$

$$+ F_x(t_i, X(t_i))[X(t_{i+1}) - X(t_i)]$$

$$+ \frac{1}{2} F_{xx}(z_i)[X(t_{i+1}) - X(t_i)]^2$$

for some $\theta_i \in [t_i, t_{i+1}]$ and z_i between $X(t_i)$ and $X(t_{i+1})$. We find that

$$F(t, X(t)) - F(0, 0) = \sum_{i=0}^{n-1} F_t(t_i, X(t_i))[t_{i+1} - t_i]$$

$$+ \sum_{i=0}^{n-1} (F_t(\theta_i, X(t_i)) - F_t(t_i, X(t_i)))[t_{i+1} - t_i]$$

$$+ \sum_{i=0}^{n-1} F_x(t_i, X(t_i))[X(t_{i+1}) - X(t_i)]$$

$$+ \frac{1}{2} \sum_{i=0}^{n-1} F_{xx}(t_i, z_i)[X(t_{i+1}) - X(t_i)]^2.$$

The first sum approximates the integral $\int_0^t F_t(s, X(s))ds$ and the second goes to zero as a result of continuity of F_t. The remaining sums are dealt with in the same way as in the proof of Theorem 4.7. □

The next task is concerned with removing the assumption that F vanishes outside some finite interval $[-M, M]$. This is important, since at the present stage we cannot use the Itô formula even for elementary functions like $F(x) = x^2$. Clearly, we need to make the limit passage $M \to \infty$ in some sense. To show that this is tricky, we give an appealing, but **wrong** argument. The error is subtle but actually quite deep since it touches the heart of the definition of the stochastic integral. It is instructive to follow the steps below to see if one can find the weak spot to appreciate the effort required in the next section to rectify matters.

False argument. Consider the simplest version of Theorem 4.5. Let

$$B_n = \{\omega \in \Omega : |W(t, \omega)| \le n \text{ for } t \in [0, T]\}.$$

Almost all paths of W are continuous – say that this holds for $\omega \in \Omega'$, $P(\Omega') = 1$. We have

$$\bigcup B_n \supset \Omega'$$

since if a path is continuous it is bounded on the interval $[0, T]$ so belongs to $[-n, n]$ for some n. We claim that

$$F(W(t)) - F(0) = \int_0^t F'(W(s))dW(s) + \frac{1}{2} \int_0^t F''(W(s))ds \qquad (4.8)$$

holds for all $\omega \in \Omega'$ for an arbitrary function F with continuous F''. Fix $\omega_0 \in \Omega'$ and take n such that $\omega_0 \in B_n$. Take a C^2 function F_n satisfying $F_n(x) = F(x)$ for $x \in [-n.n]$ and $F_n(x) = 0$ for $x \notin [-n-1, n+1]$. We know that the Itô formula holds for F_n :

$$F_n(W(t)) - F_n(0) = \int_0^t F'_n(W(s))dW(s) + \frac{1}{2} \int_0^t F''_n(W(s))ds. \qquad (4.9)$$

This is an equality of random variables which holds in particular for our ω_0 (possibly, at this stage we have to exclude some set of ωs of probability zero, which is not a problem since we need the formula to hold almost surely).

But then $|W(t, \omega_0)| \le n$ so $F_n(W(t, \omega_0)) = F(W(t, \omega_0))$, the same it true for the first and the second derivative, hence (4.9) reduces to (4.8).

Explaining the mistake. The argument contained in the last sentence is wrong in the part related to the stochastic integral, which is not defined pathwise. The value of the integral at a particular ω_0 depends in principle on all $\omega \in \Omega$ because of the involved construction: approximation of a process by simple processes gives a sequence produced globally on Ω, depending in general on the values of the integrand at all, not just some, ω. We cannot say, trying to fix the bug, that we restrict our attention to B_n as a new probability space, since the Wiener process does not live on B_n.

To overcome this problem we have to introduce some new ideas of considerable importance in their own right. This technique aims to find a proper meaning of the word 'some' used above: the integral for 'some' ω

will depend on the integrand at these ω (which explains the term 'localisation' used in this context).

The technique will also allow us to relax the unrealistic and unduly restrictive assumptions that all the processes concerned are bounded, so that we will finally be able to apply the Itô formula to a wider class of functions and also extend the definition of stochastic integral to a wider class of processes, relevant from a practical point of view.

4.5 Localising stopping times

Consider a stochastic process $X(t)$ with continuous paths, $t \in [0, T]$. In deriving properties of X it is often convenient to assume that the process is bounded, that is $|X(t, \omega)| \leq M$ for all t and almost all ω. However, this is a very restrictive assumption. To allow unbounded processes in situations where the argument used in a proof requires a bounded process, we employ the following simple idea.

We observe the paths $t \to X(t, \omega)$ for each $\omega \in \Omega$. Once the path touches one of the end points of the interval $[-M, M]$, we freeze the process and from this time on it remains constant. This time instant depends on the path, hence on ω

$$\tau_M(\omega) = \inf\{t \leq T : |X(t, \omega)| \geq M\},$$

with the convention that we take $\inf \emptyset = T$. So the random variable τ_M stops the process from growing beyond a given bound M. If the process X is adapted to a filtration $\mathcal{F}_t$, path-continuity ensures that $\{\tau_M > t\} = \bigcap_{q \leq t, q \in \mathbb{Q}}\{|X(q)| < M\}$ belongs to $\mathcal{F}_t$, so that τ_M is a stopping time (see Definition 2.36).

We define a slight variation of the stopped process $X_{\tau_M}(t) = X(t \wedge \tau_M)$ (see Definition 2.39) by setting

$$X_M(t) = \begin{cases} X(t) \text{ if } t \leq \tau_M, \\ M \text{ if } t \geq \tau_M, \end{cases}$$

which is of course bounded by M, so we can apply tools available for bounded processes. If M goes to infinity, the process X_M becomes the original one and all we have to do is to pass to the limit.

If a path is continuous, then it is bounded on a bounded interval. If we take M larger than this bound, the set of times in the definition of τ_M will

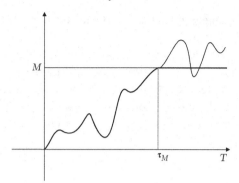

Figure 4.1

be empty so $\tau_M = T$. In other words, if the process is below M, there is no need to stop (Figure 4.1).

$$|X_M(t)| \leq M \text{ for all } t \in [0, T].$$

We can also use different stopping criteria, for instance the size of the integral of some function f:

$$\tau_M = \inf\left\{t : \int_0^t |f(s)|ds \geq M\right\}.$$

If the integral $\int_0^T |f(s)|ds < \infty$ is finite, then we take M larger than this integral and there is no need to stop the process, thus $\tau_M = T$ for large M (Figure 4.2).

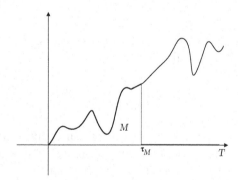

Figure 4.2

Similarly, we define the stopped process in this case as

$$f_M(t) = \begin{cases} f(t) \text{ if } t \le \tau_M, \\ 0 \text{ if } t \ge \tau_M, \end{cases}$$

and this process has finite integral

$$\int_0^T |f_M(s)|ds \le M.$$

In this example, the continuity of the integral (as a function of its upper limit) ensures that τ_M is a stopping time.

Exercise 4.3   Prove the last claim.

For stochastic calculus, a convenient space of integrands is $\mathcal{M}^2$, so we distinguish a class of stopping times which guarantee that stopping a given process provides a process in $\mathcal{M}^2$. Let $X : [0, T] \times \Omega \to \mathbb{R}$ be a stochastic process.

Definition 4.13
A sequence τ_n of stopping times is **localising for X in $\mathcal{M}^2$** if:
1. it is increasing: for each $n \ge 1$, $\tau_n \le \tau_{n+1}$,
2. for each $n \ge 1$, $\mathbf{1}_{\{t \le \tau_n\}} X \in \mathcal{M}^2$,
3. $P(\bigcup_{n=1}^{\infty}\{\omega : \tau_n(\omega) = T\}) = 1$.

The classical definition requires τ_n diverge to infinity, but our time horizon is T, so we restrict ourselves to stopping times whose range is in $[0, T]$.

4.6   Extension of the stochastic integral

The first application of these ideas will be an extension of the stochastic integral to a wider space. The role of the stochastic process X is now taken by the integrand in a (Lebesgue) integral, so we write f in place of X. Define

$$\mathcal{P}^2 = \left\{ f : [0, T] \times \Omega \to \mathbb{R}, \ f\text{-adapted}, \ \int_0^T f^2(s)ds < \infty \text{ a.s.} \right\}.$$

This space contains $\mathcal{M}^2$, since if $\mathbb{E}\int_0^T f^2(s)ds < \infty$, then of course almost all integrals $\int_0^T f^2(s)ds$ are finite (if they were infinite on a set of positive probability, then the expectation would be infinite). The inclusion is strict.

Exercise 4.4   Find a process that is in $\mathcal{P}^2$ but not in $\mathcal{M}^2$.

Proposition 4.14

If $f \in \mathcal{P}^2$, then the sequence of stopping times defined for $n \geq 1$ by

$$\tau_n = \inf\left\{ s : \int_0^s f^2(u)du \geq n \right\},$$

with the convention that $\inf \emptyset = T$, is a localising sequence for f in $\mathcal{M}^2$.

Before we prove this, note that the criterion for stopping is the size of the integral $\int_0^s f^2(u)du$ so the process X mentioned at the beginning of this section is $X(s) = \int_0^s f^2(u)du$. It may happen that for some paths $\int_0^T f^2(u)du < n$, then the convention about the infimum of the empty set applies, as on these paths we do not have to stop at all.

Proof   The sequence τ_n is clearly increasing. Next, for each ω,

$$\int_0^T f^2(s,\omega)\mathbf{1}_{\{s \leq \tau_n(\omega)\}}ds = \int_0^{\tau_n(\omega)} f^2(s,\omega)ds \leq n$$

so

$$\mathbb{E}\left(\int_0^T f^2(s)\mathbf{1}_{\{s \leq \tau_n\}}ds \right) \leq n$$

and condition 2 is verified: $\mathbf{1}_{\{t \leq \tau_n\}}f \in \mathcal{M}^2$.

If, for some $\omega \in \Omega$ we have $\int_0^T f^2(s,\omega) < \infty$, then $\int_0^T f^2(s,\omega) \leq n$ for some $n \in \mathbb{N}$, so that $\tau_n(\omega) = T$. So

$$\left\{ \omega : \int_0^T f^2(s,\omega) < \infty \right\} \subset \bigcup_{n=1}^{\infty} \{\omega : \tau_n(\omega) = T\}$$

but the set on the left has probability one so condition 3 holds as well.   □

We now describe how to extend the stochastic integral to the larger space. Take $f \in \mathcal{P}^2$ and take a localising sequence for f in $\mathcal{M}^2$. There exist continuous martingales $M_n(t)$ such that

$$M_n(t) = \int_0^T \mathbf{1}_{[0,t]}(s)f(s)\mathbf{1}_{[0,\tau_n]}(s)dW(s). \tag{4.10}$$

The next theorem, which is the main result of this section, allows us to give the formal definition:

Definition 4.15

The stochastic integral of a process $f \in \mathcal{P}^2$ is the process

$$\int_0^t f(s)dW(s) = \lim_{n\to\infty} M_n(t),$$

where M_n are defined by (4.10).

This is important from the point of view of applications. For instance, for a continuous function F and a process X with continuous paths we can now integrate the process $F(X(t))$ since the integral $\int_0^T F(X(t))^2 dt$ is finite almost surely.

The use of the letter X below (instead of M, as may seem more natural) is deliberate: it serves to emphasise that the limit does not have to be a martingale for such general integrands f.

Theorem 4.16

There exists a continuous process $X(t)$ such that $X(t) = \lim_n M_n(t)$ almost surely and the limit does not depend on the choice of the localising sequence τ_n used to define M_n.

The proof of this important result makes repeated use of a general result relating stopping times to the definition of the integral. This apparently obvious result is not as trivial as it may seem. The difficulty lies in the fact that, while the integral is defined pathwise for simple functions, its definition involves a limit process for more general integrands. However, as we now show, if for some $\omega \in \Omega$ the values of two processes remain equal up to a stopping time τ, then for almost all such ω the same will hold for their stochastic integrals up to any time $t \leq \tau(\omega)$, and other points of Ω do not interfere, even though the integral is not a pathwise one.

Proposition 4.17

If $f, g \in \mathcal{M}^2$ and τ is a stopping time such that $f(t, \omega) = g(t, \omega)$ whenever $t \leq \tau(\omega)$, then $\int_0^t f(s)dW(s) = \int_0^t g(s)dW(s)$ for almost all ω satisfying $t \leq \tau(\omega)$.

Proof See page 148. □

Proof of Theorem 4.16 The set $\Omega' = \bigcup_{n=1}^\infty \{\omega : \tau_n(\omega) = T\}$ has probability 1 since τ_n is localising. Take Ω'' to be the set of all ω for which, for all $n \geq 1$, the paths $t \mapsto M_n(t, \omega)$ are continuous. Thus $\Omega'' = \bigcap_{n\geq 1} \Omega_n$ where Ω_n is the set of full probability such that for $\omega \in \Omega_n$ the paths $t \mapsto M_n(t, \omega)$ are continuous. The union of the complements $\Omega \setminus \Omega_n$ has measure zero, so $P(\Omega'') = 1$ and the same is true of $\Omega' \cap \Omega''$.

Let $\omega \in \Omega' \cap \Omega''$. Then for some n, $\tau_n(\omega) = T$. Take the smallest such n and denote it by $N(\omega)$.

To see that the sequence $M_n(t)$ converges, we apply Proposition 4.17, which allows us to conclude that for (t, ω) such that $t \leq \tau_n(\omega)$ we have $M_n(t, \omega) = M_{n+1}(t, \omega)$. Indeed, let us write

$$g(t, \omega) = f(t, \omega)\mathbf{1}_{[0,\tau_n(\omega)]}(t),$$
$$h(t, \omega) = f(t, \omega)\mathbf{1}_{[0,\tau_{n+1}(\omega)]}(t)$$
$$\tau = \tau_n$$

and observe that for (t, ω) such that $t \leq \tau(\omega)$ we have $g(t, \omega) = h(t, \omega)$ as the result of the fact that the sequence τ_n is increasing. Then Proposition 4.17 says that for (t, ω) with $t \leq \tau(\omega)$

$$\int_0^t g(s)dW(s) = \int_0^t h(s)dW(s),$$

so, in other words, $M_n(t, \omega) = M_{n+1}(t, \omega)$ as claimed.

This will be sufficient, since if $\omega \in \Omega' \cap \Omega''$, for $n \geq N(\omega)$, $\tau_n(\omega) = T$ so for all $t \leq T$, $M_n(t, \omega) = M_{n+1}(t, \omega)$, which means that the sequence $M_n(t, \omega)$ is eventually constant and we can write $X(t, \omega) = M_n(t, \omega)$, the right-hand side being the same for each sufficiently large n. The continuity of the paths of $X(t)$ comes for free from the continuity of the paths of $M_n(t)$.

The final touch is to show that X is independent of the localising sequence. So let v_n be another localising sequence for f in $\mathcal{M}^2$, and consider the continuous martingale $M'_n(t) = \int_0^t f(s)\mathbf{1}_{[0,v_n]}(s)dW(s)$. Our goal is to show that $\lim_n M_n(t) = \lim_n M'_n(t)$ – by the above argument applied to M' instead of M we know that M'_n converges almost surely. The question is whether the limits are equal. Let

$$\Omega^* = \bigcup_n \{\omega : \tau_n(\omega) = T \text{ and } v_n(\omega) = T\},$$

which has full probability since both sequences are localising. We again apply Proposition 4.17, this time with

$$g(t, \omega) = f(t, \omega)\mathbf{1}_{[0,\tau_n(\omega)]}(t),$$
$$h(t, \omega) = f(t, \omega)\mathbf{1}_{[0,v_n(\omega)]}(t),$$
$$\eta_n = \min\{\tau_n, v_n\},$$

for $n \geq N(\omega)$. By Proposition 2.37, η_n is a stopping time, and obviously $g(t, \omega) = h(t, \omega)$ for all ω satisfying $t \leq \eta_n(\omega)$. Proposition 4.17 therefore shows that we have $M_n(t) = M'_n(t)$ for all ω satisfying the same condition:

$t \le \eta_n(\omega)$. For $\omega \in \Omega^*$, this condition reads $t \le T$ so $M_n(t) = M'_n(t)$ for all $t \le T$, almost surely, since $P(\Omega^*) = 1$. But if $M_n = M'_n$, their limits, which we know to exist, must be the same, which concludes the proof. □

We can now extend the notion of Itô processes by allowing more general stochastic integrands.

Definition 4.18
Given processes a, b with $\int_0^T |a(s)|ds < \infty$ and $\int_0^T b^2(s)ds < \infty$ almost surely, the process

$$X(t) = X(0) + \int_0^t a(s)ds + \int_0^t b(s)dW(s)$$

is called an **Itô process,** the above equation written conveniently as before in the differential form $dX = adt + bdW$.

Let us emphasise again that even if the drift a is zero, the process X does not have to be a martingale unless $b \in \mathcal{M}^2$.

Next, we show that Proposition 4.17 also holds in the larger space of integrands.

Proposition 4.19
If τ is a stopping time, $g, h \in \mathcal{P}^2$, and $g(t, \omega) = h(t, \omega)$ for $t \le \tau(\omega)$, then

$$\int_0^t g(s)dW(s) = \int_0^t h(s)dW(s)$$

for almost all ω satisfying $t \le \tau(\omega)$.

Proof See page 150. □

All this can be summarised as follows: if certain paths of the integrands are equal, then the same paths of the stochastic integral are equal. The bogus proof of the Itô formula for more general functions F given above lacked this property, and it again illustrates how paths play a central role in the theory. We now have all the tools to put things right and make the argument rigorous.

Before giving the general versions of the Itô formula we briefly review the relevance of the more general space of integrands. Recall that, given a, b with $\int_0^T |a(s)|ds < \infty$ and $b \in \mathcal{P}^2$, the Itô process X takes the form

$$X(t) = X(0) + \int_0^t a(s)ds + \int_0^t b(s)dW(s).$$

In financial applications, we wish to use the Itô formula, so in particular the stochastic integral $\int_0^t F_x(s, X(s))b(s)dW(s)$ must be well defined. From this point of view working in $\mathcal{M}^2$ is not convenient since, if $b \in \mathcal{M}^2$, the process $F_x(t, X(t))b(t)$ does not have to be in $\mathcal{M}^2$ in general. It will of course belong to this space if we assume that F_x is bounded, for then we would have $F_x(t, X(t))b(t) \in \mathcal{M}^2$, since

$$\mathbb{E} \int_0^T F_x(s, X(s))^2 b^2(s)ds \le C\mathbb{E} \int_0^T b^2(s)ds < \infty.$$

Such a restriction is not practical for the applications we seek, since there the functions F will emerge from modelling requirements, where proving such a bound may be impossible. In the space $\mathcal{P}^2$, it is sufficient to require that X and F_x are continuous since then the path $t \mapsto F_x(t, X(t))$ is bounded on $[0, T]$ and so

$$\int_0^T F_x^2(s, X(s))b^2(s)ds < \infty.$$

However, the price we must pay for this is that for such b the process $\int_0^t b(s)dW(s)$ is in general not a martingale.

Remark 4.20
(Beware of hidden pitfalls) The expectation of a stochastic integral of an $\mathcal{M}^2$ process is zero, we know that, but what about the expectation in the larger class? We do not know if it exists in the first place, so one could get infinity as the result of an attempted computation. However, it can be much worse than that. There are examples[1] showing that such an integral may be finite and positive. With applications in view, such an integral may represent the value of an investment, and it makes quite a difference if the expectation is zero or not.

4.7   The Itô formula for general integrands

Theorem 4.21 (Itô formula)
If $F : \mathbb{R} \to \mathbb{R}$ is of class C^2, then

$$F(W(t)) - F(0) = \int_0^t F'(W(s))dW(s) + \frac{1}{2} \int_0^t F''(W(s))ds. \qquad (4.11)$$

[1] See R. S. Liptser and A. N. Shiryaev, *Statistics of Random Processes I: General Theory*, Springer 1977, Example 8, p. 224.

Proof First of all, note that the stochastic integral has to be considered here in the larger space $\mathcal{P}^2$, since with general F we do not know if $F'(W(s))$ is in $\mathcal{M}^2$.

The argument follows the incomplete proof given earlier, up to the final stage. Let

$$B_n = \{\omega \in \Omega : |W(t, \omega)| \le n \text{ for } t \in [0, T]\}.$$

There is a set Ω' of full probability such that the paths $W(t, \omega)$ are continuous for $\omega \in \Omega'$, $P(\Omega') = 1$. We have $\bigcup B_n \supset \Omega'$, since if a path is continuous, then it is bounded on the interval $[0, T]$ so it does not leave the interval $[-n, n]$ for some n.

Fix $\omega_0 \in \Omega'$ and take n such that $\omega_0 \in B_n$.

Take a C^2 function F_n satisfying $F_n(x) = F(x)$ for $x \in [-n, n]$ and $F_n(x) = 0$ for $x \notin [-n - 1, n + 1]$. We know that the Itô formula holds for F_n :

$$F_n(W(t)) - F_n(0) = \int_0^t F_n'(W(s))dW(s) + \frac{1}{2} \int_0^t F_n''(W(s))ds. \tag{4.12}$$

Let $\tau = \min\{t : W(t, \omega) \notin (-n, n)\}$. Clearly, $F_n'(W(t)) = F'(W(t))$ for (t, ω) such that $t \le \tau(\omega)$, hence by Proposition 4.17

$$\int_0^t F_n'(W(s))dW(s) = \int_0^t F'(W(s))dW(s)$$

for such (t, ω). But for our fixed $\omega_0 \in \Omega'$ we have $\tau(\omega_0) = T$, so we obtain the Itô formula (4.11) for all t, since in the other terms we can replace F_n by F without any effort. $\square$

We have seen two different approaches to prevent a process from becoming 'too big to handle'. In the extension of the stochastic integral, we found it useful to multiply a process X by $\mathbf{1}_{\{t \le \tau\}}$ to force it to behave nicely, according to our particular needs. If $\tau = \min\{t : \int_0^t X^2(s)ds \ge C\}$, then the integral of $(\mathbf{1}_{\{t \le \tau\}}X)^2$ over $[0, T]$ is bounded by C. If $\tau = \min\{t : X(t) \ge C\}$, then $\mathbf{1}_{\{t \le \tau\}}X$ itself is bounded. Such a multiplication by $\mathbf{1}_{\{t \le \tau\}}$ is quite drastic since it makes the process vanish once it loses the nice properties we require of it.

In Chapter 2 we employed a slightly more subtle method of subduing a process: the stopped process (Definition 2.39). The idea is simply to freeze the process at the moment when it reaches some boundary. So for instance with $\tau = \min\{t : X(t) \ge C\}$ the stopped process is bounded by C. Now if $X \in \mathcal{P}^2$, then $X_\tau \in \mathcal{M}^2$ and the stochastic integral of X_τ is a martingale, so that, in particular, its expectation vanishes, which is crucial for many applications in finance. The task now is to let $C \to \infty$ and to note that X_τ converges to X, which may enable us to show properties of X by means of the properties of stopped processes; for instance, if X_τ satisfies an equality, it is often preserved in the limit. This method is called **localisation**. We shall use it to good effect in the next result.

Theorem 4.22 (Itô formula – general)

Assume that $F : [0, T] \times \mathbb{R} \to \mathbb{R}$ is in class $C^{1,2}$, and let X be an Itô process

$$dX(t) = a(t)dt + b(t)dW(t)$$

with $\int_0^T |a(t)| \, dt$ finite almost surely and $b \in \mathcal{P}^2$. Then the process $F(t, X(t))$ is an Itô process and the Itô formula holds:

$$F(t, X(t)) - F(0, 0) = \int_0^t F_t(s, X(s))ds + \int_0^t F_x(s, X(s))a(s)ds$$

$$+ \int_0^t F_x(s, X(s))b(s)dW(s)$$

$$+ \frac{1}{2} \int_0^t F_{xx}(s, X(s))b^2(s)ds.$$

Proof Take a $C^{1,2}$ function F_n satisfying $F_n(t, x) = F(t, x)$ for $x \in [-n, n]$ and $F_n(t, x) = 0$ for $x \notin [-n - 1, n + 1]$. Let

$$\tau_n(\omega) = \min\{t : X(t, \omega) \notin (-n, n) \text{ or } b(t, \omega) \in (-n, n)\}$$

so for $t \leq \tau_n(\omega)$, the process X is bounded, $|X(t, \omega)| \leq n$. In addition, by the continuity of almost all paths $t \to X(t, \omega)$ on $[0, T]$,

$$P\left(\bigcup_{n \geq 1} \{\tau_n = T\}\right) = 1.$$

Consider stopped processes $X_n = X_{\tau_n}$ satisfying $|X_n(t)| \leq n$. We claim that X_n is an Itô process

$$dX_n = a_n dt + b_n dW,$$

where $a_n = a\mathbf{1}_{[0,\tau_n]}$, $b_n = b\mathbf{1}_{[0,\tau_n]}$.

If $t \leq \tau_n(\omega)$, then $a_n(s, \omega) = a(s, \omega)$ for $s \in [0, t]$, so

$$\int_0^t a_n(s, \omega)ds = \int_0^t a(s, \omega)ds.$$

Similarly, $b_n(s, \omega) = b(s, \omega)$, so by Proposition 4.17

$$\int_0^t b_n(s)dW(s) = \int_0^t b(s)dW(s).$$

These two properties imply $X_{\tau_n} = X$.

On the other hand, if $t > \tau_n(\omega)$, then $a_n = 0$, $b_n = 0$, so $X_n(t) = X(\tau_n)$.
We know that the Itô formula holds for F_n and X_n, which is bounded:

$$F_n(t, X_n(t)) - F_n(0, 0) = \int_0^t (F_n)_t(s, X_n(s))ds + \int_0^t (F_n)_x(s, X_n(s))a_n(s)ds$$

$$+ \int_0^t (F_n)_x(s, X_n(s))b_n(s)dW(s)$$

$$+ \frac{1}{2}\int_0^t (F_n)_{xx}(s, X_n(s))b_n^2(s)ds. \tag{4.13}$$

Recall that for $x \in [-n, n]$, $F_n(t, x) = F(t, x)$ and $(F_n)_x(t, X_n(s))b_n(s) = F_x(t, X(t))b(s)$ if $t \leq \tau_n(\omega)$ so

$$\int_0^t (F_n)_x(s, X_n(s))b_n(s)dW(s) = \int_0^t F_x(s, X(s))b(s)dW(s) \text{ if } t \leq \tau_n(\omega).$$

The other terms are easy to handle since they involve pathwise integrals, so if $t \leq \tau_n(\omega)$, in (4.13) we can replace F_n by F, X_n by X, a_n by a, b_n by b getting

$$F(t, X(t)) - F(0, 0) = \int_0^t F_t(s, X(s))ds + \int_0^t F_x(s, X(s))a(s)ds$$

$$+ \int_0^t F_x(s, X(s))b(s)dW(s)$$

$$+ \frac{1}{2}\int_0^t F_{xx}(s, X(s))b^2(s)ds. \tag{4.14}$$

Since $P(\bigcup\{\tau_n = T\}) = 1$, (4.14) holds a.s. $\qquad\square$

Remark 4.23

Facts proved for bounded processes in the previous chapter now can be generalised, in particular the form of the quadratic variation of an Itô process. In each case, we must take care in our choice of localising sequence, to ensure that the stopped process satisfies the boundedness condition needed for the earlier proof.

Exercise 4.5 Show that the Itô process $dX(t) = a(t)dt + b(t)dW(t)$ has quadratic variation $[X, X](t) = \int_0^t b^2(s)ds$.

> **Exercise 4.6** Show that the characteristics of an Itô process are uniquely defined by the process, that is prove that $X = Y$ implies $a_X = a_Y$, $b_X = b_Y$, by applying Ito formula to find the form of $(X(t) - Y(t))^2$.

> **Exercise 4.7** Suppose that the Itô process $dX(t) = a(t)dt + b(t)dW(t)$ is positive for all t and find the characteristic of the processes $Y(t) = 1/X(t)$, $Z(t) = \ln X(t)$.

> **Exercise 4.8** Find the characteristics of $\exp\{at + X(t)\}$, given the form of an Itô process X.

4.8 Local martingales

Having allowed general processes $f \in \mathcal{P}^2$ under the stochastic integral we have lost the martingale property of the emerging process $\int_0^t f(s)dW(s)$. Our goal here is to see that localisation gives us at least a partial way out of our misery.

Definition 4.24
The process $X(t)$ adapted to $\mathcal{F}_t$ is a **local martingale** if there exists a sequence $(\tau_n)_{n\geq 1}$ of stopping times such that for each ω there is $N(\omega)$ so that $n \geq N(\omega)$ implies $\tau_n(\omega) \geq T$ (we say $\tau_n \geq T$ almost surely eventually) and such that for each n, $X_{\tau_n}(t)$ is a martingale with respect to $\mathcal{F}_t$.

This describes the 'martingale' property that we can rescue for our stochastic integrals with integrands from $\mathcal{P}^2$:

Proposition 4.25
For $f \in \mathcal{P}^2$,

$$X(t) = \int_0^t f(s)dW(s)$$

is a local martingale.

Proof Recall that the stochastic integral in the space $\mathcal{P}^2$ was constructed as the limit

$$X(t) = \lim_n M_n(t),$$

where

$$M_n(t) = \int_0^T \mathbf{1}_{[0,t]}(s)f(s)\mathbf{1}_{[0,\tau_n]}(s)dW(s)$$

are martingales (which follows from the localising nature of the times τ_n). This holds for any localising sequence, for example

$$\tau_n = \inf\{t \leq T : \int_0^t f^2(s)ds \geq n\}$$

with the convenction $\inf \emptyset = T$ (in other words, if the integral is below n, there no need to stop the process). We will prove that the stopped process X_{τ_n} is a martingale for each n :

$X_{\tau_k}(t) = X(t \wedge \tau_k)$ (definition of the stopped process)

$$= \lim_n M_n(t \wedge \tau_k)$$

$$= \lim_n \int_0^T \mathbf{1}_{[0,t\wedge\tau_k]}(s)f(s)\mathbf{1}_{[0,\tau_n]}(s)dW(s) \quad \text{(definition of } M_n)$$

$$= \lim_n \int_0^T \mathbf{1}_{[0,t]}(s)\mathbf{1}_{[0,\tau_k]}f(s)\mathbf{1}_{[0,\tau_n]}(s)dW(s) \quad \text{(properties of indicators)}$$

$$= \int_0^T \mathbf{1}_{[0,t]}(s)\mathbf{1}_{[0,\tau_k]}f(s)(s)dW(s) \quad \text{(as } \tau_n \geq \tau_k \text{ for } n \geq k)$$

$$= M_k(t).$$

$\square$

In further applications, we shall need some facts about local martingales. The main thread is concerned with identifying simple conditions guaranteeing that a local martingale is a martingale.

Proposition 4.26
Any bounded local martingale is a martingale.

Proof Let $X(t)$ be a local martingale. There exists $\tau_n \geq T$ eventually almost surely such that $X_{\tau_n}(t) = X(\tau_n \wedge t))$ is a martingale. For $s < t \leq T$,

$$\mathbb{E}(X(\tau_n \wedge t)|\mathcal{F}_s) = X(\tau_n \wedge s).$$

For all $A \in \mathcal{F}_s$,

$$\mathbb{E}(\mathbf{1}_A X(\tau_n \wedge t)) = \mathbb{E}(\mathbf{1}_A X(\tau_n \wedge s)). \tag{4.15}$$

Since τ_n hits T eventually, for $t \leq T$ we have $\tau_n \wedge t = t$ for large enough n, so

$$X(\tau_n \wedge t) = X(t), \quad X(\tau_n \wedge s) = X(s) \quad \text{eventually almost surely}$$

We assumed X is bounded so for some deterministic constant C

$$|X(\tau_n \wedge t)| \leq C.$$

This guarantees that the convergence is dominated in each case and so the expectations (i.e. integrals) converge

$$\mathbb{E}(\mathbf{1}_A X(\tau_n \wedge t)) \to \mathbb{E}(\mathbf{1}_A X(t)), \quad \mathbb{E}(\mathbf{1}_A X(\tau_n \wedge s)) \to \mathbb{E}(\mathbf{1}_A X(s)).$$

The equality (4.15) is preserved in the limit so

$$\mathbb{E}(\mathbf{1}_A X(t)) = \mathbb{E}(\mathbf{1}_A X(s)),$$

hence by the definition of the conditional expectation $\mathbb{E}(X(t)|\mathcal{F}_s) = X(s)$ as claimed. □

Next we consider non-negative local martingales. Here we need a generalisation of the classical Fatou lemma to conditional expectations.

Lemma 4.27 (Conditional Fatou)
If $Y_n \geq 0$, then for any sub-σ-field $\mathcal{G}$ or $\mathcal{F}$

$$\mathbb{E}(\liminf_{n \to \infty} Y_n | \mathcal{G}) \leq \liminf_{n \to \infty} \mathbb{E}(Y_n | \mathcal{G}).$$

Proof See page 150. □

This will enable us to see that for non-negative local martingales we only need to check the initial and final expectations to ensure that we have a martingale – first we obtain:

Proposition 4.28
Any non-negative local martingale is a supermartingale.

Proof Let $X(t)$ be a local martingale. There exists a sequence of stopping times such that $\tau_n \geq T$ eventually almost surely and $X_{\tau_n}(t) = X(\tau_n \wedge t)$ is a martingale. This means that for $s < t \leq T$

$$\mathbb{E}(X(\tau_n \wedge t)|\mathcal{F}_s) = X(\tau_n \wedge s).$$

Next, for n large enough we have $\tau_n \wedge t = t$, so that

$$\liminf X(\tau_n \wedge t) = X(t), \quad \liminf X(\tau_n \wedge s) = X(s) \quad \text{almost surely.}$$

The conditional Fatou lemma with $Y_n = X(\tau_n \wedge t)$, $\mathcal{G} = \mathcal{F}_s$ now gives

$$\begin{aligned}
\mathbb{E}(X(t)|\mathcal{F}_s) &= \mathbb{E}(\liminf X(\tau_n \wedge t)|\mathcal{F}_s) \\
&\leq \liminf \mathbb{E}(X(\tau_n \wedge t)|\mathcal{F}_s) \\
&= \liminf X(\tau_n \wedge s) \\
&= X(s).
\end{aligned}$$

$\square$

Corollary 4.29
Any non-negative local martingale with $\mathbb{E}(X(T)) = X(0)$ is a martingale.

Proof By the previous proposition we know that X is a supermartingale so

$$\mathbb{E}(X(t)|\mathcal{F}_s) \leq X(s).$$

Applying the expectation on both sides we get

$$\mathbb{E}(\mathbb{E}(X(t)|\mathcal{F}_s)) = \mathbb{E}(X(t)) \leq \mathbb{E}(X(s)).$$

Similarly,

$$\mathbb{E}(X(T)) \leq \mathbb{E}(X(t)) \leq \mathbb{E}(X(s)) \leq X(0)$$

and employing the assumption we get

$$\mathbb{E}(X(t)) = \mathbb{E}(X(s)).$$

This fact excludes the possibility of the strict inequality

$$\mathbb{E}(X(t)|\mathcal{F}_s) < X(s)$$

on a set of positive probability. $\square$

A different, but quite powerful condition ensuring the martingale property is the following:

Proposition 4.30
Any local martingale with $\mathbb{E}(\sup_{t\in[0,T]} |X_t|) < \infty$ is a martingale.

Proof There exists $\tau_n \geq T$ eventually almost surely such that $X_{\tau_n}(t) = X(\tau_n \wedge t)$ is a martingale. For $s < t \leq T$, this gives, as above,

$$\mathbb{E}(X(\tau_n \wedge t)|\mathcal{F}_s) = X(\tau_n \wedge s)$$

We have almost surely convergence, that is

$$\lim_n X(\tau_n \wedge t) = X(t) \quad \text{almost surely.}$$

If $\sup_t |X(t)|$ is integrable, this convergence is dominated, so in the limit we get the result

$$\mathbb{E}(X(t)|\mathcal{F}_s) = X(s).$$

□

4.9   Applications of the Itô formula

Exponential martingale

The first property follows immediately from the Itô formula by direct inspection. It is related to the considerations of the previous section.

Theorem 4.31
If $dX = adt + bdW(t)$, with deterministic a, b, and the $C^{1,2}$ – function $F(t, x)$ satisfies the PDE

$$F_t = -\frac{1}{2}b^2 F_{xx} - aF_x, \qquad (4.16)$$

then $F(t, X(t))$ is a local martingale. If additionally $F_x(t, X(t))$ is in $\mathcal{M}^2$, then $F(t, X(t))$ is a martingale.

Proof   Note that the process $F(t, X(t))$ does not have to be in $\mathcal{M}^2$, but always lies in $\mathcal{P}^2$.
   By Theorem 4.22

$$F(t, X(t)) - F(0, 0) = \int_0^t F_t(s, X(s))ds + \int_0^t F_x(s, X(s))a(s)ds$$
$$+ \int_0^t F_x(s, X(s))b(s)dW(s)$$
$$+ \frac{1}{2}\int_0^t F_{xx}(s, X(s))b^2(s)ds.$$

Our assumption ensures that the first term on the right cancels with the second and fourth. So

$$F(t, X(t)) - F(0, 0) = \int_0^t F_x(s, X(s))b(s)dW(s) \qquad (4.17)$$

and under the additional assumption that $F_x(t, X(t))$ is in $\mathcal{M}^2$, it is a martingale by Proposition 4.30.   □

   This provides an alternative proof of the last part of Theorem 2.32.

Corollary 4.32

The process $M(t) = e^{\sigma W(t) - \frac{1}{2}\sigma^2 t}$ is a martingale.

Proof We can write $M(t) = F(t, W(t))$ where $F(t, x) = e^{\sigma x - \frac{1}{2}\sigma^2 t}$ and (4.16) with $a(t) = 0$ and $b(t) = 1$ can be directly verified. We have to show that $\sigma e^{\sigma W(t) - \frac{1}{2}\sigma^2 t} \in \mathcal{M}^2$:

$$\mathbb{E} \int_0^T \left(\sigma e^{\sigma W(t) - \frac{1}{2}\sigma^2 t} \right)^2 dt = \mathbb{E} \int_0^T \sigma^2 e^{2\sigma W(t) - \sigma^2 t} dt$$

$$\leq \sigma^2 \mathbb{E} \int_0^T e^{2\sigma W(t)} dt \quad (\text{since } e^{2\sigma W(t) - \sigma^2 t} \leq e^{2\sigma W(t)})$$

$$= \sigma^2 \int_0^T \mathbb{E} e^{2\sigma W(t)} dt$$

$$= \sigma^2 \int_0^T e^{2\sigma^2 t} dt < \infty$$

by Fubini's theorem and using the fact that if X has normal distribution with $\mathbb{E}(X) = 0$, then $\mathbb{E}(e^X) = e^{\frac{1}{2} \text{Var}(X)}$ applied to $X = W(t)$, $\text{Var}(2\sigma W(t)) = 4\sigma^2 t$. $\qquad \square$

Exercise 4.9 Find a version of this corollary for the case where σ is a deterministic function of time.

Feynman–Kac formula

The next theorem provides a very useful link between partial differential equations and stochastic processes.

Theorem 4.33 (Feynman–Kac formula)

Assume that for a given function $\phi(x)$, X is an Itô process with

$$dX(t) = a(t)dt + b(t)dW(t)$$

$$F_t(t, x) = -\frac{1}{2}b^2(t)F_{xx}(t, x) - a(t)F_x(t, x)$$

$$F(T, x) = \phi(x)$$

and that $F_x(t, X(t))b(t) \in \mathcal{M}^2$. Then

$$F(t, X(t)) = \mathbb{E}(\phi(X(T))|\mathcal{F}_t).$$

Proof   We know that

$$\phi(X(T)) - F(0,0) = \int_0^T F_x(s, X(s))b(s)dW(s)$$

$$F(t, X(t)) - F(0,0) = \int_0^t F_x(s, X(s))b(s)dW(s)$$

so subtracting gives (taking into account $F(T, X(T)) = \phi(X(T))$)

$$\phi(X(T)) - F(t, X(t)) = \int_t^T F_x(s, X(s))b(s)dW(s).$$

Next we take the conditional expectation on both sides. The expectation of the stochastic integral is zero since the integrand is in the space $\mathcal{M}^2$, so

$$\mathbb{E}(\phi(X(T)) - F(t, X(t))|\mathcal{F}_t) = \mathbb{E}\left(\int_t^T F_x(s, X(s))b(s)dW(s)|\mathcal{F}_t\right) = 0.$$

But $F(t, X(t))$ is $\mathcal{F}_t$-measurable so

$$\mathbb{E}(F(t, X(t))|\mathcal{F}_t) = F(t, X(t)).$$

$\square$

Consider a particular case. Fix $t \in [0, T]$, $x > 0$ and our goal is to express $F(t, x)$ by means of the stochastic process X.

Take $X(0) = x$, $a(t) = b(t) = 0$ on $[0, t]$ so that $X(s) = x$ for $s \in [0, t]$, and the filtration $(\mathcal{F}_t)_{t \geq 0}$ generated by X. Then $\mathcal{F}_t = \{\Omega, \emptyset\}$ since X is constant up to time t, so the σ-field generated is trivial. Then the conditional expectation is just the ordinary expectation:

$$F(t, x) = \mathbb{E}(\phi(X(T))).$$

As we will see later, this formula will give as a consequence the Black–Scholes formula for option pricing (see [BSM]).

Integration by parts

We conclude this chapter with an analogue of the classical integration by parts formula. We begin with a simple case.

Proposition 4.34
If g is a real function of class C^1, then

$$\int_a^b g'(t)W(t)dt = g(t)W(t)|_a^b - \int_a^b g(t)dW(t).$$

Proof Consider $F(t, x) = xg(t)$ so that $F_t = xg'$, $F_x = g$, $F_{xx} = 0$. Then writing $Y(t) = F(t, W(t))$ the Itô formula reduces to

$$dY(t) = g'(t)W(t)dt + g(t)dW(t),$$

which written in the integral form proves the claim. □

We are nearly ready for a more general version of this result, but first we record a simple consequence of the Itô formula:

Lemma 4.35
If $dX(t) = a(t)dt + b(t)dW(t)$, then

$$dX^2 = 2XdX + b^2dt.$$

Proof This is an immediate application of Itô formula to $Y(t) = F(X(t))$, where $F(x) = x^2$, $F_t = 0$, $F_x = 2x$, $F_{xx} = 2$, so that

$$dY = 2Xadt + 2XbdW(t) + \frac{1}{2}2b^2dt = 2XdX + b^2dt.$$

□

We can now deduce our integration by parts result:

Theorem 4.36
Given Itô processes X, Y with

$$dX(t) = a_X(t)dt + b_Y(t)dW(t),$$
$$dY(t) = a_Y(t)dt + b_Y(t)dW(t),$$

then their product XY is also an Itô process with

$$d(XY) = XdY + YdX + b_Xb_Ydt.$$

Proof Applying the Itô formula to $(X + Y)^2$, X^2, and Y^2 we find

$$(X(t) + Y(t))^2 = (X(0) + Y(0))^2 + 2\int_0^t (X(s) + Y(s))d(X(s) + Y(s))$$
$$+ \int_0^t (b_X(s) + b_Y(s))^2 ds$$
$$X^2(t) = X^2(0) + 2\int_0^t X(s)dX(s) + \int_0^t b_X^2(s)ds$$
$$Y^2(t) = Y^2(0) + 2\int_0^t Y(s)dY(s) + \int_0^t b_Y^2(s)ds$$

so subtracting the last two from the first identity and comparing the two sides gives what is needed

$$X(t)Y(t) = X(0)X(0) + \int_0^t X(s)dY(s) + \int_0^t Y(s)dX(s) + \int_0^t b_X(s)b_Y(s)ds.$$

$\square$

Exercise 4.10   Find the characteristic of the process $e^{-rt}X(t)$.

Exercise 4.11   Find the form of the process X/Y using Exercise 4.7.

4.10   Proofs

Proposition 4.17

If $f, g \in M^2$ and τ is a stopping time such that $f(t, \omega) = g(t, \omega)$ whenever $t \leq \tau(\omega)$, then

$$\int_0^t f(s)dW(s) = \int_0^t g(s)dW(s)$$

for almost all ω satisfying $t \leq \tau(\omega)$.

Proof   By linearity this reduces to showing that for $t \leq \tau(\omega)$, if $f(t, \omega) = 0$, then $\int_0^t f(s)dW(s) = 0$.
Step 1. Suppose first that $f \in M^2$ is simple

$$f(t, \omega) = \xi_0(\omega)\mathbf{1}_{\{0\}}(t) + \sum_{k=1}^{N} \xi_k(\omega)\mathbf{1}_{(t_k, t_{k+1}]}(t).$$

For any particular ω, $\tau(\omega) \in (t_m, t_{m+1}]$ for some m. For f to vanish on $t \leq \tau(\omega)$, the coefficients $\xi_k(\omega)$ must be zero if $k \leq m$. The stochastic integral can be easily computed: let $t \in (t_n, t_{n+1}]$ and by definition

$$\left(\int_0^t f(s)dW(s) \right)(\omega)$$

$$= \sum_{k=1}^{n-1} \xi_k(\omega)[W(t_{k+1}, \omega) - W(t_k, \omega)] + \xi_n(\omega)[W(t, \omega) - W(t_n, \omega)].$$

If $t \leq \tau(\omega)$, $\xi_k(\omega) = 0$ for $k \leq n$ so the above sum vanishes.

Step 2. Take a bounded f and a sequence of simple processes f_n converging to f in $\mathcal{M}^2$. The difficulty in applying the first part of the proof lies in the fact that f_n do not have to vanish for $t \le \tau(\omega)$ even if f does. However if we truncate f_n by forcing it to be zero for those t by $f_n(t, \omega)\mathbf{1}_{(\tau(\omega),T]}(t)$, this is not a simple process. So we write

$$g_n(t, \omega) = \xi_0(\omega)\mathbf{1}_{\{0\}}(t) + \sum_{k=1}^{N} \xi_k(\omega)\mathbf{1}_{(t_k, t_{k+1}]}(t)\mathbf{1}_{(\tau(\omega),T]}(t_k).$$

The idea is that this should mean no harm as f_n is going to zero anyway in $[0, \tau]$, so we are just speeding this up a bit. We have $\mathbf{1}_{(\tau(\omega),T]}(t_k) = 1$ if $\tau \le t_k$, which belongs to $\mathcal{F}_{t_k}$ since τ is a stopping time. So g_n is an adapted simple process, clearly $g_n = 0$ on $\{t \le \tau\}$, and Step 1 applies to give

$$\int_0^t g_n(s)dW(s) = 0 \text{ if } t \le \tau.$$

The convergence $f_n \to f$ in $\mathcal{M}^2$ implies that $f_n \mathbf{1}_{(\tau,T]} \to f\mathbf{1}_{(\tau,T]} = f$ in this space so to see that $g_n \to f$, all we have to do is to show that the difference $g_n - f_n \mathbf{1}_{(\tau,T]}$ goes to zero in $\mathcal{M}^2$. Due to the form of g_n, with $\tau(\omega) \in (t_{m(\omega)}, t_{m(\omega)+1}]$ we have

$$\int_0^T (g_n(s, \omega) - f_n(s, \omega)\mathbf{1}_{(\tau(\omega),T]}(s))^2 \, ds = \int_{t_{m(\omega)}}^{t_{m(\omega)+1}} \xi_{m(\omega)}^2 (1 - \mathbf{1}_{(\tau,T]}(s))^2 ds$$

$$\le C \max_k (t_{k+1} - t_k) \to 0$$

as needed. Then

$$\int_0^t g_n(s)dW(s) \to \int_0^t f(s)dW(s) \quad \text{in } L^2(\Omega),$$

thus a subsequence converges almost surely, hence $\int_0^t f(s)dW(s) = 0$ if $t \le \tau$ holds on a set Ω_t of full probability. Taking rational times q we get

$$\int_0^q f(s)dW(s) = 0 \text{ on } \bigcup_{q \in \mathbb{Q} \cap [0,T]} \Omega_q,$$

which by continuity of stochastic integral extends to all $t \in [0, T]$.

Step 3. For an arbitrary $f \in \mathcal{M}^2$, let $f_n(t, \omega) = f(t, \omega)\mathbf{1}_{\{|f(t,\omega)|\le n\}}(\omega)$. Clearly, $f_n \to f$ pointwise and by the dominated convergence theorem this convergence is also in the norm of $\mathcal{M}^2$. By the Itô isometry, it follows that $\int_0^t f_n(s)dW(s) \to \int_0^t f(s)dW(s)$ in $L^2(\Omega)$. But f_n is bounded, it is zero if $t \le \tau(\omega)$, so $\int_0^t f_n(s)dW(s) = 0$ by Step 2, and consequently $\int_0^t f(s)dW(s) = 0$. $\square$

Proposition 4.19

If τ is a stopping time, $g, h \in \mathcal{P}^2$, and $g(t, \omega) = h(t, \omega)$ for $t \leq \tau(\omega)$, then

$$\int_0^t g(s)dW(s) = \int_0^t h(s)dW(s) \text{ for almost all } \omega \text{ satisfying } t \leq \tau(\omega).$$

Proof Take $f \in \mathcal{P}^2$; we show that if $f(t, \omega) = 0$ for $t \leq \tau(\omega)$, then $\int_0^t f(s)dW(s) = 0$ for $t \leq \tau(\omega)$, which is sufficent for the general purpose by the linearity of the stochastic integral. Let

$$\tau_n(\omega) = \min\{t : \int_0^t f^2(s, \omega)ds \geq n\}$$

which is a localising sequence for f in $\mathcal{M}^2$. The sequence

$$M_n(t) = \int_0^t f(s)\mathbf{1}_{\{t \leq \tau_n\}}(s)dW(s)$$

converges by Theorem 4.16.

For $t \leq \tau(\omega)$ we have $f(t, \omega)\mathbf{1}_{\{t \leq \tau_n(\omega)\}}(t) = 0$ so by the equality of the integrals for processes in $\mathcal{M}^2$ we obtain

$$\int_0^t f(s)\mathbf{1}_{\{t \leq \tau_n\}}(s)dW(s) = 0 \text{ for } t \leq \tau(\omega).$$

Hence $X(t, \omega) = 0$ if $t \leq \tau(\omega)$. □

Lemma 4.27

If $Y_n \geq 0$, then

$$\mathbb{E}(\liminf_{n \to \infty} Y_n | \mathcal{G}) \leq \liminf_{n \to \infty} \mathbb{E}(Y_n | \mathcal{G}).$$

Proof Write $Z_k = \inf_{n \geq k} Y_n$, which is an increasing sequence. The expectations $\mathbb{E}(Z_k | \mathcal{G})$ are also increasing. Write $Y = \liminf Y_n = \lim Z_k$ and note that $\mathbb{E}(Y | \mathcal{G}) = \mathbb{E}(\lim Z_k | \mathcal{G})$. We will show that

$$\mathbb{E}(\lim Z_k | \mathcal{G}) = \lim \mathbb{E}(Z_k | \mathcal{G}) \tag{4.18}$$

which is the conditional version of the monotone convergence thoerem. Take $A \in \mathcal{G}$ and we have to show

$$\mathbb{E}(\mathbf{1}_A \lim Z_k) = \mathbb{E}(\mathbf{1}_A \lim \mathbb{E}(Z_k | \mathcal{G})).$$

By the classical monotone convergence theorem

$$\mathbb{E}(\mathbf{1}_A \lim Z_k) = \lim \mathbb{E}(\mathbf{1}_A Z_k)$$
$$= \lim \mathbb{E}(\mathbf{1}_A \mathbb{E}(Z_k | \mathcal{G})).$$

using the definition of conditional expectation. By monotone convergence once more

$$\lim \mathbb{E}(\mathbf{1}_A \mathbb{E}(Z_k|\mathcal{G})) = \mathbb{E}(\mathbf{1}_A \lim \mathbb{E}(Z_k|\mathcal{G}))$$

which completes the proof of (4.18).

Clearly, by the definition of Z_k, for $n \geq k\,\mathbb{E}(Z_k|\mathcal{G}) \leq \mathbb{E}(Y_n|\mathcal{G})$ so also

$$\mathbb{E}(Z_k|\mathcal{G}) \leq \inf_{n \geq k} \mathbb{E}(Y_n|\mathcal{G}).$$

Going back to Y we have

$$\mathbb{E}(Y|\mathcal{G}) = \lim \mathbb{E}(Z_k|\mathcal{G}) \quad \text{(by (4.18))}$$
$$\leq \liminf_{k \ \ n \geq k} \mathbb{E}(Y_n|\mathcal{G}) \quad \text{(by the above inequality)}$$
$$= \liminf \mathbb{E}(Y_n|\mathcal{G}).$$

$\square$

5

Stochastic differential equations

Classical calculus has its origins in models of the dynamics of physical objects, assumed to be governed by physical laws such as Newton's second law of motion, which find mathematical expression in differential equations that express a relationship between a function and some of its derivatives. In many models of dynamic phenomena based upon such equations, the independent variable is assumed to represent the passage of time. For a simple model of population growth, for example, we might postulate that the rate of growth is proportional to the total population $n(t)$ at time $t \geq 0$, which is expressed as $\frac{dn}{dt} = \alpha n$, or (formally) in differential form as $dn(t) = \alpha n(t)dt$ for some proportionality constant α, and we then seek functions $n(t)$ that solve (satisfy) this equation, typically on some interval. A natural task is therefore to find conditions under which differential equations of a given class have unique solutions on some prescribed domain. The formal equation is then understood as an integral equation satisfied by the solution. In our example, this becomes: $n(t) = \alpha \int_0^t n(s)ds + c$ for some constant c.

With the Itô calculus to hand we can extend such models to include an additional random term, described by means of the Wiener process, as in our first example below. Quite generally, we must then interpret a formal expression of the form

$$dX(t) = a(t, X(t))dt + b(t, X(t))dW(t), \tag{5.1}$$

where $a(t, x)$ and $b(t, x)$ are given as functions $\mathbb{R}^2 \to \mathbb{R}$, as an integral equation

$$X(t) = X(0) + \int_0^t a(s, X(s))ds + \int_0^t b(s, X(s))dW(s).$$

Here the first integral is of (Riemann or) Lebesgue type and the second is an Itô integral. An equation of the form (5.1) is called a **stochastic differential equation (SDE).** We will find sufficient conditions on the coefficient functions a, b to ensure that a unique solution X of (5.1) can be found.

5.1 Examples

We first discuss several examples of stochastic differential equations that arise in finance, beginning with the best-known and most widely used one.

The Black–Scholes equation

Recall our motivation at the beginning of Chapter 3, where an argument based on approximation via binomial trees suggested the process $S(t) = S(0)e^{mt+\sigma W(t)}$ (interpreted in finance as the price of a risky asset, such as a stock) as a solution to the so-called **Black–Scholes equation**, which is the basis of their famous model,

$$dS(t) = \mu S(t)dt + \sigma S(t)dW(t) \qquad (5.2)$$

with $\mu = m + \frac{1}{2}\sigma^2$. The starting point is the initial value, which is a given positive number $S(0) = S_0 > 0$. We can now solve this equation rigorously, but first we make sure that the stochastic integral makes sense.

Proposition 5.1
The process

$$S(t) = S(0)\exp\left\{\mu t - \frac{1}{2}\sigma^2 t + \sigma W(t)\right\} \qquad (5.3)$$

belongs to $\mathcal{M}^2$.

Proof According to the definition, we have to analyse

$$\mathbb{E}\int_0^T \left(\exp\left\{\mu t - \frac{1}{2}\sigma^2 t + \sigma W(t)\right\}\right)^2 dt.$$

The inner integral cannot be computed so the first step is to change the order of integration. To see that this is legitimate, we will show that the integral resulting from such a change is finite and since the measures are finite (Lebesgue on $[0, T]$ and P on Ω), Fubini's theorem applies (see [PF]). So we compute

$$\int_0^T \mathbb{E}\exp\{2\mu t - \sigma^2 t + 2\sigma W(t)\}dt = \int_0^T \exp\{2\mu t - \sigma^2 t\}\mathbb{E}\exp\{2\sigma W(t)\}dt$$

but $\mathbb{E}\exp\{X\} = \exp\{\frac{1}{2}\text{Var}(X)\}$ if X is normal with zero expectation, so $\mathbb{E}\exp\{2\sigma W(t)\} = \exp\{2\sigma^2 t\}$ and inserting this above we get $\int_0^T \exp\{2\mu t + \sigma^2 t\}dt$, which is of course finite. □

Theorem 5.2
The process (5.3) solves the Black–Scholes equation (5.2).

Proof   We can write $S(t) = F(t, W(t))$ where $F(t, x) = S(0)\exp\{\mu t - \frac{1}{2}\sigma^2 t + \sigma x\}$. Direct differentiation gives

$$F_t(t, x) = (\mu - \frac{1}{2}\sigma^2)S(0)\exp\left\{\mu t - \frac{1}{2}\sigma^2 t + \sigma x\right\}$$

$$F_x(t, x) = \sigma S(0)\exp\left\{\mu t - \frac{1}{2}\sigma^2 t + \sigma x\right\}$$

$$F_{xx}(t, x) = \sigma^2 S(0)\exp\left\{\mu t - \frac{1}{2}\sigma^2 t + \sigma x\right\}$$

so by the Itô formula

$$dS(t) = \left(\mu - \frac{1}{2}\sigma^2\right)S(0)\exp\left\{\mu t - \frac{1}{2}\sigma^2 t + \sigma W(t)\right\}dt$$

$$+\sigma S(0)\exp\left\{\mu t - \frac{1}{2}\sigma^2 t + \sigma W(t)\right\}dW(t)$$

$$+\frac{1}{2}\sigma^2 S(0)\exp\left\{\mu t - \frac{1}{2}\sigma^2 t + \sigma W(t)\right\}dt$$

$$= \mu S(t)dt + \sigma S(t)dW(t)$$

as claimed. □

Exercise 5.1   Find an equation satisfied by $X(t) = S(0)\exp\{\mu t + \sigma W(t)\}$.

Exercise 5.2   Find the equations for the functions $t \mapsto \mathbb{E}(S(t))$, $t \mapsto \text{Var}(S(t))$.

This is not the whole story yet, since we have to make sure that there are no other solutions. The following uniqueness result will in fact follow from a general theorem which we will prove later. But the main idea of this general case is similar, so it is instructive to analyse a simple situation first.

Proposition 5.3
The following equation has at most one solution in $\mathcal{M}^2$:

$$dS(t) = \mu S(t)dt + \sigma S(t)dW(t),$$
$$S(0) = S_0.$$

Proof Suppose S_1, S_2 solve

$$S_i(t) = S_0 + \int_0^t \mu S_i(u)du + \int_0^t \sigma S_i(u)dW(u), \quad i = 1, 2.$$

Then

$$S_1(t) - S_2(t) = \int_0^t \mu[S_1(u) - S_2(u)]du + \int_0^t \sigma[S_1(u) - S_2(u)]dW(u)$$

(subtraction ensures cancellation of the common initial value) and using $(a + b)^2 \leq 2a^2 + 2b^2$ we have

$$(S_1(t) - S_2(t))^2$$
$$= \left(\int_0^t \mu[S_1(u) - S_2(u)]du + \int_0^t \sigma[S_1(u) - S_2(u)]dW(u) \right)^2$$
$$\leq 2\left(\int_0^t \mu[S_1(u) - S_2(u)]du \right)^2 + 2\left(\int_0^t \sigma[S_1(u) - S_2(u)]dW(u) \right)^2.$$

Take the expectation on both sides

$$\mathbb{E}(S_1(t) - S_2(t))^2 \leq 2\mathbb{E}\left(\int_0^t \mu[S_1(u) - S_2(u)]du \right)^2$$
$$+ 2\mathbb{E}\left(\int_0^t \sigma[S_1(u) - S_2(u)]dW(u) \right)^2.$$

The next step needs some preparation. First note that the Itô isometry (Theorem 3.13 with $[a, b] = [0, t]$) gives us

$$\mathbb{E}\left(\int_0^t \sigma(S_1(u) - S_2(u))dW(u) \right)^2 = \mathbb{E} \int_0^t \sigma^2(S_1(u) - S_2(u))^2 du.$$

Next, exchange the order of integration in the integral on the right, which is legitimate, since we are working with a class of processes where Fubini's theorem applies. Thus if we set

$$f(t) = \mathbb{E}(S_1(t) - S_2(t))^2,$$

the inequality in question takes the form

$$f(t) \le 2\mathbb{E}\left(\int_0^t \mu[S_1(u) - S_2(u)]du\right)^2 + 2\sigma^2 \int_0^t f(u)du.$$

It would be nice to introduce f into the term involving μ, and for this we need to compare $\mathbb{E}[(\int_0^t \mu(S_1(u) - S_2(u))du)^2]$ with

$$\mathbb{E}\int_0^t \mu^2(S_1(u) - S_2(u))^2 du = \int_0^t \mu^2 \mathbb{E}[(S_1(u) - S_2(u))^2]du,$$

which boils down to comparing $(\int_0^t \mu(S_1(u) - S_2(u))du)^2$ with $\int_0^t \mu^2(S_1(u) - S_2(u))^2 du$.

The Cauchy–Schwarz inequality ([PF]), which in the present context says that

$$\left(\int_0^t g(u)h(u)du\right)^2 \le \int_0^t g^2(u)du \int_0^t h^2(u)du,$$

can be applied to $g(t) = \mu$, $h(t) = S_1(t) - S_2(t))$, to give

$$\left(\int_0^t \mu(S_1(u) - S_2(u))du\right)^2 \le t\mu^2 \int_0^t (S_1(u) - S_2(u))^2 du$$

$$\le T\mu^2 \int_0^t (S_1(u) - S_2(u))^2 du.$$

Now take the expectation on both sides and exchange the order of integration on the right, so that

$$\mathbb{E}\left(\int_0^t \mu(S_1(u) - S_2(u))du\right)^2 \le T\mu^2 \int_0^t \mathbb{E}[(S_1(u) - S_2(u))^2]du).$$

Hence we have

$$f(t) \le 2(\mu^2 T + \sigma^2) \int_0^t f(u)du.$$

Observe that f is zero at time zero. The point is that this estimate does not allow f to grow. We can now use an important and frequently used inequality, as expressed by the Gronwall lemma given immediately below (we use this with $a = 0$). Hence $f(t) = 0$, that is $S_1(t) = S_2(t)$. □

Lemma 5.4 (Gronwall)

If $f : [0, T] \rightarrow \mathbb{R}$ is integrable, $b \geq 0$ and

$$f(t) \leq a + b \int_0^t f(s)ds,$$

then

$$f(t) \leq ae^{bt}.$$

Proof   See page 174.   □

The Black–Scholes equation can easily be generalised to variable coefficients.

Exercise 5.3   Show that the linear equation

$$dS(t) = \mu(t)S(t)dt + \sigma(t)S(t)dW(t)$$

with continuous deterministic functions $\mu(t)$ and $\sigma(t)$ has a unique solution

$$S(t) = S(0) \exp\left\{ \int_0^t \left(\mu(s) - \frac{1}{2}\sigma^2(s) \right) ds + \int_0^t \sigma(s)dW(s) \right\}.$$

Counterexamples

Unique solutions of stochastic differential equations over a given interval are not always available. We consider two situations where a unique solution cannot be found by providing simple counterexamples.

Example 5.5 (The solution does not exist)
It is well known that a solution to a differential equation may not exist over a predetermined interval – the solution may blow up prematurely. For instance, the equation $\frac{d}{dt}x(t) = x^2(t)$, $x(0) = c > 0$, has solution $x(t) = \frac{1}{c-t}$ which lives on $[0, c)$ only. This example obviously covers the stochastic equation by taking $b = 0$. We can use this idea to design a similar example of a stochastic differential equation by taking the process $X(t) = \frac{1}{c-W(t)}$ which starts at c and goes to infinity over any interval $[0, h]$ with positive probability (this probability is greater than $P(W(h) \geq c) > 0$). To find the

candidate for the equation we informally use the Itô formula with $F(x) = \frac{1}{1-x}$ (the function F is not sufficiently regular so this is not rigorous) to get

$$dX(t) = X^3(t)dt + X^2(t)dW(t).$$

Now suppose this equation has a strictly positive solution living on some interval $[0, T]$. Applying the Itô formula with $F(x) = \frac{1}{x}$ we easily find out that $dF(X(t)) = -dW(t)$, which with the initial condition $X(0) = c > 0$ gives $X(t) = \frac{1}{c-W(t)}$. We have a contradition with the assumption that X is well defined on $[0, T]$.

Example 5.6 (The solution is not unique)

A classical example of an ordinary differential equation with many solutions is given by $\frac{d}{dt}x(t) = x^{2/3}(t)$, $x(0) = 0$ since this equation is satisfied by any function of the form

$$x_a(t) = \begin{cases} 0 & \text{for } t \in [0, a] \\ (t - a)^3 & \text{for } t > a. \end{cases}$$

Inspired by the above success we try to design a stochastic example by taking

$$X_a(t) = \begin{cases} 0 & \text{for } t \in [0, a] \\ (W(t) - a)^3 & \text{for } t > a. \end{cases}$$

For fixed a, we use the Itô formula with $F(x) = (x - a)^3$, so for $t \geq a$

$$X_a(t) - X_a(a) = \int_a^t 3X_a^{1/3}(s)ds + \int_a^t 3X_a^{2/3}(s)dW(s)$$

and this also holds over intervals $[0, t]$ for $t < a$ by the fundamental principle that $0 = 0$. So the equation

$$dX = 3X^{1/3}dt + 3X^{2/3}dW$$

has infinitely many solutions starting from the same initial value $X(0) = 0$.

Further examples

We restrict ourselves to just a few more examples. Some intuition for solving stochastic equations by educated guesswork can be gathered by simple applications of the Itô formula and deriving equations satisfied by various proceess.

Exercise 5.4 Find the equation solved by the process $\sin W(t)$.

Exercise 5.5 Find a solution to the equation $dX = -\sqrt{1 - X^2}dW + \frac{1}{2}Xdt$ with $X(0) = 1$.

Exercise 5.6 Find a solution to the equation $dX(t) = 3X^2(t)dt - X^{3/2}(t)dW(t)$ bearing in mind the above derivation of $dX(t) = X^3(t)dt + X^2(t)dW(t)$.

Proposition 5.7
A solution to the equation

$$dX(t) = \mu X(t)dt + \sigma dW(t)$$

(called the Langevin equation) is the process

$$X(t) = X(0)e^{\mu t} + \int_0^t e^{\mu(t-s)}\sigma dW(s),$$

called the Ornstein–Uhlenbeck process.

Proof We use integration by parts to compute

$$d(e^{-\mu t}X(t)) = -\mu e^{-\mu t}X(t)dt + e^{-\mu t}dX(t)$$
$$= -\mu e^{-\mu t}X(t)dt + e^{-\mu t}\mu X(t)dt + e^{-\mu t}\sigma dW(t)$$
$$= e^{-\mu t}\sigma dW(t)$$

so

$$e^{-\mu t}X(t) = X(0) + \int_0^t e^{-\mu s}\sigma dW(s)$$

and multiplying both sides by $e^{\mu t}$ gives the result. □

The following extension of the above equation is relevant in the theory of stochastic interest rates. It can be solved by a modification of the method applied in the proof.

Exercise 5.7   Solve the following Vasicek equation $dX(t) = (a - bX(t))dt + \sigma dW(t)$.

The next exercise produces an equation also used for modelling interest rates.

Exercise 5.8   Find the equation solved by the process X^2 where X is the Ornstein–Uhlenbeck process.

5.2   Existence and uniqueness of solutions

Consider an equation of the form

$$dX(t) = a(t, X(t))dt + b(t, X(t))dW(t), \quad t \in (0, T], \qquad (5.4)$$
$$X(0) = X_0,$$

where the initial condition X_0 is a random variable with $\mathbb{E}X_0^2 < \infty$. In practice, the initial condition is deterministic, but paradoxically, the above case, although more general, will be easier to tackle. The equation is of course understood as an integral equation.

Theorem 5.8
Suppose that the coefficients are Lipschitz continuous with respect to the second variable, uniformly with respect to the first, so that there exists $K > 0$ such that for all $t \in (0, T]$ and real numbers x, y

$$|a(t, x) - a(t, y)| + |b(t, x) - b(t, y)| \le K|x - y|,$$

and have linear growth, so that there is a $C > 0$ with

$$|a(t, x)| + |b(t, x)| \le C(1 + |x|) \quad for\ x \in \mathbb{R},\ t \in [0, T].$$

Then (5.4) has a unique solution with continuous paths, which satisfies $\mathbb{E}(\int_0^T X^2(t)dt) < \infty$.

Proof   The integral form of our equation reads as follows:

$$X(t) = X_0 + \int_0^t a(s, X(s))ds + \int_0^t b(s, X(s))dW(s)$$
$$= \Phi(X)(t)$$

– here the right-hand side is regarded as a process depending on the process X and as we know this process has continuous paths. In this way the right-hand side defines a mapping from processes to processes, a mapping denoted by Φ.

The solution of the equation is therefore a process X satisfying the equation

$$\Phi(X) = X,$$

that is X is a fixed point of Φ. We will exploit the idea of the contraction mapping principle, also known as the Banach fixed-point theorem, and find a solution of our SDE as the fixed point of the operator Φ, defined on the following space

$$\mathcal{Z}_T = \{X(t) : X \text{ is adapted, } \mathbb{E}\left(\int_0^T X^2(t)dt\right) < \infty\}$$

with the norm

$$\|X\|_T = \left(\mathbb{E}\left(\int_0^T X^2(t)dt\right)\right)^{\frac{1}{2}}.$$

This space equipped with this norm is complete since this is a closed subspace of the space $L^2([0,T] \times \Omega)$ of functions of two variables $(t,\omega) \in [0,T] \times \Omega$ that are square-integrable with respect to the product measure $m \times P$ (see [PF]).

The proof we present goes along the following scheme:

Step 1. For any T, Φ maps $\mathcal{Z}_T$ into $\mathcal{Z}_T$.

Step 2. Φ is a contraction on $\mathcal{Z}_{T_1}$ if T_1 is sufficiently small and T_1 depends only on the data, that is the coefficients of the equation, but does not depend on the initial condition. In other words, we then have

$$\|\Phi(X) - \Phi(Y)\|_{T_1} \leq c\|X - Y\|_{T_1},$$

where $c < 1$.

Step 3. The sequence of consecutive approximations

$$X_1(t) = X_0,$$
$$X_{n+1}(t) = \Phi(X_n)(t)$$

is convergent in $\mathcal{Z}_{T_1}$, and the limit is a solution of the equation.

Step 4. The solution is unique in $\mathcal{Z}_{T_1}$.

Step 5. The solution can be extended to $[0,T]$.

Step 6. Every solution is equal to the solution obtained in Step 5 and uniqueness follows.

Next we proceed to the detailed arguments for each step.

Proof of Step 1. We will show that $\Phi : \mathcal{Z}_T \to \mathcal{Z}_T$ so let $X \in \mathcal{Z}_T$. To prove that $\Phi(X) \in \mathcal{Z}_T$ we have to show $\mathbb{E}(\int_0^T [\Phi X(t)]^2 dt) < \infty$, but due to Fubini it is sufficient to show $\int_0^T \mathbb{E}[\Phi X(t)]^2 dt < \infty$. We begin by estimating the square of the process $\Phi(X(t))$:

$$[\Phi X(t)]^2 = \left(X_0 + \int_0^t a(s, X(s)) ds + \int_0^t b(s, X(s)) dW(s) \right)^2$$

$$\leq 3X_0^2 + 3 \left(\int_0^t a(s, X(s)) ds \right)^2 + 3 \left(\int_0^t b(s, X(s)) dW(s) \right)^2$$

using $(a + b + c)^2 \leq 3(a^2 + b^2 + c^2)$.

The first term on the right is easy because the initial condition X_0 is a square-integrable random variable and does not depend on time

$$\int_0^T \mathbb{E}(3X_0^2) dt \leq 3T \mathbb{E}(X_0^2) < \infty.$$

The second term can be tackled by the Cauchy–Schwarz inequality

$$\left(\int_0^T g(u) h(u) du \right)^2 \leq \int_0^T g^2(u) du \int_0^T h^2(u) du,$$

with $g(t) = \mathbf{1}_{[0,t]}(s) a(s, X(s))$, $h(t) = 1$, to give

$$\left(\int_0^t a(s, X(s)) ds \right)^2 \leq T \int_0^t a^2(s, X(s)) ds$$

$$\leq T \int_0^T a^2(s, X(s)) ds.$$

The linear growth of a is used next

$$\int_0^T a^2(s, X(s)) ds \leq \int_0^T C^2 (1 + |X(s)|)^2 ds,$$

and for some constants c_1, c_2 we obtain

$$3 \left(\int_0^t a(s, X(s)) ds \right)^2 \leq c_1 + c_2 \int_0^T X^2(s) ds.$$

Integrating with respect to t and taking the expectation we obtain

$$3 \int_0^T \mathbb{E} \left(\int_0^t a(s, X(s)) ds \right)^2 dt \leq T c_1 + T c_2 \mathbb{E} \int_0^T X^2(s) ds$$

$$= T c_1 + T c_2 \|X\|_T^2 < \infty.$$

For the final term, we have to begin with the expectation, but first we check that this is legitimate, namely we verify that $b(t, X(t)) \in \mathcal{M}^2$, which uses the linear growth of b :

$$\mathbb{E}(3 \int_0^T b^2(s, X(s))ds) \leq \mathbb{E}(3 \int_0^T C^2(1 + |X(s)|)^2 ds)$$

$$\leq c_1 + c_2 \|X\|_T^2 < \infty.$$

Now the Itô isometry gives

$$\mathbb{E}\left(\int_0^t b(s, X(s))dW(s) \right)^2 = \mathbb{E}(\int_0^t b^2(s, X(s))ds)$$

and using the previous estimate we get the same bound as for the second term

$$3 \int_0^T \mathbb{E}\left(\int_0^t b(s, X(s))dW(s) \right)^2 dt \leq Tc_1 + Tc_2\|X\|_T^2 < \infty.$$

Putting these together we can conlude that for some constants d_1, d_2

$$\int_0^T \mathbb{E}[\Phi X(t)]^2 dt \leq d_1 + d_2 \|X\|_T^2 < \infty.$$

Proof of Step 2. We wish to show that for small enough T we have $\|\Phi(X) - \Phi(Y)\|_T \leq c\|X - Y\|_T$ for some $c < 1$. Employing the form of Φ and using the linearity of integration we have

$$\|\Phi(X) - \Phi(Y)\|_T^2 = \int_0^T \mathbb{E}\left(\int_0^t (a(s, X(s)) - a(s, Y(s)))ds \right.$$

$$\left. + \int_0^t (b(s, X(s)) - b(s, Y(s)))dW(s) \right)^2 dt.$$

Using the elementary fact $(a + b)^2 \leq 2a^2 + 2b^2$ the problem reduces to analysing two resulting terms on the right.

For the first one we use the Cauchy–Schwarz trick as above

$$2 \int_0^T \mathbb{E}\left(\int_0^t (a(s, X(s)) - a(s, Y(s)))ds \right)^2 dt$$

$$\leq 2 \int_0^T \mathbb{E}(T \int_0^T [a(s, X(s)) - a(s, Y(s))]^2 ds)dt$$

$$= 2T^2\mathbb{E} \int_0^T K^2|X(s)) - Y(s)|^2 ds$$

$$= 2T^2K^2 \|X - Y\|_T^2 .$$

The second requires the Itô isometry and then the estimation is again routine

$$2 \int_0^T \mathbb{E} \left(\int_0^t (b(s, X(s)) - b(s, Y(s))) dW(s) \right)^2 dt$$

$$= 2 \int_0^T \mathbb{E} \left(\int_0^t [b(s, X(s)) - b(s, Y(s))]^2 ds \right) dt$$

$$\leq 2k^2 \int_0^T \mathbb{E} \int_0^T |X(s) - Y(s)|^2 ds dt$$

$$= 2T K^2 \|X - Y\|_T^2 .$$

The conclusion is

$$\|\Phi(X) - \Phi(Y)\|_T^2 \leq 2K^2 T(T + 1) \|X - Y\|_T^2 .$$

Finally, choose T_1 such that $c^2 = 2K^2 T(T + 1) < 1$, we have a contraction in the corresponding space $\mathcal{Z}_{T_1}$:

$$\|\Phi(X) - \Phi(Y)\|_{T_1} \leq c \|X - Y\|_{T_1} .$$

Proof of Step 3. Since the space $\mathcal{Z}_T$ is complete, to obtain convergence we only need to show that the sequence X_n is Cauchy. So we consider

$$\|X_{n+1} - X_n\| = \|\Phi(X_n) - \Phi(X_{n-1})\|$$

$$= \|\Phi(X_n - X_{n-1})\|$$

$$\leq c \|X_n - X_{n-1}\|$$

and by induction

$$\|X_{n+1} - X_n\| \leq c^n \|X_1 - X_0\| .$$

This gives for $n < m$.

$$\|X_m - X_n\| = \|X_m - X_{m-1} + X_{m-1} - X_{m-2} + \cdots + X_{n+1} - X_n\|$$

$$\leq \|X_m - X_{m-1}\| + \|X_{m-1} - X_{m-2}\| + \cdots + \|X_{n+1} - X_n\|$$

$$\leq (c^{m-1} + c^{m-2} + \cdots + c^n) \|X_1 - X_0\| .$$

The series $\sum c^n$ is convergent, that is the sequence of partial sums $s_m = \sum_{n=0}^m c^m$ converges, and $c^m + c^{m-1} + \cdots + c^{n+1} = s_m - s_n$ can be made as small as we please by chosing n, m large enough.

So the sequence X_n converges to some $X \in \mathcal{Z}_{T_1}$, so $\Phi(X_n) \to \Phi(X)$ as Φ is continuous. Passing to the limit on both sides of the recursive definition $X_{n+1} = \Phi(X_n)$, we get

$$X = \Phi(X)$$

so X solves the SDE.

Proof of Step 4. We argue abstractly (the argument holds for any contraction) to show that there is at most one fixed point of Φ. For, if $\Phi(X) = X$, $\Phi(Y) = Y$, then

$$\|\Phi(X) - \Phi(Y)\|_{T_1} < \|X - Y\|_{T_1} = \|\Phi(X) - \Phi(Y)\|_{T_1},$$

a contradiction unless $X = Y$.

Proof of Step 5. We have solved the equation on $[0, T_1]$ with initial condition $X(0)$. We will make sure that $\mathbb{E}(X^2(T_1))$ is finite to solve the equation in $[T_1, 2T_1]$ with (random) initial value $X(T_1)$. Arguing as in Step 1, employing the Itô isometry and linear growth, we get for $t \le T_1$

$$\mathbb{E}(X^2(t)) \le 3\mathbb{E}(X_0^2) + 3\mathbb{E}\left(\int_0^t a(s, X(s))ds\right)^2 + 3\mathbb{E}\left(\int_0^t b(s, X(s))dW(s)\right)^2$$

$$\le 3\mathbb{E}(X_0^2) + C \int_0^t (1 + \mathbb{E}(X^2(s))ds$$

$$= C_1 + C_2 \int_0^t \mathbb{E}(X^2(s))ds,$$

so the function $f(t) = \mathbb{E}(X^2(t))$ satisfies the assumption of the Gronwall lemma and as a result $f(T_1)$ is finite.

In the same way, we can solve the equation in $[2T_1, 3T_1]$ with initial value $X(2T_1)$ and so on until $nT_1 \ge T$. At the last stage, we work in $[(n-1)T_1, T]$, so the solution is defined on $[0, T]$. This construction guarantees that the resulting process is continuous. At each stage (bar the last) the length of the interval for which we can extend the solution is the same since it does not depend on the initial condition, which here is different for each stage. This process can be continued as long as the coefficients of the equation are defined, that is up to the moment when T_1 exceeds T. So the extension will cover the whole interval $[0, T]$. Here we see that it was very convenient to allow the initial condition to be random though in fact in practice X_0 will be a deterministic number.

Proof of Step 6. Uniqueness: if we show that every possible solution is in $\mathcal{Z}_T$, any solution must be equal to the solution obtained above by the Banach theorem, hence the SDE has a unique solution.

Let X be any solution, that is an Itô process satisfying the equation. The main problem in proving the regularity needed is concerned with the stochastic term. To estimate this term, we need the Itô isometry. This was easy above, since we had the necessary information about the process under the integral. With arbitrary X, we cannot be sure that $b(t, X(t)) \in \mathcal{M}^2$. A remedy is (of course) a suitable localisation procedure. There are many ways of attacking this; we will take the most natural sequence of stopping times

$$\tau_n = \inf\left\{t \geq 0 : \int_0^t b^2(s, X(s))ds \geq n\right\},$$

which, as we know, localise the process $b(t, X(t))$ in $\mathcal{M}^2$. Consider the stopped process $X_n(t) = X(t \wedge \tau_n)$ (recall that $t \wedge \tau_n = \min\{t, \tau_n\}$). We have

$$X_n(t) = X_0 + \int_0^{t \wedge \tau_n} a(s, X(s))ds + \int_0^{t \wedge \tau_n} b(s, X(s))dW(s)$$

so, as before,

$$\mathbb{E}(X_n^2(t)) = \mathbb{E}\left(X_0 + \int_0^{t \wedge \tau_n} a(s, X(s))ds + \int_0^{t \wedge \tau_n} b(s, X(s))dW(s)\right)^2$$

$$\leq 3\mathbb{E}(X_0^2) + 3\mathbb{E}\left(\int_0^{t \wedge \tau_n} a(s, X(s))ds\right)^2$$

$$+ 3\mathbb{E}\left(\int_0^{t \wedge \tau_n} b(s, X(s))dW(s)\right)^2. \tag{5.5}$$

Next, we estimate the second term

$$\mathbb{E}\left(\int_0^{t \wedge \tau_n} a(s, X(s))ds\right)^2 \leq T\mathbb{E}\left(\int_0^{t \wedge \tau_n} a^2(s, X(s))ds\right) \text{ (Cauchy–Schwarz)}$$

$$\leq TC^2\mathbb{E}\left(\int_0^{t \wedge \tau_n} (1 + X(s))^2 ds\right) \text{ (linear growth)}$$

$$\leq T^2C^2 + TC^2\mathbb{E}\left(\int_0^{t \wedge \tau_n} X^2(s)ds\right).$$

Now, if $\tau_n(\omega) < t$, then we have

$$\int_0^{\tau_n(\omega)} X^2(s, \omega)ds \leq \int_0^{\tau_n(\omega)} X^2(s, \omega)ds + \int_{\tau_n(\omega)}^t X^2(\tau_n(\omega), \omega)ds$$

$$= \int_0^t X_n^2(s, \omega)ds$$

but if $t < \tau_n(\omega)$, then $X_n(t, \omega) = X(t, \omega)$ so

$$\int_0^t X^2(s, \omega)ds = \int_0^t X_n^2(s, \omega)ds.$$

The inequality is preserved by the expectation

$$\mathbb{E}\int_0^{t\wedge\tau_n} X^2(s)ds \le \mathbb{E}\int_0^t X_n^2(s)ds,$$

which gives the estimate

$$\text{2nd term in (5.5)} \le c_1 + c_2\int_0^t \mathbb{E}(X_n^2(s))ds.$$

In the third term, we can apply Itô isometry

$$\mathbb{E}\left(\int_0^{t\wedge\tau_n} b(s,X(s))dW(s)\right)^2 = \mathbb{E}\left(\int_0^t \mathbf{1}_{[0,\tau_n]}(s)b(s,X(s))dW(s)\right)^2$$

$$= \mathbb{E}\int_0^t \mathbf{1}_{[0,\tau_n]}(s)b^2(s,X(s))ds \text{ (Itô isometry)}$$

$$\le \mathbb{E}\int_0^{t\wedge\tau_n} b^2(s,X(s))ds$$

$$\le \mathbb{E}\int_0^{t\wedge\tau_n} C^2(1+|X(s)|)^2 ds \text{ (linear growth)}$$

$$\le C^2T + C^2\mathbb{E}\int_0^{t\wedge\tau_n} X^2(s)ds$$

$$\le C^2T + C^2\mathbb{E}\int_0^t X_n^2(s)ds \text{ (as in 2}^{\text{nd}}\text{ term)},$$

which gives

$$\text{3rd term in (5.5)} \le c_3 + c_4\int_0^t \mathbb{E}(X_n^2(s))ds.$$

Bearing in mind that the first term in (5.5) is a constant, writing

$$f_n(t) = \mathbb{E}(X_n^2(t))$$

we finally get

$$f_n(t) \le c_5 + c_6\int_0^t f_n(s)ds$$

for some constants independent of n. This enables us to apply the Gronwall Lemma 5.4 and so

$$f_n(T) \le c = c_5(e^{c_6 T}),$$

where the constant c does not depend on n. Letting $n \to \infty$ we have

$$\sup_n f_n(T) < \infty$$

and finally by Fatou's lemma, $(\mathbb{E}(\lim X_n^2) \leq \lim \mathbb{E}(X_n^2)$, see [PF]), $\mathbb{E}(X^2(t))$ is bounded, hence Lebesgue-integrable over $[0, T]$, so $X \in \mathcal{Z}_T$ as claimed.

□

Exercise 5.9   Prove uniqueness using the method of Proposition 5.3 for a general equation with Lipschitz coefficients (take any two solutions and estimate the square of their difference to show that it is zero).

Exercise 5.10   Prove that the solution depends continuously on the initial value in the L^2 norm, namely show that if X, Y are solutions of (5.4) with initial conditions X_0, Y_0, respectively, then for all t we have $\mathbb{E}(X(t) - Y(t))^2 \leq c\mathbb{E}(X_0 - Y_0)^2$. Find the form of the constant c.

Solutions have continuous paths so for (almost) all ω, $\sup_{t \in [0,T]} X^2(t, \omega) < \infty$. We also know that for all t, $\mathbb{E}X^2(t) < \infty$. However, the claim of the next proposition, needed later, does not follow from these facts and requires a separate proof.

Proposition 5.9
For any solution X, any $t \leq T$,

$$\mathbb{E} \sup_{s \in [0,t]} X^2(s) < \infty.$$

Proof   Take $\tau_n = \inf\{s \geq 0 : |X(s)| \geq n\}$. Recalling that τ_n and hence $t \wedge \tau_n = \min(t, \tau_n)$ are stopping times for the underlying filtration $\mathcal{F}_t^W$, define

$$f_n(t) = \mathbb{E} \sup_{s \in [0, t \wedge \tau_n]} X^2(s).$$

The restriction to the stopping time guarantees that this function is well defined. Next

$$\sup_{u \in [0, \tau_n]} |X(u)|^2 = \sup_{u \in [0,t]} \mathbf{1}_{\{u \leq \tau_n\}} \left(X_0 + \int_0^u a(s, X(s))ds + \int_0^u b(s, X(s))dW(s) \right)^2$$

$$\leq 3X_0^2 + 3 \int_0^\tau a^2(s, X(s))ds + 3 \sup_{[0,t]} \mathbf{1}_{\{u \leq \tau_n\}} \left(\int_0^u b(s, X(s))dW(s) \right)^2.$$

Note that if $u \leq \tau_n$, then $f_n(u) = \mathbf{1}_{\{u \leq \tau_n\}} f_n(u)$, so by Proposition 4.17

$$\int_0^u f_n(s)dW(s) = \int_0^u \mathbf{1}_{\{u \leq \tau_n\}} f_n(s)dW(s)$$

on $\{u \leq \tau_n\}$ and

$$\mathbf{1}_{u \leq \tau_n} \left| \int_0^u f_n(s) dW(s) \right|^2 = \left| \int_0^u \mathbf{1}_{u \leq \tau_n} f_n(s) dW(s) \right|^2 .$$

In this way, using the Itô isometry again, we obtain

$$f_n(t) \leq c_1 + c_2 \int_0^t \mathbb{E}(\mathbf{1}_{s \leq \tau_n} X^2(s)) ds \leq c_1 + c_2 \int_0^t f_n(s) ds$$

which enables us to apply the Gronwall Lemma 5.4, which gives $f_n(t) \leq c$. Passing with n to ∞ we have proved the claim, as the estimate does not depend on n. □

5.3 Markov property

In this section we discuss solutions to stochastic equations with coefficients satisfying a Lipschitz condition and having linear growth, which therefore have a unique solution with continuous paths. If we restrict attention to any subinterval $[s, u] \subset [0, T]$, the theory we have developed applies here as well. Given any $\mathcal{F}_s^W$-measurable random variable X_s, a unique solution exists, since it is independent of the relevant σ-field $\mathcal{F}_{[s,u]}^W$ generated by the increments $W(t) - W(s)$, $s < t \leq u$. We denote the solution by $X_{s,X_s}(t)$, where $X_{s,X_s}(s) = X_s$. In particular, the unique solution discussed above can be written as $X(t) = X_{0,X_0}(t)$. Note also that when $X_s = x$ is deterministic, the solution is written as $X_{s,x}(t)$. In the next proposition, we use deterministic initial values.

Proposition 5.10
Given real numbers x, y, there exists $C > 0$ such that

$$\mathbb{E} \sup_{t \in [s,T]} (X_{s,x}(t) - X_{s,y}(t))^2 \leq C|x - y|^2.$$

Proof Since both $X_{s,x}(t)$ and $X_{s,y}(t)$ are solutions to the equation, subtracting, squaring and using $(a + b + c)^2 \leq 3a^2 + 3b^2 + 3c^2$ we have

$$\mathbb{E} \sup_{r \in [s,t]} (X_{s,x}(r) - X_{s,y}(r))^2$$

$$\leq 3(x - y)^2 + 3\mathbb{E} \sup_{r \in [s,t]} \left(\int_s^r [a(u, X_{s,x}(u)) - a(u, X_{s,y}(u))] du \right)^2 \quad (5.6)$$

$$+ 3\mathbb{E} \sup_{r \in [s,t]} \left(\int_s^r [b(u, X_{s,x}(u)) - b(u, X_{s,y}(u))] dW(s) \right)^2 .$$

Write the left-hand side as

$$f(t) = \mathbb{E} \sup_{r \in [s,t]} (X_{s,x}(r) - X_{s,y}(r))^2,$$

which is integrable by Proposition 5.9, since it is bounded by $f(T)$.

We estimate the second term on the right of (5.6):

$$\mathbb{E} \sup_{r \in [s,t]} \left(\int_s^r [a(u, X_{s,x}(u)) - a(u, X_{s,y}(u))]du \right)^2$$

$$\leq (t - s)\mathbb{E} \sup_{r \in [s,t]} \int_s^r [a(u, X_{s,x}(u)) - a(u, X_{s,y}(u))]^2 du \text{ (Cauchy–Schwarz)}$$

$$\leq (t - s)\mathbb{E} \sup_{r \in [s,t]} \int_s^r K[X_{s,x}(u) - X_{s,y}(u)]^2 du \text{ (Lipschitz condition)}$$

$$\leq TK\mathbb{E} \int_s^t [X_{s,x}(u) - X_{s,y}(u)]^2 du$$

$$\leq TK\mathbb{E} \int_s^t \sup_{r \in [s,u]} [X_{s,x}(r) - X_{s,y}(r)]^2 du$$

$$= TK \int_s^t \mathbb{E} \sup_{r \in [s,u]} [X_{s,x}(r) - X_{s,y}(r)]^2 du \text{ (Fubini)}$$

$$= TK \int_s^t f(u)du.$$

For the stochastic term, write

$$M(r) = \int_s^r [b(u, X_{s,x}(u)) - b(u, X_{s,y}(u))]dW(s),$$

which is a martingale so Doob's L^2-inequality can be applied:

$$\mathbb{E} \sup_{r \in [s,t]} M^2(r) \leq 4\mathbb{E}(M^2(t))$$

$$= 4\mathbb{E} \left(\int_s^t [b(u, X_{s,x}(u)) - b(u, X_{s,y}(u))]dW(s) \right)^2$$

$$= 4\mathbb{E} \int_s^t [b(u, X_{s,x}(u)) - b(u, X_{s,y}(u))]^2 ds \text{ (Itô isometry)}$$

$$\leq 4TK \int_s^t f(u)du$$

using the same arguments as for the term involving a.

Putting all the estimates together, we obtain

$$f(t) \leq 3(x - y)^2 + 15TK \int_s^t f(u)du$$

and the Gronwall lemma (Lemma 5.4) gives the result:

$$f(t) \le 3e^{15TK}(x - y)^2.$$

$\square$

We can solve our equation for each initial x but the solution is a process defined only on a set of full probability. If we want to analyse the regularity of the solution with respect to the starting point, we need a common function which produces all solutions by inserting the initial value. Such a function is sometimes called a **flow** of solutions, and it is produced by the next proposition.

Proposition 5.11

For any fixed $s \in [0, T]$, there exists a function $\phi_s(x, t, \omega)$ defined on $\mathbb{R} \times [s, T] \times \Omega$, measurable with respect to $\mathcal{B}(\mathbb{R}) \times \mathcal{B}([s, T]) \times \mathcal{F}_{[s,T]}^W$ and continuous with respect to x for all t and almost all ω, and such that $\phi_s(x, t, w) = X_{s,x}(t, w)$ a.s.

Proof For any fixed m, consider the collection of dyadic rationals $\frac{k}{2^m}$ with $k \in \mathbb{Z}$. Consider the solutions to the stochastic equation over $[s, T]$ started at these rationals, $X_{s, \frac{k}{2^m}}(t)$, to build each approximate flow $\phi^{(m)}$ as a piecewise constant function of x :

$$\phi_s^{(m)}(x, t, \omega) = \sum_k X_{s, \frac{k}{2^m}}(t, \omega) \mathbf{1}_{[\frac{k}{2^m}, \frac{k+1}{2^m})}(x).$$

Measurability of $\phi^{(m)}$ with respect to (x, t, ω) follows directly from its form and it is preserved in the limit (the upper limit always exists)

$$\phi_s(x, t, \omega) = \limsup_{n \to \infty} \phi_s^{(m)}(x, t, \omega).$$

We wish to prove that the sequence $\phi^{(m)}$ actually converges, the limit is the solution $X_{s,x}(t, \omega)$, and convergence is uniform in t, for all $x \in \mathbb{R}$, for almost all $\omega \in \Omega$. This requires that the set

$$A = \{\omega : \sup_{t \in [s,T]} |\phi_s^{(m)}(x, t, \omega) - X_{s,x}(t, \omega)| \to 0\}$$

has probability one. From this point of view we can distinguish favourable events, for any $\varepsilon > 0$, of the form

$$A_\varepsilon^{(m)} = \{\omega : \sup_{t \in [s,T]} |\phi_s^{(m)}(x, t, \omega) - X_{s,x}(t, \omega)| < \varepsilon\}.$$

The inequalities should be satisfied from a certain N on, so we consider

$$A_\varepsilon = \bigcup_{N=1}^{\infty} \bigcap_{m=N}^{\infty} A_\varepsilon^{(m)}$$

and if we show that $P(A_\varepsilon) = 1$, this will complete the argument since the sets A_ε are decreasing when $\varepsilon \searrow 0$, so

$$P(A) = P\left(\bigcap_{\varepsilon > 0} A_\varepsilon\right) = \lim_{\varepsilon \searrow 0} P(A_\varepsilon) = 1.$$

By the Borel–Cantelli lemma (see [PF]) it is sufficient to show that for $B^{(m)} = \Omega \setminus A^{(m)}$

$$\sum_{m=1}^{\infty} P(B^{(m)}) < \infty.$$

Proposition 5.10 allows us to handle this series:

$$P(B^{(m)}) = P(\{\omega : \sup_{t \in [s,T]} |X_{s,\frac{k}{2m}}(t, \omega) - X_{s,x}(t, \omega)| \geq \varepsilon\})$$

$$\leq \varepsilon^2 \mathbb{E} \sup_{t \in [s,T]} |X_{s,\frac{k}{2m}}(t, \omega) - X_{s,x}(t, \omega)|^2 \text{ (Chebyshev inequality, see [PF])}$$

$$\leq \varepsilon^2 C \left|\frac{k}{2^m} - x\right|^2 \leq \varepsilon^2 C \frac{1}{2^{2m}}.$$

The required regularity now follows from the above considerations.   □

The idea of the next proposition is quite simple: a solution at time t can be produced by solving the equation in one step over the interval $[0, t]$, or equivalently by a two-stage procedure:

1. Solve the equation in $[0, s]$.
2. Solve the equation in $[s, t]$ (using a Wiener process defined over this interval) with the starting point equal to the terminal value obtained at stage one.

This can be written as

$$X_{0,x_0}(t) = X_{s,X_{0,x_0}(s)}(t)$$

or, as below, in flow notation, which is perhaps less evident but also less clumsy – for notational convenience we also suppress the dependence on ω.

Proposition 5.12
For all $s \leq t$,

$$\phi_0(X_0, t) = \phi_s(\phi_0(X_0, s), t). \tag{5.7}$$

Proof The left-hand side process satisfies the equation over $[0, t]$ so

$$\phi_0(X_0, t) = X_0 + \int_0^t a(u, \phi_0(X_0, u))du + \int_0^t b(u, \phi_0(X_0, u))dW(u)$$

$$= \phi_0(X_0, s) + \int_s^t a(u, \phi_0(X_0, u))du + \int_s^t b(u, \phi_0(X_0, u))dW(u)$$

by the additivity of integrals. We have to show that the process on the right of (5.7) solves the equation over $[s, t]$ with initial value $\phi_0(X_0, s)$, that is

$$\phi_s(\phi_0(X_0, s), t) = \phi_0(X_0, s) + \int_s^t a(u, \phi_s(\phi_0(X_0, s), u))du$$

$$+ \int_0^t b(u, \phi_s(\phi_0(X_0, s), u))dW(u).$$

We then have two solutions over $[s, t]$ with the same initial value so uniqueness of the solution gives the result we seek.

By Proposition 5.11, we know that for any real (deterministic) x we have a solution

$$\phi_s(x, t) = x + \int_s^t a(u, \phi_s(x, u))du + \int_s^t b(u, \phi_s(x, u))dW(u)$$

and we would like to insert $x = \phi_0(X_0, s)$. This is straightforward for the left-hand side and the first two terms on the right, but the stochastic integral is not defined pathwise, and we cannot insert a random variable directly. However, this can be done for the approximating sums, and writing

$$\psi(x, t) = \int_s^t b(u, \phi_s(x, u))dW(u),$$

we can conclude that for any $\mathcal{F}_s$-measurable random variable Z

$$\psi(Z, t) = \int_s^t b(u, \phi_s(Z, u))dW(u)$$

where the integral is computed afresh with the modified integrand (the process $b(u, \phi_s(Z, u))$ is in $\mathcal{M}^2$ by all we know about the solutions). $\quad\square$

For our final result, we need the following version of Lemma 1.43.

Lemma 5.13
If $\eta : \mathbb{R} \times \Omega \to \mathbb{R}$ is bounded and $\mathcal{B} \times \mathcal{F}^W_{[s,u]}$ measurable, Y is $\mathcal{F}^W_s$-measurable, $G(x) = \mathbb{E}(\eta(x))$, then

$$\mathbb{E}(\eta(Y)|\mathcal{F}_s) = G(Y).$$

Proof See [PF]. $\quad\square$

Theorem 5.14
The solution $X(t) = \phi_0(X_0, t)$ of our stochastic equation (with linear growth Lipschitz coefficients) has the Markov property.

Proof   We have to show that for any bounded Borel f and for all $0 \leq s \leq t \leq T$

$$\mathbb{E}(f(X(t))|\mathcal{F}_s) = \mathbb{E}(f(X(t))|\mathcal{F}_{X(s)}). \tag{5.8}$$

The left-hand side, using Proposition 5.12 takes the form

$$\mathbb{E}(f(X(t))|\mathcal{F}_s) = \mathbb{E}(f(\phi_0(X_0, t))|\mathcal{F}_s)$$
$$= \mathbb{E}(f(\phi_s(\phi_0(X_0, s), t))|\mathcal{F}_s).$$

By Lemma 5.13 with $\eta(x, \omega) = f(\phi_s(x, t, \omega))$ and $Y(\omega) = \phi_0(X_0, s, \omega)$ the right-hand side above

$$= G(\phi_0(X_0, s))$$
$$= G(X(s)) \quad \text{(recall that } X(s) = \phi_0(X_0, s)).$$

Since $G(x) = \mathbb{E}(f(\phi_s(x, t)))$ is a measurable function by Proposition 5.11, $G(X(s))$ is an $\mathcal{F}_{X(s)}$-measurable random variable and

$$G(X(s)) = \mathbb{E}(G(X(s))|\mathcal{F}_{X(s)})$$
$$= \mathbb{E}(\mathbb{E}(f(X(t))|\mathcal{F}_s)|\mathcal{F}_{X(s)}) \text{ (the above computation)}$$
$$= \mathbb{E}(f(X(t))|\mathcal{F}_{X(s)}) \text{ (tower property, } \mathcal{F}_{X(s)} \subset \mathcal{F}_s),$$

which completes the proof. $\square$

5.4   Proofs

Lemma 5.4 (Gronwall)
If $f : [0, T] \rightarrow \mathbb{R}$ is integrable, $b \geq 0$ and

$$f(t) \leq a + b \int_0^t f(s)ds,$$

then

$$f(t) \leq ae^{bt}.$$

Proof   Write

$$u(t) = a + b \int_0^t f(s)ds$$

so that the assumption reads $f(t) \leq u(t)$. Then $u'(t) = bf(t)$ (u is almost everywhere differentiable as an absolutely continuous function) so by the assumption

$$u'(t) \leq bu(t). \tag{5.9}$$

Since $(u(t)e^{-bt})' = u'(t)e^{-bt} - be^{-bt}u(t)$, (5.9) is equivalent to

$$(u(t)e^{-bt})' \leq 0.$$

So $u(t)e^{-bt}$ is non-increasing and since $u(0) = a$, we get $u(t)e^{-bt} \leq a$. Using the assumption again we have $f(t)e^{-bt} \leq a$ and the claim follows after multiplying both sides by e^{bt}.   □

Index

Printed in the United States
By Bookmasters